Space Exploration
Primary
Sources

Space Exploration
Primary Sources

Peggy Saari

Deborah J. Baker
and Sarah Hermsen,
Project Editors

U·X·L

An imprint of Thomson Gale,
a part of The Thomson Corporation

THOMSON

GALE

Detroit • New York • San Francisco • San Diego • New Haven, Conn. • Waterville, Maine • London • Munich

Space Exploration: Primary Sources
Peggy Saari

Project Editors
Deborah J. Baker and Sarah Hermsen

Rights Acquisitions and Management
Ann Taylor

Imaging and Multimedia
Dean Dauphinais, Lezlie Light, Dan Newell

Product Design
Pamela Galbreath

Composition
Evi Seoud

Manufacturing
Rita Wimberley

Library of Congress Cataloging-in-Publication Data
Saari, Peggy.
Space exploration. Primary sources / Peggy Saari.
        p. cm. – (Space exploration reference library)
        Includes bibliographical references and index.
        ISBN 0-7876-9213-1 (hardcover : alk. paper)
    1.   Astronautics–History–Sources–Juvenile literature.
I. Title.   II. Series.
    TL794.5.S23 2004
    629.4'09–dc22
                                                                        2004015879

Printed in the United States of America
10 9 8 7 6 5 4 3

Contents

Reader's Guide

Fascinating and forbidding, space has drawn the attention of humans since before recorded history. People have looked outward, driven by curiosity about the vast universe that surrounds Earth. Unaware of the meaning of the bright lights in the night sky above them, ancient humans thought they saw patterns, images in the sky of things in the landscape around them.

Slowly, humans came to realize that the lights in the sky had an effect on the workings of the planet around them. They sought to understand the movements of the Sun, the Moon, and the other, brighter objects. They wanted to know how those movements related to the changing seasons and the growth of crops.

Still, for centuries, humans did not understand what lay beyond the boundaries of Earth. In fact, with their limited vision, they saw a limited universe. Ancient astronomers relied on naked-eye observations to chart the positions of stars, planets, and the Sun. In the third century B.C.E., philosophers concluded that Earth was the center of the universe. A few dared to question this prevailing belief. In the face of overwhelming opposition and ridicule, they persisted in trying to understand the truth. This belief ruled human affairs until the scientific revolution of the seventeenth century, when scientists used the newly invented telescope to prove that the Sun is the center of Earth's galaxy.

Over time, with advances in science and technology, ancient beliefs were exposed as false. The universe ever widened with humans' growing understanding of it. The dream to explore its vast reaches passed from nineteenth-century fiction writers to twentieth-century visionaries to present-day engineers and scientists, pilots, and astronauts.

The quest to explore space intensified around the turn of the twentieth century. By that time, astronomers had built better observatories and perfected more powerful telescopes. Increasingly sophisticated technologies led to the discovery that the universe extends far beyond the Milky Way and holds even deeper mysteries, such as limitless galaxies and unexplained phenomena like black holes. Scientists, yearning to solve those mysteries, determined that one way to accomplish this goal was to penetrate space itself.

Even before the twentieth century, people had discussed ways to travel into space. Among them were science fiction writers, whose fantasies inspired the visions of scientists. Science fiction became especially popular in the late nineteenth century, having a direct impact on early twentieth-century rocket engineers who invented the fuel-propellant rocket. Initially developed as a weapon of war, this new projectile could be launched a greater distance than any human-made object in history, and it eventually unlocked the door to space.

From the mid-twentieth century until the turn of the twenty-first century, the fuel-propellant rocket made possible dramatic advances in space exploration. It was used to propel unmanned satellites and manned space capsules, space shuttles, and space stations. It launched an orbiting telescope that sent spectacular images of the universe back to Earth. During this era of intense optimism and innovation, often called the space age, people confidently went forth to conquer the distant regions of space that have intrigued humans since early times. They traveled to the Moon, probed previously uncharted realms, and contemplated trips to Mars.

Overcoming longstanding rivalries, nations embarked on international space ventures. Despite the seemingly unlimited technology at their command, research scientists, engineers, and astronauts encountered political maneuvering, lack of funds, aging spacecraft, and tragic accidents. As the world settled into the twenty-first century, space exploration faced an uncertain future. Yet, the ongoing exploration of space continued to represent the "final frontier" in the last great age of exploration.

Space Exploration: Primary Sources tells the story of humanity's quest to uncover the mysteries of space through the words of those involved. The work captures the highlights of the space age with full-text reprints and lengthy excerpts of seventeen documents that include science fiction, nonfiction, autobiography, official reports, articles, interviews, and speeches. The reader will be taken on an adventure spanning a period of more than one hundred twenty-five years, from nineteenth-century speculations about space travel through twenty-first century plans for human flights to Mars.

Format

The excerpts in *Space Exploration: Primary Sources* are divided into fifteen chapters. These include sections on Jules Verne's science fiction writings; Robert H. Goddard's landmark study on space travel; Wernher von Braun's ideas about putting a man on the Moon; the announcement of the first satellite in space; President John F. Kennedy's special message to Congress asserting that the United States must be first to send a man to the Moon; Tom Wolfe's account of America's first astronauts; Martha Ackmann's story of the women in the Mercury 13 program; John Glenn's memoirs about his long career in space travel; Michael Collins and Buzz Aldrin's recollections of being on the first manned mission to the Moon; NASA administrator James C. Fletcher and President Richard Nixon's comments on the space shuttle program; Vice President George H. W. Bush's announcement concerning the first teacher selected to go into space and President Ronald Reagan's address following the explosion of the Space Shuttle *Challenger*; Shannon Lucid's memories of living on *Mir*; NASA's strategic plan regarding the *Origins, Evolution, and Destiny of the Cosmos and Life*; the findings of the *Columbia* space shuttle accident investigation board; and President George W.

Bush's new vision for space exploration. Every chapter opens with a historical overview, followed by reprinted documents.

Each excerpt (or section of excerpts) includes the following additional features:

- **Introductory material** places the document and its author in a historical context.

- **Things to remember while reading** offers important background information about the featured text.

- **Excerpt** presents the document in its original spelling and format.

- **What happened next. . .** discusses the impact of the document and/or relevant historical events following the date of the document.

- **Did you know. . .** provides interesting facts about the document and its author.

- **Consider the following. . .** poses questions about the material for the reader to consider.

- **For More Information** offers resources for further study of the document and its author as well as sources used by the authors in writing the material.

Other features of *Space Exploration: Primary Sources* include sidebar boxes highlighting interesting, related information. More than fifty black-and-white photos illustrate the text. In addition, each excerpt is accompanied by a glossary running in the margin alongside the reprinted document that defines terms, people, and ideas. The volume begins with a timeline of events and a "Words to Know" section, and concludes with a general bibliography and subject index of people, places, and events discussed throughout *Space Exploration: Primary Sources*.

Space Exploration Reference Library

Space Exploration: Primary Sources is only one component of the three-part Space Exploration Reference Library. The other two titles in this set are:

- *Space Exploration: Almanac* (two volumes) presents, in fourteen chapters, key developments and milestones in the continuing history of space exploration. The focus ranges from ancient views of a Sun-centered universe to the scientific understanding of the laws of planetary motion and gravity, from the launching of the first artificial satellite to be placed in orbit around Earth to current robotic explorations of near and distant planets in the solar system. Also covered is the development of the first telescopes by men such as Hans Lippershey, who called his device a "looker" and thought it would be useful in war, and Galileo Galilei, who built his own device to look at the stars. The work also details the construction of great modern observatories, both on ground and in orbit around Earth, that can peer billions of light-years into space and, in doing so, peer billions of years back in time. Also examined is the development of rocketry; the work of theorists and engineers Konstantin Tsiolkovsky, Robert H. Goddard, and others; a discussion of the Cold War and its impact on space exploration; space missions such as the first lunar landing; and great tragedies, including the explosions of U.S. space shuttles *Challenger* and *Columbia.*

- *Space Exploration: Biographies* captures the height of the space age in twenty-five entries that profile astronauts, scientists, theorists, writers, and spacecraft. Included are astronauts Neil Armstrong, John Glenn, Mae Jemison, and Sally Ride; cosmonaut Yuri Gagarin; engineer Wernher von Braun; writer H. G. Wells; and the crew of the space shuttle *Challenger.* The volume also contains profiles of the Hubble Space Telescope and the International Space Station. Focusing on international contributions to the quest for knowledge about space, this volume takes readers on an adventure into the achievements and failures experienced by explorers of space.

- A cumulative index of all three titles in the Space Exploration Reference Library is also available.

Comments and Suggestions

We welcome your comments on *Space Exploration: Primary Sources* and suggestions for other topics to consider. Please write: Editors, *Space Exploration: Primary Sources*, U•X•L, 27500 Drake Rd. Farmington Hills, Michigan 48331-3535; call toll-free: 1-800-877-4253; fax to (248) 699-8097; or send e-mail via http://www.gale.com.

Timeline of Events

c. 3000 B.C.E. Sumerians produce the oldest known drawings of constellations as recurring designs on seals, vases, and gaming boards.

c. 3000 B.C.E. Construction begins on Stonehenge.

c. 700 B.C.E. Babylonians have already assembled extensive, relatively accurate records of celestial events, including charting the paths of planets and compiling observations of fixed stars.

c. 550 B.C.E. Greek philosopher and mathematician Pythagoras argues that Earth is round and develops an early system of cosmology to explain the nature and structure of the universe.

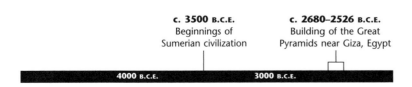

c. 3500 B.C.E.
Beginnings of
Sumerian civilization

c. 2680–2526 B.C.E.
Building of the Great
Pyramids near Giza, Egypt

4000 B.C.E.   3000 B.C.E.

c. 370 B.C.E. Eudoxus of Cnidus develops a system to explain the motions of the planets based on spheres.

c. 280 B.C.E. Greek mathematician and astronomer Aristarchus proposes that the planets, including Earth, revolve around the Sun.

c. 240 B.C.E. Greek astronomer and geographer Eratosthenes calculates the circumference of Earth with remarkable accuracy from the angle of the Sun's rays at separate points on the planet's surface.

c. 130 B.C.E. Greek astronomer Hipparchus develops the first accurate star map and star catalog covering about 850 stars, including a scale of magnitude to indicate the apparent brightness of the stars; it is the first time such a scale has been used.

140 C.E. Alexandrian astronomer Ptolemy publishes his Earth-centered or geocentric theory of the solar system.

c. 1000 The Maya build El Caracol, an observatory, in the city of Chichén Itzá.

1045 A Chinese government official publishes the *Wu-ching Tsung-yao* (*Complete Compendium of Military Classics*), which details the use of "fire arrows" launched by charges of gunpowder, the first true rockets.

1268 English philosopher and scientist Roger Bacon publishes a book on chemistry called *Opus Majus* (*Great Work*) in which he describes in detail the process of making gunpowder, becoming the first European to do so.

1543 Polish astronomer Nicolaus Copernicus publishes his Sun-centered, or heliocentric, theory of the solar system.

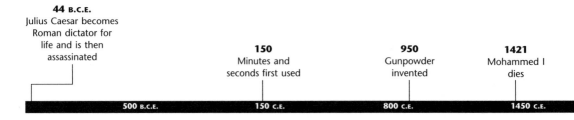

44 B.C.E.
Julius Caesar becomes Roman dictator for life and is then assassinated

150
Minutes and seconds first used

950
Gunpowder invented

1421
Mohammed I dies

500 B.C.E.　　150 C.E.　　800 C.E.　　1450 C.E.

November 1572 Danish astronomer Tycho Brahe discovers what later proves to be a supernova in the constellation of Cassiopeia.

1577 German armorer Leonhart Fronsperger writes a book on firearms in which he describes a device called a *roget* that uses a base of gunpowder wrapped tightly in paper. Historians believe this resulted in the modern word "rocket."

c. late 1500s German fireworks maker Johann Schmidlap invents the step rocket, a primitive version of a multistage rocket.

1608 Dutch lens-grinder Hans Lippershey creates the first optical telescope.

1609 German astronomer Johannes Kepler publishes his first two laws of planetary motion.

1609 Italian mathematician and astronomer Galileo Galilei develops his own telescope and uses it to discover four moons around Jupiter, craters on the Moon, and the Milky Way.

1633 Galileo is placed under house arrest for the rest of his life by the Catholic Church for advocating the heliocentric theory of the solar system.

1656 French poet and soldier Savinien de Cyrano de Bergerac publishes a fantasy novel about a man who travels to the Moon in a device powered by exploding firecrackers.

1687 English physicist and mathematician Isaac Newton publishes his three laws of motion and his law of universal gravitation in the much-acclaimed *Philosophiae Naturalis Principia Mathematica* (*Mathematical Principles of Natural Philosophy*).

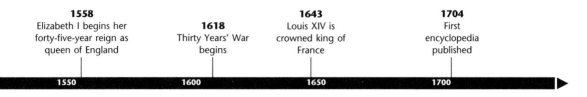

1558 Elizabeth I begins her forty-five-year reign as queen of England

1618 Thirty Years' War begins

1643 Louis XIV is crowned king of France

1704 First encyclopedia published

1550   1600   1650   1700

1781   English astronomer William Herschel discovers the planet Uranus using a reflector telescope he had made.

1804   English artillery expert William Congreve develops the first ship-fired rockets.

1844   English inventor William Hale invents the stickless, spin-stabilized rocket.

1865   French writer Jules Verne publishes *From the Earth to the Moon,* the first of two novels he would write about traveling to the Moon.

1895   Russian rocket scientist Konstantin Tsiolkovsky describes travel to the Moon, other planets, and beyond in "Dreams of the Earth and Sky and the Effects of Universal Gravitation." He also introduces the concept of an artificial Earth.

1897   The Yerkes Observatory in Williams Bay, Wisconsin, which houses the largest refractor telescope in the world, is completed.

1903   Russian scientist and rocket expert Konstantin Tsiolkovsky publishes an article titled "Exploration of the Universe with Reaction Machines," in which he presents the basic formula that determines how rockets perform.

1919   American scientist Robert H. Goddard publishes "**A Method of Reaching Extreme Altitudes**," an article about propelling rockets into space. In the conclusion he suggests the possibility of sending a multi-stage rocket to the Moon.

1923   German physicist Hermann Oberth publishes a ninety-two-page pamphlet titled *Die Rakete zu den Planetenräumen* (*The Rocket into Interplanetary Space*) in which he explains the mathematical theory of rock-

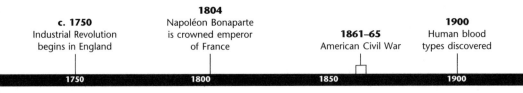

c. 1750
Industrial Revolution
begins in England

1804
Napoléon Bonaparte
is crowned emperor
of France

1861–65
American Civil War

1900
Human blood
types discovered

1750   1800   1850   1900

etry, speculates on the effects of spaceflight on the human body, and theorizes on the possibility of placing satellites in space.

1924   Using the 100-inch telescope at Mount Wilson near Los Angeles, California, American astronomer Edwin Hubble observes billions of galaxies beyond the Milky Way.

March 16, 1926 American physicist and space pioneer Robert H. Goddard launches the world's first liquid-propellant rocket.

1929   Using the Hooker Telescope at the Mount Wilson Observatory in southern California, U.S. astronomer Edwin Hubble develops what comes to be known as Hubble's law, which describes the rate of expansion of the universe.

1929   Konstantin Tsiolkovsky writes about placing rockets into space by arranging them in packets, or "cosmic rocket trains." This becomes known as "rocket staging."

1930   The International Astronomical Union (IAU) sets the definitive boundaries of the eighty-eight recognized constellations.

1942   German rocket scientist Wernher von Braun leads the Peenemünde team in the first successful launch of the V-2 rocket. By the end of World War II, Germany has fired approximately six thousand V-2s on Allied targets.

September 8, 1944 Germany launches V-2 rockets, the first true ballistic missiles, to strike targets in Paris, France, and London, England.

1947 The 200-inch-diameter Hale Telescope becomes operational at the Palomar Observatory in southern California.

1952 Wernher von Braun publishes **"Man on the Moon: The Journey,"** the first in a series of articles on space travel in *Collier's* magazine.

March 9, 1955 German-born American engineer Wernher von Braun appears on "Man in Space," the first of three space-related television shows he and American movie producer Walt Disney create for American audiences.

July 1, 1957, to December 31, 1958 During this eighteen-month period, known as the International Geophysical Year, more than ten thousand scientists and technicians representing sixty-seven countries engage in a comprehensive series of global geophysical activities.

October 4, 1957 The Soviet newspaper *Pravda* releases **"Announcement of the First Satellite,"** revealing that *Sputnik 1* had been launched the previous day. This event, which catches the world by surprise, intensifies the space race between the Soviets and the United States.

January 31, 1958 *Explorer 1,* the United States's first successful artificial satellite, is launched into space.

March 17, 1958 The U.S. Navy launches the small, artificial satellite *Vanguard 1.* The oldest human-made object in space, it remains in orbit around Earth.

October 1, 1958 The National Aeronautics and Space Administration (NASA) begins work.

January 2, 1959 The Soviet Union launches the space probe *Luna 1,* which becomes the first human-made object to escape Earth's gravity.

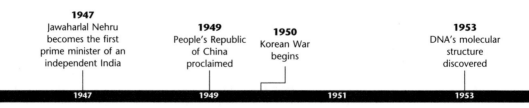

1947
Jawaharlal Nehru becomes the first prime minister of an independent India

1949
People's Republic of China proclaimed

1950
Korean War begins

1953
DNA's molecular structure discovered

1947   1949   1951   1953

April 9, 1959 NASA announces the selection of the first American astronauts—the Mercury 7 astronauts: M. Scott Carpenter, Leroy G. "Gordo" Cooper Jr., John Glenn, Virgil I. "Gus" Grissom, Walter M. "Wally" Schirra Jr., Alan B. Shepard Jr., and Donald K. "Deke" Slayton.

September 13, 1959 The Soviet space probe *Luna 2* becomes the first human-made object to land on the Moon when it makes a hard landing east of the Sea of Serenity.

1960 The first of the Mercury 13 women aviators secretly begin testing for the Mercury astronaut training program.

August 18, 1960 The United States launches *Discoverer 14*, its first spy satellite.

October 23, 1960 More than one hundred Soviet technicians are incinerated when a rocket explodes on a launch pad. Known as the Nedelin catastrophe, it is the worst accident in the history of the Soviet space program.

1961 NASA cancels the women's astronaut testing program.

April 12, 1961 Soviet cosmonaut Yuri Gagarin orbits Earth aboard *Vostok 1*, becoming the first human in space.

May 5, 1961 U.S. astronaut Alan Shepard makes a suborbital flight in the capsule *Freedom 7*, becoming the first American to fly into space.

May 25, 1961 U.S. President John F. Kennedy delivers his speech, **"Urgent National Needs,"** in which he announces that the United States will put a man on the Moon by the end of the decade.

1962 A Congressional hearing is held on discrimination against women in the U.S. space program. NASA announces that the Mercury 13 did not qualify as astronauts because they had not received jet-pilot training. No American woman travels in space until 1983.

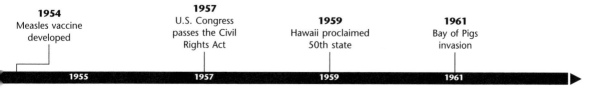

1954
Measles vaccine
developed

1957
U.S. Congress
passes the Civil
Rights Act

1959
Hawaii proclaimed
50th state

1961
Bay of Pigs
invasion

1955   1957   1959   1961

February 20, 1962 U.S. astronaut John Glenn becomes the first American to circle Earth when he makes three orbits in the *Friendship 7* Mercury spacecraft.

August 27, 1962 *Mariner 2* is launched into orbit, becoming the first interplanetary space probe.

June 16, 1963 Soviet cosmonaut Valentina Tereshkova rides aboard *Vostok 6,* becoming the first woman in space.

November 1, 1963 The world's largest single radio telescope, at Arecibo Observatory in Puerto Rico, officially begins operation.

March 18, 1965 During the Soviet Union's *Voskhod 2* orbital mission, cosmonaut Alexei Leonov performs the first spacewalk, or extravehicular activity (EVA).

February 3, 1966 The Soviet Union's *Luna 9* soft-lands on the Moon and sends back to Earth the first images of the lunar surface.

January 27, 1967 The Project Apollo mission begins tragically when astronauts Virgil "Gus" Grissom, Roger Chaffee, and Edward White die aboard ***Apollo 1.*** Their deaths are caused by a fire that ignites in the spacecraft on the launch pad during a practice session at Kennedy Space Center, Florida.

April 24, 1967 Soviet cosmonaut Vladimir Komarov becomes the first fatality during an actual spaceflight when the parachute from *Soyuz 1* fails to open and the capsule slams into the ground after reentry.

December 24, 1968 *Apollo 8,* with three U.S. astronauts aboard, becomes the first manned spacecraft to enter orbit around the Moon.

July 20, 1969 U.S. astronaut Neil Armstrong becomes the first human to set foot on the Moon. He is followed by fellow astronaut Edwin Eugene "Buzz" Aldrin.

1963
U.S. president
John F. Kennedy
is assassinated

1964
Supercomputer
debuts

1965
Malcolm X
assassinated

1966
U.S. Department
of Transportation
founded

1963   1964   1965   1966

April 14, 1970 An oxygen tank in the *Apollo 13* service module explodes while the craft is in space, putting the lives of the three U.S. astronauts onboard into serious jeopardy.

December 14, 1970 U.S. astronauts Eugene Cernan and Harrison Schmitt lift off from the Moon after having spent seventy-five hours on the surface. They are the last humans to have set foot on the Moon as of the early twenty-first century.

December 15, 1970 The Soviet space probe *Venera 7* arrives at Venus, making the first-ever successful landing on another planet.

1971 NASA administrator James C. Fletcher publishes "**The Space Shuttle,**" an article in which he presents the argument for a U.S. space shuttle program.

April 19, 1971 The Soviet Union launches *Salyut 1,* the first human-made space station.

November 13, 1971 The U.S. probe *Mariner 9* becomes the first spacecraft to orbit another planet when it enters orbit around Mars.

January 5, 1972 In "**The Statement by President Nixon,**" U.S. president Richard M. Nixon announces the initiation of a space shuttle program as NASA's follow-up human space flight effort.

May 14, 1973 *Skylab,* the first and only U.S. space station, is launched.

December 4, 1973 The U.S. space probe *Pioneer 10* makes the first flyby of Jupiter.

March 29, 1974 The U.S. space probe *Mariner 10* makes the first of three flybys of Mercury.

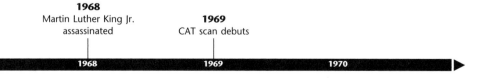

1968
Martin Luther King Jr. assassinated

1969
CAT scan debuts

1967   1968   1969   1970

July 15 to 24, 1975 The Apollo-Soyuz Test Project is undertaken as an international docking mission between the United States and the Soviet Union.

July 20, 1976 The lander of the U.S. space probe *Viking 1* makes the first successful soft landing on Mars.

September 17, 1976 The first space shuttle orbiter, known as OV-101, rolls out of an assembly facility in Palmdale, California.

January 26, 1978 NASA launches the International Ultraviolet Explorer, considered the most successful UV satellite and perhaps the most productive astronomical telescope ever.

1979 American writer Tom Wolfe publishes ***The Right Stuff,*** a book about the U.S. space program in the 1950s and early 1960s.

July 11, 1979 *Skylab* falls into Earth's atmosphere and burns up over the Indian Ocean.

October 1979 The United Kingdom Infrared Telescope, the world's largest telescope dedicated solely to infrared astronomy, begins operation in Hawaii near the summit of Mauna Kea.

November 12, 1980 The U.S. probe *Voyager 1* makes a flyby of Saturn and sends back the first detailed photographs of the ringed planet.

April 12, 1981 U.S. astronauts John W. Young and Robert L. Crippen fly the space shuttle *Columbia* on the first orbital flight of NASA's new reusable spacecraft.

1983 *The Right Stuff,* the movie version of Tom Wolfe's bestselling book of the same title, becomes a hit in the United States.

1971
Microprocessor
introduced

1973
General Motors
offers automobile
airbag

1977
Star Wars is
released

1978
Test-tube
baby born

1972   1974   1976   1978

June 18, 1983 U.S. astronaut Sally Ride becomes America's first woman in space when she rides aboard the space shuttle *Challenger.*

August 30, 1983 U.S. astronaut Guy Bluford flies aboard the space shuttle *Challenger,* becoming the first African American in space.

January 25, 1984 U.S. president Ronald Reagan directs NASA to develop a permanently manned space station within a decade.

1985 In **"Remarks of the Vice President Announcing the Winner of the Teacher-in-Space Project,"** U.S. vice president George H. W. Bush announces that grade-school teacher Christa McAuliffe has been selected to become the first civilian in space. She will travel aboard the space shuttle *Challenger.*

January 28, 1986 The space shuttle *Challenger* explodes seventy-three seconds after launch because of poorly sealing O-rings on the booster rocket, killing all seven astronauts aboard.

January 28, 1986 President Ronald Reagan mourns the loss of the *Challenger* crew in his **"Address to the Nation on the Explosion of the Space Shuttle Challenger."**

February 1986 Former U.S. astronaut Neil Armstrong is appointed deputy chair of the Rogers Commission to investigate the explosion of the space shuttle *Challenger.*

February 20, 1986 The Soviet Union launches the core module of its new space station, *Mir,* into orbit.

June 6, 1986 The Rogers Commission releases a report stating that the *Challenger* explosion was caused by defective O-rings. It recommends major changes at NASA, and an American shuttle is not launched again until 1988.

1979–80
Fifty-two Americans are held hostage in Iran

1981
AIDS is first recognized

1983
U.S. invades Grenada

1985
DNA fingerprinting developed

1980   1982   1984   1986

May 4, 1989 The space shuttle *Atlantis* lifts off carrying the *Magellan* probe, the first planetary explorer to be launched by a space shuttle.

April 25, 1990 Astronauts aboard the space shuttle *Discovery* deploy the Hubble Space Telescope.

April 7, 1991 The Compton Gamma Ray Observatory is placed into orbit by astronauts aboard the space shuttle *Atlantis.*

December 1993 Astronauts aboard the space shuttle *Endeavour* complete repairs to the primary mirror of the Hubble Space Telescope.

February 3, 1995 The space shuttle *Discovery* lifts off under the control of U.S. astronaut Eileen M. Collins, the first female pilot on a shuttle mission.

December 2, 1995 The Solar and Heliospheric Observatory is launched to study the Sun.

December 7, 1995 The U.S. space probe *Galileo* goes into orbit around Jupiter, dropping a mini-probe to the planet's surface.

March 24, 1996 U.S. astronaut Shannon Lucid begins her 188-day stay aboard *Mir,* a U.S. record for spaceflight endurance at that time.

October 1996 The second of the twin 33-foot Keck telescopes on Mauna Kea, Hawaii, the world's largest optical and infrared telescopes, begins science observations. The first began observations three years earlier.

1997 NASA publishes *The Space Science Enterprise Strategic Plan: Origins, Evolution, and Destiny of the Cosmos and Life,* which outlines questions to be addressed in future space science missions.

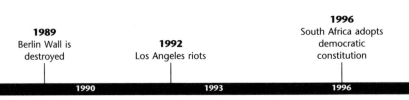

1989
Berlin Wall is
destroyed

1992
Los Angeles riots

1996
South Africa adopts
democratic
constitution

1987   1990   1993   1996

July 2, 1997 The U.S. space probe *Mars Pathfinder* lands on Mars and releases *Sojourner,* the first Martian rover.

October 15, 1997 The *Cassini-Huygens* spacecraft, bound for Saturn, is launched.

1998 In ***Apollo Expeditions to the Moon,*** *Apollo 11* crew members Michael Collins and Edwin "Buzz" Aldrin reminisce about their flight to the Moon.

1998 In **"Interview with Shannon Lucid,"** astronaut Shannon Lucid discusses her record-setting stay on the *Mir.*

January 6, 1998 NASA launches the *Lunar Prospector* probe to improve understanding of the origin, evolution, current state, and resources of the Moon.

October 29, 1998 At age seventy-seven, U.S. senator John Glenn, one of the original Mercury astronauts, becomes the oldest astronaut to fly into space when he lifts off aboard the space shuttle *Discovery.*

November 11, 1998 Russia launches Zarya, the control module and first piece of the International Space Station, into orbit.

1999 Former U.S. astronaut John Glenn publishes ***John Glenn: A Memoir,*** an autobiography in which he recounts his two historic space flights: as the first American to orbit Earth and then as the oldest person to travel in space.

July 23, 1999 The Chandra X-ray Observatory is deployed from the space shuttle *Columbia.*

February 21, 2001 The U.S. space probe *NEAR Shoemaker* becomes the first spacecraft to land on an asteroid.

March 23, 2001 After more than 86,000 orbits around Earth, Russia takes the *Mir* out of service. Most of the space

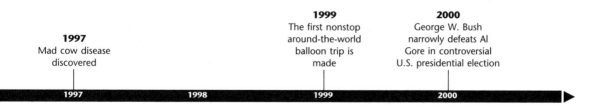

1997
Mad cow disease
discovered

1999
The first nonstop
around-the-world
balloon trip is
made

2000
George W. Bush
narrowly defeats Al
Gore in controversial
U.S. presidential election

1997　　　1998　　　1999　　　2000

station burns up over the Pacific Ocean, and the remaining remnants crash into the Pacific Ocean in 2004.

April 28, 2001 U.S. investment banker Dennis Tito, the world's first space tourist, lifts off aboard a Soyuz spacecraft for a week-long stay on the International Space Station.

2003 American author Martha Ackmann publishes *The Mercury 13: The True Story of Thirteen Women and the Dream of Space Flight.* In the book she gives an account of the pioneering efforts of the women who wanted to become astronauts.

February 1, 2003 The space shuttle *Columbia* breaks apart in flames above Texas, sixteen minutes before it is supposed to touch down in Florida, because of damage to the shuttle's thermal-protection tiles. All seven astronauts aboard are killed.

February 2, 2003 NASA administrator Sean O'Keefe appoints the Columbia Accident Investigation Board (CAIB) to determine the causes of the *Columbia* accident.

June 2003 The Canadian Space Agency launches MOST, its first space telescope successfully launched into space and also the smallest space telescope in the world.

August 25, 2003 NASA launches the Space Infrared Telescope Facility, subsequently renamed the Spitzer Space Telescope, the most sensitive instrument ever to look at the infrared spectrum in the universe.

August 26, 2003 The CAIB releases its official findings on August 26 in the "**Columbia Accident Investigation Board Report.**" The report calls for sweeping changes in NASA's organization and the way the agency con-

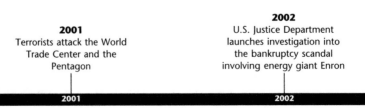

2001
Terrorists attack the World
Trade Center and the
Pentagon

2001

2002
U.S. Justice Department
launches investigation into
the bankruptcy scandal
involving energy giant Enron

2002

ducts its flights. The CAIB recommends grounding shuttle flights until safety procedures are reviewed.

October 15, 2003 Astronaut Yang Liwei lifts off aboard the spacecraft *Shenzhou 5,* becoming the first Chinese to fly into space.

2004 The Mars rovers Spirit and Opportunity begin sending back to Earth pictures of craters, hills, and empty landscape on Mars. Scientists seek to determine the existence of life on Mars.

January 14, 2004 U.S. president George W. Bush outlines a new course for U.S. space exploration in **"Remarks by the President on U.S. Space Policy,"** including plans to send future manned missions to the Moon and Mars.

June 21, 2004 Civilian pilot Mike Melvill flies the rocket plane *SpaceShipOne* to an altitude of more than 62.5 miles, becoming the first person to pilot a privately built craft beyond the internationally recognized boundary of space.

June 30, 2004 The *Cassini-Huygens* spacecraft becomes the first exploring vehicle to orbit Saturn.

2003
The United States
declares war on Iraq

2003   2004

Words to Know

A

Allies: Alliances of countries in military opposition to another group of nations. In World War II, the Allied powers included Great Britain, the Soviet Union, and the United States.

antimatter: Matter that is exactly the same as normal matter, but with the opposite spin and electrical charge.

apogee: The point in the orbit of an artificial satellite or Moon that is farthest from Earth.

artificial satellite: A human-made device that orbits Earth and other celestial bodies and that follows the same gravitational laws that govern the orbit of a natural satellite.

asterism: A collection of stars within a constellation that forms an apparent pattern.

astrology: The study of the supposed effects of celestial objects on the course of human affairs.

astronautics: The science and technology of spaceflight.

astronomy: The scientific study of the physical universe beyond Earth's atmosphere.

atomic bomb: An explosive device whose violent power is due to the sudden release of energy resulting from the splitting of nuclei of a heavy chemical element (plutonium or uranium), a process called fission.

aurora: A brilliant display of streamers, arcs, or bands of light visible in the night sky, chiefly in the polar regions. It is caused by electrically charged particles from the Sun that are drawn into the atmosphere by Earth's magnetic field.

B

ballistic missile: A missile that travels at a velocity less than what is needed to place it in orbit and that follows a curved path (trajectory) back to Earth's surface once it has reached a given altitude.

bends: A painful and sometimes fatal disorder caused by the formation of gas bubbles in the blood stream and tissues when a decrease in air pressure occurs too rapidly.

big bang theory: The theory that explains the beginning of the universe as a tremendous explosion from a single point that occurred about thirteen billion years ago.

Big Three: The trio of U.S. president Franklin D. Roosevelt, Soviet leader Joseph Stalin, and British prime minister Winston Churchill; also refers to the countries of the United States, the Soviet Union, and Great Britain.

binary star: A pair of stars orbiting around one another, linked by gravity.

black hole: The remains of a massive star that has burned out its nuclear fuel and collapsed under tremendous gravitational force into a single point of infinite mass and gravity from which nothing escapes, not even light.

Bolshevik: A member of the revolutionary political party of Russian workers and peasants that became the Communist Party after the Russian Revolution of 1917.

brown dwarf: A small, cool, dark ball of matter that never completes the process of becoming a star.

C

capitalism: An economic system in which property and businesses are privately owned. Prices, production, and distribution of goods are determined by competition in a market relatively free of government intervention.

celestial mechanics: The scientific study of the influence of gravity on the motions of celestial bodies.

celestial sphere: An imaginary sphere of gigantic radius with Earth located at its center.

Cepheid variable: A pulsating star that can be used to measure distance in space.

chromatic aberration: Blurred coloring of the edge of an image when visible light passes through a lens, caused by the bending of the different wavelengths of the light at different angles.

Cold War: A prolonged conflict for world dominance from 1945 to 1991 between the two superpowers: the democratic, capitalist United States and the Communist Soviet Union. The weapons of conflict were commonly words of propaganda and threats.

Communism: A system of government in which the nation's leaders are selected by a single political party that controls almost all aspects of society. Private ownership of property is eliminated and government directs all economic production. The goods produced and wealth accumulated are, in theory, shared relatively equally by all. All religious practices are banned.

concave lens: A lens with a hollow bowl shape; it is thin in the middle and thick along the edges.

constellation: One of eighty-eight recognized groups of stars that seems to make up a pattern or picture on the celestial sphere.

convex lens: A lens with a bulging surface like the outer surface of a ball; it is thicker in the middle and thinner along the edges.

corona: The outermost and hottest layer of the Sun's atmosphere that extends out into space for millions of miles.

cosmic radiation: High-energy radiation coming from all directions in space.

D

dark matter: Virtually undetectable matter that does not emit or reflect light and that is thought to account for 90 percent of the mass of the universe, acting as a "cosmic glue" that holds together galaxies and clusters of galaxies.

democracy: A system of government that allows multiple political parties. Members of the parties are elected to various government offices by popular vote of the people.

détente: A relaxing of tensions between rival nations, marked by increased diplomatic, commercial, and cultural contact.

docking system: Mechanical and electronic devices that work jointly to bring together and physically link two spacecraft in space.

E

eclipse: The obscuring of one celestial object by another.

ecliptic: The imaginary plane of Earth's orbit around the Sun.

electromagnetic radiation: Radiation that transmits energy through the interaction of electricity and magnetism.

electromagnetic spectrum: The entire range of wavelengths of electromagnetic radiation.

epicycle: A small secondary orbit incorrectly added to the planetary orbits by early astronomers to account for periods in which the planets appeared to move backward with respect to Earth.

escape velocity: The minimum speed that an object, such as a rocket, must have in order to escape completely from the gravitational influence of a planet or a star.

exhaust velocity: The speed at which the exhaust material leaves the nozzle of a rocket engine.

F

flyby: A type of space mission in which the spacecraft passes close to its target but does not enter orbit around it or land on it.

focus: The position at which rays of light from a lens converge to form a sharp image.

force: A push or pull exerted on an object by an outside agent, producing an acceleration that changes the object's state of motion.

G

galaxy: A huge region of space that contains billions of stars, gas, dust, nebulae, and empty space all bound together by gravity.

gamma rays: Short-wavelength, high-energy radiation formed either by the decay of radioactive elements or by nuclear reactions.

geocentric model: The flawed theory that Earth is at the center of the solar system, with the Sun, the Moon, and the other planets revolving around it. Also known as the Ptolemaic model.

geosynchronous orbit: An orbit in which a satellite revolves around Earth at the same rate at which Earth rotates on its axis; thus, the satellite remains positioned over the same location on Earth.

gravity: The force of attraction between objects, the strength of which depends on the mass of each object and the distance between them.

gunpowder: An explosive mixture of charcoal, sulfur, and potassium nitrate.

H

hard landing: The deliberate, destructive impact of a space vehicle on a predetermined celestial object.

heliocentric model: The theory that the Sun is at the center of the solar system and all planets revolve around it. Also known as the Copernican model.

heliosphere: The vast region permeated by charged particles flowing out from the Sun that surrounds the Sun and extends throughout the solar system.

Hellenism: The culture, ideals, and pattern of life of ancient Greece.

hydrocarbon: A compound that contains only two elements, carbon and hydrogen.

hydrogen bomb: A bomb more powerful than the atomic bomb that derives its explosive energy from a nuclear fusion reaction.

hyperbaric chamber: A chamber where air pressure can be carefully controlled; used to acclimate divers, astronauts, and others gradually to changes in air pressure and air composition.

I

inflationary theory: The theory that the universe underwent a period of rapid expansion immediately following the big bang.

infrared radiation: Electromagnetic radiation with wavelengths slightly longer than that of visible light.

interferometer: A device that uses two or more telescopes to observe the same object at the same time in the same wavelength to increase angular resolution.

interplanetary: Between or among planets.

interplanetary medium: The space between planets including forms of energy and dust and gas.

interstellar: Between or among the stars.

interstellar medium: The gas and dust that exists in the space between stars.

ionosphere: That part of Earth's atmosphere that contains a high concentration of particles that have been ionized, or electrically charged, by solar radiation. These particles help reflect certain radio waves over great distances.

J

jettison: To eject or discard.

L

light-year: The distance light travels in the near vacuum of space in one year, about 5.88 trillion miles (9.46 trillion kilometers).

liquid-fuel rocket: A rocket in which both the fuel and the oxidizing agent are in a liquid state.

M

magnetic field: A field of force around the Sun and the planets generated by electrical charges.

magnetism: A natural attractive energy of iron-based materials for other iron-based materials.

magnetosphere: The region of space around a celestial object that is dominated by the object's magnetic field.

mass: The measure of the total amount of matter in an object.

meteorite: A fragment of extraterrestrial material that makes it to the surface of a planet without burning up in the planet's atmosphere.

microgravity: A state where gravity is reduced to almost negligible levels, such as during spaceflight; commonly called weightlessness.

micrometeorite: A very small meteorite or meteoritic particle with a diameter less than a 0.04 inch (1 millimeter).

microwaves: Electromagnetic radiation with a wavelength longer than infrared radiation but shorter than radio waves.

moonlet: A small artificial or natural satellite.

N

natural science: A science, such as biology, chemistry, or physics, that deals with the objects, occurrences, or laws of nature.

neutron star: The extremely dense, compact, neutron-filled remains of a star following a supernova.

nuclear fusion: The merging of two hydrogen nuclei into one helium nucleus, accompanied by a tremendous release of energy.

O

observatory: A structure designed and equipped to observe astronomical phenomena.

oxidizing agent: A substance that can readily burn or promote the burning of any flammable material.

ozone layer: An atmospheric layer that contains a high proportion of ozone molecules that absorb incoming ultraviolet radiation.

P

payload: Any cargo launched aboard a spacecraft, including astronauts, instruments, and equipment.

perigee: The point in the orbit of an artificial satellite or Moon that is nearest to Earth.

physical science: Any of the sciences—such as astronomy, chemistry, geology, and physics—that deal mainly with nonliving matter and energy.

precession: The small wobbling motion Earth makes about its axis as it spins.

probe: An unmanned spacecraft sent to explore the Moon, other celestial bodies, or outer space; some probes are programmed to return to Earth while others are not.

propellant: The chemical mixture burned to produce thrust in rockets.

pulsar: A rapidly spinning, blinking neutron star.

Q

quasars: Extremely bright, star-like sources of radio waves that are found in remote areas of space and that are the oldest known objects in the universe.

R

radiation: The emission and movement of waves of atomic particles through space or other media.

radio waves: The longest form of electromagnetic radiation, measuring up to 6 miles (9.7 kilometers) from peak to peak in the wave.

Red Scare: A great fear among U.S. citizens in the late 1940s and early 1950s that communist influences were infiltrating U.S. society and government and could eventually lead to the overthrow of the American democratic system.

redshift: The shift of an object's light spectrum toward the red end of the visible light range, which is an indication that the object is moving away from the observer.

reflector telescope: A telescope that directs light from an opening at one end to a concave mirror at the far end, which reflects the light back to a smaller mirror that directs it to an eyepiece on the side of the telescope.

refractor telescope: A telescope that directs light waves through a convex lens (the objective lens), which bends the waves and brings them to a focus at a concave lens (the eyepiece) that acts as a magnifying glass.

retrofire: The firing of a spacecraft's engine in the direction opposite to which the spacecraft is moving in order to cut its orbital speed.

rover: A remote-controlled robotic vehicle.

S

sidereal day: The time for one complete rotation of Earth on its axis relative to a particular star.

soft landing: The slow-speed landing of a space vehicle on a celestial object to avoid damage to or the destruction of the vehicle.

solar arrays: Groups of solar cells or other solar collectors arranged to capture energy from the Sun and use it to generate electrical power.

solar day: The average time span from one noon to the next.

solar flare: Temporary bright spot that explodes on the Sun's surface, releasing an incredible amount of energy.

solar prominence: A tongue-like cloud of flaming gas projecting outward from the Sun's surface.

solar wind: Electrically charged subatomic particles that flow out from the Sun.

solid-fuel rocket: A rocket in which the fuel and the oxidizing agent exist in a solid state.

solstice: Either of the two times during the year when the Sun, as seen from Earth, is farthest north or south of the equator; the solstices mark the beginning of the summer and winter seasons.

space motion sickness: A condition similar to ordinary travel sickness, with symptoms that include loss of appetite, nausea, vomiting, gastrointestinal disturbances, and fatigue. The precise cause of the condition is not fully understood, though most scientists agree the problem originates in the balance organs of the inner ear.

space shuttle: A reusable winged spacecraft that transports astronauts and equipment into space and back.

space station: A large orbiting structure designed for long-term human habitation in space.

spacewalk: Technically known as an EVA, or extravehicular activity, an excursion outside a spacecraft or space station by an astronaut or cosmonaut wearing only a pressurized spacesuit and, possibly, some sort of maneuvering device.

spectrograph: A device that separates light by wavelengths to produce a spectrum.

splashdown: The landing of a manned spacecraft in the ocean.

star: A hot, roughly spherical ball of gas that emits light and other forms of electromagnetic radiation as a result of nuclear fusion reactions in its core.

stellar scintillation: The apparent twinkling of a star caused by the refraction of the star's light as it passes through Earth's atmosphere.

stellar wind: Electrically charged subatomic particles that flow out from a star (like the solar wind, but from a star other than the Sun).

sunspot: A cool area of magnetic disturbance that forms a dark blemish on the surface of the Sun.

supernova: The massive explosion of a relatively large star at the end of its lifetime.

T

telescope: An instrument that gathers light or some other form of electromagnetic radiation emitted by distant sources, such as celestial bodies, and brings it to a focus.

thrust: The forward force generated by a rocket.

U

ultraviolet radiation: Electromagnetic radiation of a wavelength just shorter than the violet (shortest wavelength) end of the visible light spectrum.

United Nations: An international organization, composed of most of the nations of the world, created in 1945 to preserve world peace and security.

V

Van Allen belts: Two doughnut-shaped belts of high-energy charged particles trapped in Earth's magnetic field.

X

X rays: Electromagnetic radiation of a wavelength just shorter than ultraviolet radiation but longer than gamma rays that can penetrate solids and produce an electrical charge in gases.

Y

Yalta Conference: A 1944 meeting between Allied leaders Joseph Stalin, Winston Churchill, and Franklin D. Roosevelt in anticipation of an Allied victory in Europe over the Nazis during World War II (1939–45). The leaders discussed how to manage lands conquered by Germany, and Roosevelt and Churchill urged Stalin to enter the Soviet Union in the war against Japan.

Text Credits

Following is list of the copyright holders who have granted us permission to reproduce excerpts from primary source documents in *Space Exploration: Primary Sources*. Every effort has been made to trace copyright; if omissions have been made, please contact us.

Copyrighted excerpts reproduced from the following books:

Ackermann, Martha. From *The Mercury 13: The Untold Story of Thirteen American Women and the Dream of Space Flight*. Random House, 2003. Copyright © 2003 by Martha Ackermann. All rights reserved. Reproduced by permission of Random House, Inc.

Glenn, John with Nick Taylor. From *John Glenn: A Memoir*, Bantam Books, 1999. Copyright © 1999 by John Glenn. All rights reserved. Reproduced by permission of Bantam Books, a division of Random House, Inc.

von Braun, Wernher. From "Man on the Moon: The Journey," in *Collier's* October 18, 1952. Reproduced by permission.

Space Exploration
Primary
Sources

Jules Verne

Excerpt from "Chapter 8—History of the Cannon," in **From the
Earth to the Moon: Passage Direct in Ninety-seven Hours
and Twenty Minutes**

Published in 1865; available at *Space Educators' Handbook, Johnson
Space Center,* NASA (Web site)

Science fiction is imaginative literature that is based on scientific principles. This literary genre, or distinct type of literature, is unlike fantasy literature such as *The Lord of the Rings* by J. R. R. Tolkien (1892–1973), which portrays fantastical events that have no basis in the real world. Science fiction emerged in the nineteenth century after science became increasingly important to society. It was not until the early part of the twentieth century, however, that a large number of authors began to write science fiction, mainly in the form of short stories. Magazines such as *Amazing Stories* and *Astounding Science Fiction,* both founded in the 1930s, brought science fiction into the homes of millions of readers. After the end of World War II (1939–45) there was a great boom in this kind of literature. The terrible devastation caused by the atomic bomb, dropped by the United States on Japan to end the war, prompted writers to imagine the advances, and the destruction, that could be created by science. Science fiction also became a popular subject in movies. By the 1950s science fiction was taken seriously as a literary and cinematic art form.

French author Jules Verne (1828–1905) is generally considered the father of science fiction. His immense catalogue of work, containing over forty science-fiction and adventure novels, has been translated from French into dozens of languages and has been read by people around the world. Although Verne wrote in the nineteenth century, his works foresaw the use of numerous scientific marvels, such as the submarine, television, the Aqua-Lung™ (a device used for breathing under water), and, most importantly, space travel. That all of these phenomena were later invented or achieved conveys that Verne's work was not fantasy, but rather a realistic glimpse into the future based on scientific speculation.

Born in Nantes, France, in 1828, Verne was a product of his time. In the nineteenth century people began to question traditional ways of looking at the world around them. The Christian Church was losing its traditional authority, and many people began to listen less often to their priest or pastor and more often to news of discoveries made by scientists. The average person was more interested in politics and individual rights than ever before. People debated how society should be organized, what role government should have in individual life, and what economic system best served the nation. Verne was a socialist (one who believes in communal ownership of property and a strong central government), but he did not follow the teachings of German political philosopher Karl Marx (1818–1883), who is considered the founder of socialism. Rather, Verne embraced the ideas of the French philosopher Henri Saint-Simon (1720–1825), believing that universal industrial and scientific production would unify the world. He was captivated by this vision and wove themes of harmonious industrial cooperation into his works.

Verne was fascinated by science. His most notable novels, such as *Journey to the Center of the Earth* (1872) and *Twenty Thousand Leagues under the Sea* (1873), have scientific principles at their core. Although Verne's stories contain elements of adventure tales, they were completely different from any other fiction being written at the time. Typically, Verne put his characters in specific places at specific times, requiring that they draw upon their knowledge of science to overcome obstacles within the natural world.

By using a mixture of imagination, practicality, and scientific training, Verne created visions of the future that, decades later, did not seem so fantastical as they did during the time when he was writing.

Verne wrote his most political book, *From the Earth to the Moon: Passage Direct in Ninety-seven Hours and Twenty Minutes,* during the American Civil War (1861–65). He wondered how the American economy, which was completely dependent on the war industry, could survive after the war. More importantly, he wondered how the American people, who were putting all their energies into destroying one another, would redirect their energy when peace was declared. In the book he depicts the adventures of a group of Civil War veterans who organize the Baltimore Gun Club. Led by club president Impey Barbicane, the club members theorize that by melting down all the cannons left

Jules Verne.

over from the war, they will be able to make a cannon that is large enough to launch a projectile (a rocket-like object projected by external force and continuing in motion) carrying human cargo to the Moon. From the Moon they will be able to travel to other planets. The men call the cannon the *Columbiad,* and they draw up plans that attract international attention. Receiving funds from groups around the world, the club members soon build the cannon and a large telescope to monitor the projectile's flight in space. After a huge cooperative effort, the *Columbiad* launches the projectile into space carrying humans bound for interplanetary travel. The projectile does not land on the Moon but instead is drawn into the Moon's gravitational pull. At the end of the book it is unclear whether the projectile will be destroyed or will remain forever in orbit.

H. G. Wells

The English author H. G. Wells (1866–1946) was another influential nineteenth-century science-fiction writer. Like Jules Verne, Wells was a committed socialist. Calling his novels "scientific romances," he depicted the dark side of human nature and warned about the misuse of technology. In these works he predicted devastating global conflicts, the development of atomic weaponry, and the advent of chemical warfare. Among his most popular early science-fiction novels were *The Time Machine, The War of the Worlds, The Invisible Man,* and *The Island of Doctor Moreau.* Today, Wells is perhaps best known for *The War of the Worlds* (1898), which describes a Martian invasion of Earth. This novel was the basis of one of the more memorable events of the twentieth century: On an October evening in 1938, the American actor Orson Welles (1915–1985) and his Mercury Theater players broadcast a live radio dramatization of *The War of the Worlds.* The performance was so realistic that listeners in New Jersey fled their homes in panic, believing they were actually being invaded by Martians.

Things to remember while reading an excerpt from "Chapter 8—History of the Cannon," in *From the Earth to the Moon:*

- Notice that Barbicane's committee members are skeptical about his ideas for a space rocket. They ask him detailed questions that require him to explain how it will be built, the materials they will use, and the ability of the finished product to remain aloft in space.

- Verne wrote *From the Earth to the Moon* almost one hundred years before the flight of *Apollo 11,* the first mission to the Moon (see Michael Collins and Edwin E. Aldrin Jr. entry). He firmly believed that human beings could and would travel into space.

- Although Verne's cannon seems fantastical, notice that he discusses many of the same issues that National Aeronautics and Space Administration (NASA) scientists had to consider when making the rockets that carried the *Apollo* spacecraft: the length of the apparatus, the materials needed to construct the vessel, the cost of the project, and the type of fuel needed to send the vessel into orbit.

Excerpt from "Chapter 8—History of the Cannon," in From the Earth to the Moon

*The resolutions passed at the last meeting produced a great effect out of doors. Timid people took fright at the idea of a shot weighing 20,000 pounds being launched into space; they asked what cannon could ever transmit a sufficient **velocity** to such a mighty mass. The minutes of the second meeting were destined triumphantly to answer such questions. The following evening the discussion was renewed.*

*"My dear colleagues," said Barbicane, without further **preamble**, "the subject now before us is the construction of the engine, its length, its composition, and its weight. It is probable that we shall end by giving it gigantic dimensions; but however great may be the difficulties in the way, our mechanical genius will readily **surmount** them. Be good enough, then, to give me your attention, and do not hesitate to make objections at the close. I have no fear of them. The problem before us is how to communicate an initial force of 12,000 yards per second to a shell of 108 inches in diameter, weighing 20,000 pounds. Now when a projectile is launched into space, what happens to it? It is acted upon by three independent forces: the resistance of the air, the attraction of the earth, and the force of **impulsion** with which it is **endowed**. Let us examine these three forces. The resistance of the air is of little importance. The atmosphere of the earth does not exceed forty miles. Now, with the given rapidity, the projectile will have **traversed** this in five seconds, and the period is too brief for the resistance of the medium to be regarded otherwise than as insignificant. Proceding [sic], then, to the attraction of the earth, that is, the weight of the shell, we know that this weight will diminish in the **inverse** ratio of the square of the distance. When a body left to itself falls to the surface of the earth, it falls five feet in the first second; and if the same body were removed 257,542 miles further off, in other words, to the distance of the moon, its fall would be reduced to about half a line in the first second. That is almost equivalent to a state of perfect rest. Our business, then, is to overcome progressively this action of **gravitation**. The mode of accomplishing that is by the force of impulsion."*

"There's the difficulty," broke in the major.

"True," replied the president; "but we will overcome that, for the force of impulsion will depend on the length of the engine and the

Velocity: Quickness of motion; speed.

Preamble: Introductory statement.

Surmount: Overcome.

Impulsion: Forward motion.

Endowed: Granted or given; contain.

Traversed: Crossed.

Inverse: Opposite in order, nature, or effect.

Gravitation: A force manifested by acceleration of two free material particles or bodies toward each other.

Illustration from *From the Earth to the Moon.* *(© Bettmann/Corbis)*

powder employed, the latter being limited only by the resisting power of the former. Our business, then, today is with the dimensions of the cannon."

"Now, up to the present time," said Barbicane, "our longest guns have not exceeded twenty-five feet in length. We shall therefore astonish the world by the dimensions we shall be obliged to adopt. It must evidently be, then, a gun of great range, since the length of the piece will increase the **detention** of the gas accumulated behind the projectile; but there is no advantage in passing certain limits."

"Quite so," said the major. "What is the rule in such a case?"

"Ordinarily the length of a gun is twenty to twenty-five times the diameter of the shot, and its weight two hundred and thirty-five to two hundred and forty times that of the shot."

"That is not enough," cried J. T. Maston **impetuously.**

"I agree with you, my good friend; and, in fact, following this proportion for a projectile nine feet in diameter, weighing 30,000 pounds, the gun would only have a length of two hundred and twenty-five feet, and a weight of 7,200,000 pounds."

"Ridiculous!" rejoined Maston. "As well take a pistol."

"I think so too," replied Barbicane; "that is why I propose to **quadruple** that length, and to construct a gun of nine hundred feet."

The general and the major offered some objections; nevertheless, the **proposition**, actively supported by the secretary, was definitely adopted.

"But," said Elphinstone, "what thickness must we give it?"

"A thickness of six feet," replied Barbicane.

"You surely don't think of mounting a mass like that upon a carriage?" asked the major.

"It would be a superb idea, though," said Maston.

"But **impracticable**," replied Barbicane. "No, I think of sinking this engine in the earth alone, binding it with hoops of wrought iron, and finally surrounding it with a thick mass of masonry of stone and cement. The piece once cast, must be **bored** with great precision, so as to preclude any possible **windage.** So there will be no loss whatever of gas, and all the expansive force of the powder will be employed in the propulsion."

"One simple question," said Elphinstone: "is our gun to be **rifled**?"

"No, certainly not," replied Barbicane; "we require an enormous initial velocity; and you are well aware that a shot quits a rifled gun less rapidly than it does a smooth-bore."

"True," rejoined the major.

The committee here adjourned for a few minutes to tea and sandwiches.

Detention: Confinement.

Impetuously: Without consideration or forethought.

Quadruple: Make four times as great or as many.

Proposition: Suggestion.

Impracticable: Impossible.

Bored: Make a cylindrical hole by digging away.

Windage: Space between the projectile of a smoothbore gun (an unrifled gun; that is, one without spiral grooves cut into the bore) and the surface of the bore.

Rifled: Cut spiral groves into a bore, or cylindrical hollow part, of a gun.

Illustration of the projectile approaching the Moon, from _From the Earth to the Moon._ _(© Bettmann/Corbis)_

Tenacity: Persistence or firmness.

Infusible: Incapable of being fused or joined.

Indissoluble: Incapable of being broken or undone; permanent.

Inoxidable: Cannot be oxidized, or combined with oxygen.

Corrosive: Wearing away; able to corrode.

On the discussion being renewed, "Gentlemen," said Barbicane, "we must now take into consideration the metal to be employed. Our cannon must be possessed of great **tenacity**, great hardness, be **infusible** by heat, **indissoluble**, and **inoxidable** by the **corrosive** action of acids."

"There is no doubt about that," replied the major; "and as we shall have to employ an immense quantity of metal, we shall not be at a loss for choice."

"Well, then," said Morgan, "I propose the best **alloy hitherto** known, which consists of one hundred parts of copper, twelve of tin, and six of brass."

"I admit," replied the president, "that this composition has yielded excellent results, but in the present case it would be too expensive, and very difficult to work. I think, then, that we ought to adopt a material excellent in its way and of low price, such as cast iron. What is your advice, major?"

"I quite agree with you," replied Elphinstone.

"In fact," continued Barbicane, "cast iron costs ten times less than bronze; it is easy to cast, it runs readily from the moulds of sand, it is easy of manipulation, it is at once economical of money and of time. In addition, it is excellent as a material, and I well remember that during the war, at the siege of Atlanta, some iron guns fired one thousand rounds at intervals of twenty minutes without injury."

"Cast iron is very brittle, though," replied Morgan.

"Yes, but it possesses great resistance. I will now ask our worthy secretary to calculate the weight of a cast-iron gun with a bore of nine feet and a thickness of six feet of metal."

"In a moment," replied Maston. Then, dashing off some algebraical formulae with marvelous facility, in a minute or two he declared the following result:

"The cannon will weigh 68,040 tons. And, at two cents a pound, it will cost—"

"Two million five hundred and ten thousand seven hundred and one dollars."

Maston, the major, and the general regarded Barbicane with uneasy looks.

"Well, gentlemen," replied the president, "I repeat what I said yesterday. Make yourselves easy; the millions will not be wanting."

With this assurance of their president the committee separated, after having fixed their third meeting for the following evening.

Alloy: Substance composed of two or more metals.

Hitherto: Up to this point.

What happened next . . .

Jules Verne went on to write dozens of successful and popular novels, including *Around the World in Eighty Days*. In 1892 he was inducted as an officer into the French Foreign Legion of Honor. Several successful films have been made from Verne's novels, including *Twenty Thousand Leagues under the Sea*, (1916 and 1954), *The Mysterious Island,* (1929 and 1961), *Journey to the Center of the Earth* (1959), and *Around the World in Eighty Days* (1956 and 2004).

Did you know . . .

- The term "science fiction" was not coined until 1926, when author Hugo Gernsback (1884–1967) used the term to describe the stories published in *Amazing Stories* magazine, a periodical dedicated exclusively to science fiction.

- Preeminent twentieth-century authors such as Aldous Huxley (1894–1963), C. S. Lewis (1898–1963), and Kurt Vonnegut (1922–) wrote science fiction in addition to their many other works. These "crossover" works by noted "serious" authors helped lend credibility to the genre of science fiction.

Consider the following . . .

- Jules Verne wrote his novels and stories before the invention of the automobile, telephone, airplane, television, and submarine—to name a few—yet his plots often involved such inventions. With all the advancements made in science today, can you think of an invention that might seem unthinkable today but could be used in everyday life one hundred years from now?

- Science fiction is still popular. Who is your favorite science-fiction writer? Explain the reasons for your choice.

For More Information

Books

Lottmann, Herbert R. *Jules Verne: An Exploratory Biography*. New York: St. Martin's Press, 1996.

Verne, Jules. *De la terre a la lune: Trajet direct en 97 heures 20 minutes*. Hetzel, 1865. Translated as *From the Earth to the Moon: Passage Direct in Ninety-seven Hours and Twenty Minutes*. New York: Newark Printing and Publishing, 1869.

Periodicals

Seelhorst, Mary. "Jules Verne." *Popular Mechanics* (July 2003): pp. 36–37.

Web Sites

"Jules Verne." *The Literature Network*. http://www.online-literature.com/verne/ (accessed on July 15, 2004).

Science Fiction Weekly. http://www.scifi.com/sfw/ (accessed on July 15, 2004).

Verne, Jules. "Chapter 8—History of the Cannon," in *From the Earth to the Moon. Space Educators' Handbook, Johnson Space Center/NASA* http://www.jsc.nasa.gov/er/seh/chapter8.htm (accessed on July 15, 2004).

Robert H. Goddard

Excerpt from **A Method of Reaching Extreme Altitudes**
Published by the Smithsonian Institution in 1919; also available at
Clark University **(Web site)**

Since the late seventeenth century, scientists have been fascinated with the idea of space travel. The initial scientific work that allowed scientists to dream about traveling to the stars was performed by Sir Isaac Newton (1642–1727). His ideas were built upon in the eighteenth and nineteenth centuries, allowing for the development of primitive rockets—not for space travel, however, but for use in wartime. These rockets changed the face of modern warfare, but they were so inaccurate that large numbers were required to destroy a single target. By the end of the nineteenth century, warfare rockets momentarily became obsolete. Once again, some scientists turned their attention to the sky, believing rockets were the perfect vehicles to explore the cosmos. However, a majority of scientists believed that no rocket could travel outside of the upper atmosphere of Earth. American scientist Robert Hutchings Goddard (1882–1945) challenged this view.

Goddard had dreamed of space travel since he was a young boy. He trained as a physicist and in 1908 obtained a doctor of philosophy degree (Ph.D.) from the prestigious Worchester Polytechnic Institute in Worchester, Massachusetts. The following year, he joined the faculty at the Institute and began work that revolutionized the field of space travel. In 1912 he developed the complicated and detailed mathematical theory of rocket propulsion; that is, what conditions and elements are required to propel a rocket successfully into space. In 1914 he received two patents for rockets: one for a rocket that used solid fuel and one for a rocket that used liquid fuel. In 1915 he publicly declared that space travel was possible. Although his work was sound, many of his fellow scientists continued to doubt him.

Despite skepticism, in 1916 the Smithsonian Institution granted Goddard funds to continue his work on rockets. He began his research as World War I (1914–18) raged across Europe, and, like his predecessors, he developed rocket technology for use on the battlefield. His development of several types of solid-fuel rockets that could be fired from handheld devices or from devices mounted on tripods (three-legged supports) forever changed mod-

Robert H. Goddard. *(AP/Wide World Photos)*

ern warfare. The bazooka (a portable military weapon consisting of a tube from which antitank rockets are launched) and the immensely powerful rockets used in World War II (1939–45) were developed as a result of Goddard's work.

Goddard's most important work was not in the field of weapons development, but in space travel. In 1916 he used the funds awarded him by the Smithsonian Institute and began work on liquid rocket propulsion. He initially felt that liquid hydrogen and liquid oxygen were the best fuels for rocket propulsion, but after conducting extensive research, he concluded that oxygen and gasoline, because of their less volatile (less explosive) compositions, were superior. He theorized that using these fuels in a properly designed apparatus (a rocket), the upper atmosphere, which was impossible to reach by hot-air balloon, could be reached. The rocket would have to travel at the speed of 6.95 miles (11.18 kilometers) per second (in a vacuum without air resistance) to overcome the pull of Earth's gravity and soar into space. He also stated that, by using his calculations, human beings could reach the Moon. In 1919, he published these findings in the classic study *A Method of Reaching Extreme Altitudes.*

Goddard was ridiculed by his fellow scientists and the popular media. The *New York Times* was extremely critical, questioning Goddard's scientific training and dismissing him as a misled dreamer in an editorial published on January 18, 1920. The following is an excerpt of Goddard's revolutionary paper, *A Method of Reaching Extreme Altitudes.*

Things to remember while reading an excerpt from *A Method of Reaching Extreme Altitudes:*

- Goddard wrote during a time when space travel was an idea in science fiction. Stating that human beings could actually send someone to the Moon *and* have that person return safely was revolutionary.

- In this excerpt, Goddard discusses the amount of fuel necessary to carry a rocket away from Earth and into space. He reaches these conclusions by conducting experiments based on the amount of flash powder (powder that, once ignited, produces a large flash of light) needed to produce visible light at certain distances. With these figures he makes his fuel calculations.

Excerpt from A Method of Reaching Extreme Altitudes

It is of extreme interest to speculate upon the possibility of proving that such extreme altitudes had been reached even if they actually were attained. In general, the proving would be a difficult matter. Thus, even if a mass of flash powder, arranged to be ignited automatically after a long interval of time, were projected vertically up-

ward, the light would at best be faint, and it would be difficult to **foretell**, even approximately, the direction in which it would most likely appear.

The only reliable procedure would be to send the smallest mass of flash powder possible to the dark surface of the moon when in conjunction (i.e., the "new moon"), in such a way that it would be ignited on impact. The light would then be visible in a powerful telescope. Further, the larger the **aperture** of the telescope, the greater would be the ease of seeing the flash, from the fact that a telescope enhances the brightness of the point sources, and dims the faint background.

An experiment was performed to find the minimum mass of flash powder that should be visible at any particular distance. In order to reproduce, approximately, the conditions that would obtain at the surface of the moon, the flash powder was placed in small capsules . . . held in glass tubes, closed by rubber stoppers. The tubes were **exhausted** to a pressure of from 3 to 10 centimeters of mercury, and sealed, the stoppers being painted with wax, to preserve the **vacuum**. Two **shellacked** wires, passing to the powder, permitted the firing of the powder by an automatic spark coil.

It was found that Victor flash powder was slightly superior to a mixture of powdered **magnesium** and **sodium nitrate**, in atomic proportions, and much superior to a mixture of powdered magnesium and **potassium chlorate**, also in atomic proportions.

In the actual test, six samples of Victor flash powder, varying in weight from 0.05 gram to 0.0029 gram were placed in tubes . . . and these tubes were fastened in blackened compartments of a box. The ignition system was placed in the back of the same box. . . . This system, comprised of a spark coil, operated by three triple cells of "Ever-ready" battery, placed two by two in parallel. The charge was firing on closing the primary switch at the left. The six-point switch at the right served to connect the tubes, in order, to the high-tension side of the coil.

The flashes were observed at a distance of 2.24 miles on a fairly clear night; and it was found that a mass of 0.0029 grams of Victor flash powder was visible, and that 0.015 gram was strikingly visible, all the observations being made with the unaided eye. The minimum mass of flash powder visible is thus surprisingly small.

From these experiments, it is seen that if this flash powder were exploded on the surface of the moon, distant 220,000 miles, and a

Foretell: Predict.

Aperture: Opening.

Exhausted: Emptied.

Vacuum: A space devoid of matter; emptiness of space.

Shellacked: Sealed with a varnishlike substance.

Magnesium: Metallic element used in chemical processes.

Sodium nitrate: Form of salt used as an oxidizing (combined with oxygen) agent.

Potassium chlorate: Oxidizing agent used in explosives.

telescope of one foot aperture were used—the exit pupil being not greater than the pupil of the eye (e.g., two millimeters)—we should need a mass of flash powder of

2.67 pounds, to be just visible, and

13.82 pounds or less, to be strikingly visible.

If we consider the final mass of the last "secondary" rocket plus the mass of the flash powder and its container, to be four times the mass of the flash powder alone, we should have, for the final mass of the rocket, four times the above masses. These final masses correspond to the "one pound final mass" which has been mentioned throughout the calculations.

The "total initial masses," or the masses necessary for the start at the earth, are at once obtained from the data given in table VII [not included]. Thus if the start is made from sea-level, and the "effective **velocity** of ejection" is 7,000 feet/second, we need 602 pounds for every pound that is to be sent to "**infinity.**"

We arrive, then, at the conclusion that the "total initial masses" necessary would be

6,436 pounds or 3.21 tons; flash just visible, and 33,278 pounds or 16.63 tons (or less); flash strikingly visible.

A "total initial mass" of 8 or 10 tons would, without doubt, raise sufficient flash powder for clear visibility.

These masses could, of course, be much reduced by the employment of a larger telescope. For example, with an aperture of two feet, the masses would be reduced to one-fourth of those just given. The use of such a large telescope would, however, limit considerably the possible number of observers. In all cases, the magnification should be so low that the entire lunar disk is in the field of the telescope.

It should be added that the probability of collision of a small object with meteors of the visible type is negligible. . . .

This plan of sending the mass of flash powder to the surface of the moon, although a matter of general interest, is not of obvious scientific importance. There are, however, developments of the general method under discussion, which involve a number of important features not herein mentioned, which could lead to results of much scientific interest. These developments involve many experimental difficulties, to be sure; but they depend upon nothing that is really impossible.

Velocity: Quickness of motion; speed.

Infinity: Unlimited extent of time, space, or quantity.

Summary

1. *An important part of the atmosphere, that extends for many miles beyond the reach of sounding balloons, has up to the present time been considered inaccessible. Data of great value in **meteorology** and in **solar physics** could be obtained by recording instruments sent into this region.*

2. *The rocket, in principle, is ideally suited for reaching high altitudes, in that it carries apparatus without jar, and does not depend upon the presence of air for propulsion. A new form of rocket apparatus, which embodies a number of improvements over the common form, is described in the present paper.*

3. *A theoretical treatment of the rocket principles shows that, if the velocity of **expulsion** of the gases were considerably increased and the ratio of propellant material to the entire rocket were also increased, a tremendous increase in range would result, from the fact that these two quantities enter **exponentially** in the expression for the initial mass of the rocket necessary to raise a given mass to a given height.*

4. *Experiments with ordinary rockets show that the efficiency of such rockets is of the order of 2 percent, and the velocity of ejection of the gases, 1,000 feet/second. For small rockets the values are slightly less.*

With a special type of steel chamber and nozzle, an efficiency has been obtained with smokeless powder of over 64 percent (higher than that of any heat engine ever before tested); and a velocity of nearly 8,000 feet/second, which is the highest velocity so far obtained in any way except in electrical discharge work.

5. *Experiments were repeated with the same chamber in vacuo, (in a vacuum) which demonstrated that the high velocity of the ejected gases was a real velocity and not merely an effort of reaction against the air. In fact, experiments performed at the pressures such as probably exist at an altitude of 30 miles gave velocities even higher than those obtained in air at atmospheric pressure, the increase in velocity probably being due to a difference in **ignition**. Results of the experiments indicate also that this velocity could be exceeded, with a modified form of apparatus.*

6. *Experiments with a large chamber demonstrated that not only are large chambers operative, but that the velocities and efficiencies are higher than for small chambers.*

Meteorology: Science that deals with the weather or weather forecasting.

Solar physics: Science that deals with matter and energy and their interactions relating to the Sun.

Expulsion: Ejection.

Exponentially: Rapidly increasing in size.

Ignition: Act of igniting; starting a fire.

Robert H. Goddard stands next to his first liquid-propelled rocket in anticipation of its first flight. *(NASA)*

---

7. *A calculation based upon the theory, involving data that is in part obtained by experiments, and in part what is considered as realizable in practice, indicates that the initial mass required to raise recording instruments of the order of one*

pound, even to the extreme upper atmosphere, is moderate. The initial mass necessary is likewise not excessive, even if the effective velocity is reduced by half. Calculations show, however, that any apparatus in which ordinary rockets are used would be impracticable owing to the very large initial mass that would be required.

8. *The recovery of the apparatus, on its return, need not be a difficult matter, from the fact that the time of ascent even to great altitudes in the atmosphere will be comparatively short, due to the high speed of the rocket throughout the greater part of its course. The time of descent will also be short; but free fall can be satisfactorily prevented by a suitable parachute. A parachute will be operative for the reason that high velocities and small atmospheric densities are essentially the same as low velocities and ordinary density.*

9. *Even if a mass of the order of a pound were propelled by the apparatus under consideration until it possessed sufficient velocity to escape earth's attraction, the initial mass need not be unreasonably large, for an effective velocity of ejection which is without doubt obtainable. A method is suggested whereby the passage of a body to such an extreme altitude could be demonstrated.*

Conclusion

Although the present paper is not the description of a working model, it is believed, nevertheless, that the theory and experiments, herein described, together settle all points that could seriously be questioned, and that it remains only to perform certain necessary preliminary experiments before an apparatus can be constructed that will carry recording instruments to any desired altitude.

What happened next . . .

The negative response to Goddard's findings did not stop the scientist from conducting more work. Although he became more reclusive and was rarely seen in public, Goddard was awarded 214 patents (documents securing to an inventor for a term of years the exclusive right to make, use, or sell an invention) in the area of rocket science. He built the first

Early space rocket, designed by Robert H. Goddard, is prepared for launch near Roswell, New Mexico, in 1935. *(© Bettmann/Corbis)*

liquid-fueled rocket, and his designs for fuel pumps, motors, and other essential components provided the foundation upon which all future rockets were built. On March 16, 1926, Goddard launched his first rocket, powered by oxygen and gasoline. The apparatus took only 2.5 seconds to rise 184 feet (56 meters). Most historians regard this event as the birth of modern rocketry. Not satisfied with this accomplishment, Goddard achieved another first on July 17, 1929, near Auburn, Massachusetts, when he flew the first instrument carrying a rocket; aboard was a camera to record the readings of an aneroid (liquidless) barometer (an instrument for determining the pressure of the atmosphere and for assisting in forecasting weather and determining altitude) and a thermometer. However, the launch was a failure. After rising 90 feet (27.43 meters), the rocket crashed. The fire caused by the crash was so severe that the neighbors complained and Goddard was forbidden to launch rockets in Massachusetts in the future.

Goddard was able to continue his work, however, largely due to the interest of Charles Lindbergh (1902–1974), who conducted the first solo airplane flight across the Atlantic. Goddard was awarded fifty thousand dollars by a private philanthropist, and used the money to establish a private experiment station near Roswell, New Mexico. There, from 1930 to 1941, Goddard launched a number of rockets, each more complex and advanced than the last. He developed the technology that allows a rocket to be steered by propelling the exhaust with a rudderlike device. In 1941, Goddard achieved his greatest success when he successfully launched a rocket to an altitude of 9,000 feet (2,743 meters). That same year, he worked with the naval service to develop rockets to assist jet planes taking off from aircraft carriers. He died in Baltimore, Maryland, on August 10, 1945, but his research affected science for decades to come.

Did you know . . .

- Long before the first person walked on the Moon or even traveled in space, Goddard thought that human beings could travel to the Moon and many other planets.

- Goddard theorized that jet planes could take off from aircraft carriers with minimal runway distance. He also envisioned a rocket-borne, or transported mail and express delivery service and pioneered research into nuclear-powered rockets.

- After World War II, the United States wanted to develop its own rockets, but Goddard had died by that time. His work, however, allowed them to understand the intricacies of rocket science.

- In 1960, the U.S. government officially recognized Goddard's pioneering work by awarding his estate one million dollars for his 214 patents.

Consider the following . . .

- Imagine you are a scientist living in the first half of the twentieth century. Automobiles are still a recent invention; airplane travel is less than fifty years old; more Americans listen to the radio than watch (or own) a television. How would you respond to someone who claimed that we could travel to the Moon? Would you believe this person? Why or why not?

- Many scientists have worked closely with the armed forces to develop weapons. Some, such as Albert Einstein (1879–1955), later regretted such work. If you were a scientist, would you want to work in weapons development? Why or why not?

- Goddard's pioneering rocket research led to several advancements in space travel. If you could invent something for your own personal use that used rocket technology, what would it be?

For More Information

Books

Goddard, Robert H. *The Autobiography of Robert Hutchings Goddard, Father of the Space Age; Early Years to 1927*. Worcester, MA: A. J. St. Onge, 1966.

Goddard, Robert H. *Rockets*. Mineola, NY: Dover Publications, 2002.

Lehman, Milton. *Robert H. Goddard: Pioneer of Space Research*. New York: Da Capo, 1988.

Winter, Frank H. *Rockets into Space*. Cambridge, MA: Harvard University Press, 1990.

Periodicals

Crouch, Tom D. "Reaching Toward Space: His 1935 Rocket Was a Technological Tour de Force, But Robert H. Goddard Hid It from History." *Smithsonian* (February 2001): p. 38.

Web Sites

Goddard, Robert H. *A Method of Reaching Extreme Altitudes*. Washington, DC: Smithsonian Institution, 1919; also available at *Clark University*. http://www.clarku.edu/offices/library/archives/GoddardSources. htm (accessed on July 19, 2004).

"Robert H. Goddard: American Rocket Pioneer." *Goddard Space Flight Center, NASA.* http://www.gsfc.nasa.gov/gsfc/service/gallery/fact_sheets/general/goddard/goddard.htm (accessed on July 19, 2004).

"Robert Goddard (1882–1945)." *About.com.* http://inventors.about.com/library/inventors/blgoddard.htm (accessed on July 19, 2004).

"Robert Goddard and His Rockets." *Goddard Space Flight Center, NASA.* http://www.istp.gsfc.nasa.gov/stargaze/Sgoddard.htm (accessed on July 19, 2004).

Wernher von Braun

"Man on the Moon: The Journey"

Originally published in *Collier's,* **October 18, 1952; reprinted from**
Exploring the Unknown: Selected Documents in the History of the U.S. Civil
Space Program, Volume I: Organizing for Exploration, **published in 1995**

On March 22, 1952, *Collier's* magazine began a series of issues that outlined, in impressive detail, how humans could and would explore space, land on the Moon, and visit the planet Mars. By the time the final issue reached newsstands in April 1954, the popular imagination had been changed forever. Exploring the outer reaches of space no longer seemed a fantastical dream, but an inevitable reality. The German-born physicist Wernher von Braun (1912–1977) was a central figure in ushering in this change.

When von Braun was approached by *Collier's* magazine to contribute to their series concerning space exploration, he was already an accomplished rocket scientist who dreamed of traveling to the stars. After the conclusion of World War II (1939–45), von Braun moved from his native Germany to the United States. He brought with him 112 German engineers and scientists and one hundred V-2 rockets they had designed and developed for the Nazi military during the war. They also possessed technical data concerning rockets and detailed plans for trips to the Moon, orbiting satellites, and space stations. The U.S. government, recognizing von Braun's brilliance, provided him a research station at Fort Bliss near El Paso, Texas. He and his team of former German scientists used their expertise to advance the developing U.S. rocket program, Project Paperclip.

Von Braun was truly ahead of his time. While conducting his research for the U.S. rocket program, he photographed Earth from high altitudes and performed medical experiments with animals in space. He also wrote *The Mars Project,* in which he outlined the steps for launching a successful mission to Mars. Von Braun completed the book in 1948, but he was unable to find a publisher until much later. Consequently, long before *Collier's* editors even dreamed of publishing their groundbreaking series, von Braun had already completed an entire study on future exploration of Mars.

Wernher von Braun. *(Library of Congress)*

On March 22, 1952, *Collier's* released the first installment of its space series. Von Braun wrote the featured article, "Crossing the Last Frontier," in which he provided intricate details regarding the materials, construction design and cost, and manpower necessary for building a 24-story space station. The issue immediately captured the imagination of Americans and made von Braun a household name. Seven months later, on October 18, *Collier's* published "Man on the Moon: The Journey."

Things to remember while reading "Man on the Moon: The Journey":

- The scientists who contributed to the *Collier's* series were told to write their articles in a straightforward, readable style. Although the following excerpt sometimes reads like a science-fiction story, von Braun supports his ideas with sound scientific research.

Von Braun's Nazi Connections

Wernher von Braun's prominence in American spaceflight efforts often overshadows his responsibility in the suffering and loss of life associated with the German V-2 rocket. By the end of the war in June 1945, approximately six thousand rockets were manufactured at an underground production site named *Mittelwerk.* The factory used the slave labor of concentration-camp inmates and prisoners of war. Although von Braun always gave credit to his team for the technical success of the V-2, he clearly played a key role in the development of the missile. He and his army superior, General Walter Dornberger (1895–1980), were also successful in obtaining funding and other support for development of the rocket. Von Braun had no direct responsibility for the production, yet he was aware of the dreadful conditions in concentration camps. Moreover, he joined the Nazi Party on May 1, 1937, and in 1940 he be-

came an officer in the elite SS (an abbreviation of *Schutzstaffel,* German for "Protective Corps"). The SS started as a corps of bodyguards who protected the Nazi dictator Adolf Hitler (1889–1945). Under Heinrich Himmler (1900–1945) the SS came to control military police activities, Nazi intelligence, and the administration and maintenance of the concentration camps.

While historians note that more research is needed on this subject, available American records support von Braun's claim that he was forced to join both the Nazi Party and the SS to avoid abandoning his rocketry work. He further stated that his motivation in building army missiles was their ultimate use in space travel and scientific endeavors. He said he was arrested by the Nazis in 1944 because he was not interested in using the V-2 as a weapon.

- When writing his article, von Braun considered nearly every possible situation that could arise during a trip to the Moon. He packs tremendous detail into a few relatively short pages—everything from eating in space to sleeping arrangements to landing on the Moon.

- Each *Collier's* article was accompanied by the color illustrations of Chesley Bonestell (1888–1986), Fred Freeman (1906–1988), and Rolf Klep (1904–1981). Their artwork helped bring alive the scientists's vision and impress upon the reader the awesome scope of the missions.

"Man on the Moon: The Journey"

*For five days, the expectation speeds through space on its historic voyage—50 men on three **ungainly** craft, bound for the great unknown.*

Here is how we shall go to the moon. The pioneer expedition, 50 scientists and technicians, will take off from the space station's orbit in three clumsy-looking but highly efficient rocket ships. They won't be streamlined: all travel will be in space, where there is no air to impede motion. Two will be loaded with propellant for the five day, 239,000-mile trip and the return journey. The third, which will not return, will carry only enough propellant for a one-way trip; the extra room will be filled with supplies and equipment for the scientists' six-week stay.

On the outward journey, the rocket ships will hit a top speed of 19,500 miles per hour about 33 minutes after departure. Then the motors will be stopped and the ships will fall the rest of the way to the moon.

Such a trip takes a great deal of planning. For a beginning we must decide what flight path to follow, how to construct the ships and where to land. But the project could be completed within the next 25 years. There are no problems involved which we don't have the answers—or the ability to find them—right now.

First, where should we land? We may have a wide choice, once we have had a close look at the moon. We'll get that look on a preliminary survey flight. A small rocket ship taking off from the space station will take us to within 50 miles of the moon to get a picture of its meteor-pitted surface—including the "back" part never visible from earth.

We'll study the photographs for a suitable site. Several considerations limit our selection. Because the Moon's surface has 146,000,000 square miles—about one thirteenth that of the earth—we won't be able to explore more than a small area in detail, perhaps part of a section 500 miles in diameter. Our scientists want to see as many kinds of lunar features as possible, so we'll pick a spot of particular interest. We want radio contact with the earth, so that means we'll have to stick to the moon's "face," for radio waves won't reach across space to any point the eye won't reach.

Ungainly: Awkward or clumsy.

Wernher von Braun, holding a space vehicle, stands next to a map depicting the distance from Earth to the Moon. *(AP/Wide World Photos)*

We can't land at the moon's equator because its noonday temperatures reach an unbearable 220-degrees Fahrenheit, more than hot enough to boil water. We can't land where the surface is too rugged because we need a flat place to set down. Yet the site can't be too flat either—grain sized meteors constantly bombard the moon at speeds several miles per second; we have to set camp in a crevice where we have protection from these bullets.

There's one section of the moon that meets all of our requirements, and unless something better turns up on closer inspection that's where we land. It's an area called Sinus Roris, or "Dewy Bay" on the northern branch of a plain known as Oceanus Procellarum, or "Stormy Ocean" (so called by early astronomers who thought the moon's plains were great seas). Dr. Fred L. Whipple [1906–2004], chairman of Harvard University astronomy department, says Sinus Ro-lis *is ideal for our purposes*—about 650 miles from the lunar north pole where the daylight temperature averages a reasonably pleasant 40 de-grees and the terrain is flat enough to land on, yet irregular enough to hide in. With a satisfactory site located we start detailed planning.

To save fuel and time, we want to take the shortest practical course. The moon moves around the earth in an **elliptical** path once every 27$\frac{1}{3}$ days. The space station, our point of departure, circles the earth every two hours. Every two weeks their paths are such that a rocket ship from the space station will intercept the moon in just five days. The best conditions for the return trip will occur two weeks later, and again two weeks after that. With their stay limited to multiples of two weeks, our scientists have set themselves a six week limit for the first exploration of the moon—long enough to accomplish some constructive research, but not long enough to require a **prohibitive** supply of essentials like liquid oxygen, water and food.

Six months before our scheduled take-off, we begin piling up con-struction materials, supplies and equipment at the space station. This operation is a massive, impressive one, involving huge shuttling cargo rocket ships, scores of hard working handlers, and tremendous amounts of equipment. Twice a day pairs of sleek rocket transports from the earth sweep into the **satellite**'s orbit and swarms of work-ers unload the 36 tons of cargo each carries. With the arrival of the first shipment of material, work on the first of the three moon-going space craft gets underway, picking up intensity as more and more equipment arrives.

The supplies are not stacked inside the space station; they are just left floating in space. They don't have to be secured and here's why: the satellite is traveling around the earth at 15,840 miles per hour; at that speed, it can't be affected by the earth's gravity, so it doesn't fall, and it never slows down because there's no air resistance. The same applies to any other object brought into the orbit at the same speed: to park beside the space station a rocket ship merely adjusts its speed to 15,840 miles per hour: and it, too, becomes a satellite. Crates moved out of its hold are traveling at the same speed in rela-tion to the earth, so they also are weightless satellites.

As the weeks pass and the unloading of cargo continues, the con-struction area covers several littered square miles. Tons of equipment lie about—aluminum **girders**, collapsed nylon-and-plastic fuel tanks,

Elliptical: Oval or curved.

Prohibitive: Excessive; unreasonable.

Satellite: An object orbiting Earth, the Moon, or another celestial body.

Girders: Support structures, such as joists or beams.

rocket motor units, **turbopumps**, bundles of thin aluminum plates [and] a great many nylon bags containing smaller parts. It's a bewildering scene, but not to the moon-ship builders. All construction parts are color-coded—with blue tipped cross braces fitting into blue sockets, red joining members keyed to others of the same color and so forth. Work proceeds swiftly.

In fact, the workers accomplish wonders, considering the obstacles confronting the man forced to struggle with unwieldy objects in space. The men move clumsily, hampered by bulky pressurized suits equipped with such necessities of space-life as air conditioning, oxygen tanks, walkie-talkie radios and tiny rocket motors for propulsion. The work is laborious, for although objects are weightless they still have **inertia**. A man who shoves a one-ton girder makes it move all right but he makes himself move too. As his inertia is less than the girders he shoots backward much farther than he pushes the big piece of metal forward.

The small personal rocket motors help the workers move some of the construction parts; the big stuff is hitched to space taxis, tiny pressurized rocket vehicles used for short trips outside the space station.

As the framework of the new rocket ship takes form; big, folded nylon-and-plastic bundles are brought over. They're the personal cabins; pumped full of air, they become spherical, and plastic **astrodomes** are fitted to the top of sides of each. Other stacks are pumped full of propellant and balloon into the shapes of globes and cylinders. Soon the three moon-going ships begin to emerge in their final form. The two round-trip ships resemble an arrangement of hourglasses inside a metal framework; the one-way cargo carrier has much the same framework, but instead of hourglasses it has a central structure which looks like a great **silo**.

Dimensions of the Rocket Ship

Each ship is 160 feet long (nine feet more than the height of the Statue of Liberty) and about 110 feet wide. Each has at its base a battery of 30 rocket motors, and each is topped by the sphere which houses the crew members, scientists and technicians on five floors. Under the sphere are two long arms set on a circular track which enables them to rotate almost a full 360 degrees. These light booms, which fold against the vehicles during take-off and landing to avoid damage, carry two vital pieces of equipment: a radio antenna dish for short-wave communication and a solar mirror [for] generating power.

Turbopumps: Pumps driven by a turbine, a kind of rotary engine.

Inertia: A property of matter by which it remains at rest or in uniform motion in the same straight line unless acted upon by some external force.

Astrodomes: Transparent observation domes.

Silo: A tall cylinder sealed to keep air out.

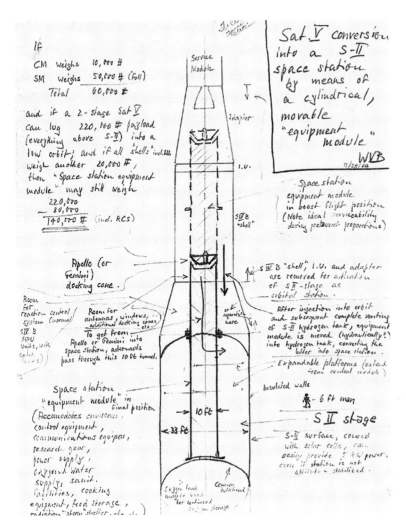

A concept sketch of one of Wernher von Braun's rockets, *Saturn 5*.
(Marshall Flight Center, NASA)

The solar mirror is a curved sheet of highly polished metal which concentrates the sun's rays on a mercury-filled pipe. The intense heat vaporizes the mercury, and the vapor drives a turbo-generator, producing 35 kilowatts of electric power—enough to run a small factory. Its work done, the vapor cools, returns to its liquid state, and starts the cycle all over again.

Under the radio and mirror booms of the passenger ships hangs 18 propellant tanks carrying nearly 800,000 gallons of ammonialike **hydrazine** (our fuel) and oxygen-rich nitric acid (the combustion

Hydrazine: A colorless, fuming corrosive used especially in fuels for rocket and jet engines.

agent). *Four of the 18 tanks are outsized spheres, more than 33 feet in diameter. They are attached to light frames on the outside of the rocket ship's structure. More than half our propellant supply—580,000 gallons—is in these large balls: that's the amount needed for take-off. As soon as it's exhausted, the big tanks will be **jettisoned**. Four other large tanks carry propellant for the landing. They will be left on the moon.*

*We also carry a supply of **hydrogen peroxide** to run the turbopumps which also force the propellant into the rocket motors. Besides the 14 cylindrical propellant tanks and the four spherical ones, eight small helium containers are strung throughout the framework. The lighter-than-air helium will be pumped into partly emptied fuel tanks to keep their shape under acceleration and to create pressure for the turbopumps.*

The cost of the propellant required for the first trip to the moon, the bulk of it used for the supply ships during the build-up period, is enormous—about $300,000,000, roughly 60 percent of the half-billion-dollar cost of the entire operation. (That doesn't count the $4,000,000,000 cost of erecting the space station, whose main purpose is strategic rather than scientific.)

The cargo ship carries only enough fuel for a one-way trip, so it has fewer tanks; four discardable spheres like those on the passenger craft, and four cylindrical containers with 162,000 gallons of propellant for the moon landing.

*In one respect, the cargo carrier is the most interesting of the space vehicles. Its big silo-like storage cabin, 75 feet long and 36 feet wide, was built to serve a double purpose. Once we reach the moon and the big cranes folded against the framework have swung out and unloaded the 285 tons of supplies in a cylinder, the silo will be detached from the rest of the rocket ship. The **winch**-driven cables slung from the cranes will then raise half of the cylinder, in sections, which it will deposit on trailers drawn by tractors. The tractors will take them to a protective crevice on the moon's surface at the place chosen for our camp. Then the other lengthwise half will be similarly moved—giving us two ready-to-use Quonset huts.*

Now that we have our space ships built and have provided ourselves with living quarters for our stay on the moon a couple of important items remain; we must protect ourselves against two of the principal hazards of space travel, flying meteors and extreme temperatures.

Jettisoned: Discarded.

Hydrogen peroxide: A compound used as an oxidizing (mixed with oxygen) and bleaching agent, an antiseptic, and a propellant.

Winch: Hoist.

For Protection Against Meteors

To guard against meteors, all vital parts of the three craft—propellant tanks, personnel spheres, cargo cabin—are given a thin covering of sheet metal, set on studs which leave at least one inch of space between this outer shield and inside wall. The covering, called meteor bumper, will take the full impact of the flying particles (we don't expect to be struck by any meteors much larger than a grain of sand) and will cause them to disintegrate before they can do damage.

For protection against excessive heat, all parts of the three rocket ships are painted white because white absorbs little of the sun's radiation. Then, to guard against cold, small black patches are scattered over the tanks and personnel spheres. The patches are covered by white blinds, automatically controlled thermostats. When the blinds on the sunny side are open, the spots absorb heat and warm the cabins and tanks. When the blinds are closed, all the white surface is exposed to the sun, permitting little heat to enter. When the blinds on the shaded sides are open, the black spots radiate heat and the temperature drops.

Now we're ready to take off from the space station's orbit to the moon.

The bustle of our departure—hurrying space taxis, the nervous last-minute checks by engineers, the loading of late cargo and finally the take-off itself—will be watched by millions. Television cameras on the space station will transmit the scene to receivers all over the world. And people on earth's dark side will be able to turn from their screens to catch a fleeting glimpse of light—high in the heavens—the combined flash of 90 rocket motors, looking from the earth like the birth of a new short lived star.

Our departure is slow. The big rocket ships rise **ponderously**, one after the other, green flames streaming from their batteries of rockets, and then they pick up speed. Actually, we don't need to gain much speed. The velocity required to get us to our destination is 19,500 miles an hour but we've had a running start, while "resting" in the space station's orbit, we are really streaking through space at 15,840 miles an hour. We need an additional 3,660 miles an hour.

Thirty-three minutes from take-off we have it. Now we cut our motors; momentum and the moon's gravity will do the rest.

The moon itself is visible to us as we coast through space, but it's so far off [to] one side that it's hard to believe we won't miss it. In the five days of the journey, though, it will travel a great distance

Ponderously: Slowly and clumsily because of weight or size.

Wernher von Braun 33

and so will we; at the end of that time we shall reach the farthest point, or apogee, of our elliptical course, and the moon shall be right in front of us.

The earth is visible, too—an enormous ball, most of it bulking pale black against the deeper black of space but with a wide crescent of day light where the sun strikes it. Within the crescent, the continents enjoying summer stand out as vast green terrain maps surrounded by the brilliant blue of the oceans. Patches of white cloud obscure some of the detail; white blobs are snow and ice on mountain ranges and polar areas.

Against the blackness of the earth's night side is a gleaming spot—the space station, reflecting the light of the sun.

Two hours and 54 minutes after departure we are 17,750 miles from the earth's surface. Our speed has dropped sharply to 10,500 miles [an] hour. Five hours and eight minutes en route, the earth is 32,950 miles away, and our speed is 8,000 miles an hour; after 20 hours, we're 132,000 miles from the earth traveling at 4,300 miles an hour.

On this first day, we discard the empty departure tanks. Engineers in protective suits step outside the cabin, stand for a moment in space, then make their way down the girders to the big spheres. They pump any remaining propellant into reserve tanks, disconnect the useless containers, and give them a gentle shove. For a while the tanks drift along beside us; soon they float out of sight. Eventually they will crash on the moon.

There is no hazard for the engineers in this operation. As a precaution they are secured to the ship by safety lines. But they could probably have done well without them. There is no air in space to blow them away.

That's just one of the peculiarities of space to which we must adapt ourselves. Lacking a natural sequence of night and day, we live by an **arbitrary** *time schedule. Because nothing has weight[,] cooking and eating are special problems. Kitchen utensils have magnetic strips or clamps so they won't float away. The heating of food is done on electric ranges. They have many advantages; they're clean, easy to operate, and their short-wave rays don't burn up precious oxygen.*

Difficulties Dining in Space
We have no knives, spoons or forks. All solid food is precut; all liquids are served in plastic bottles and forced directly into the mouth

Arbitrary: Random.

by squeezing. Our mess kits [have] spring operated covers; our only eating utensils are tonguelike devices; if we open the covers carefully, we can grab a mouthful of food without getting it all over the cabin.

From the start of the trip, the ship's crew has been maintaining a round-the-clock schedule, standing eight hour watches. Captains, navigators and radio men spend most of their time checking and rechecking our flight track, ready to start up the rockets for a change in course if an error turns up. Technicians back up this operation with reports from the complex and delicate "electronic brains"—computers, **gyroscopes**, switchboards and other instruments—on the control deck. Other specialists keep watch over the air conditioning, temperature, pressure and oxygen systems.

But the busiest crew members are the maintenance engineers and their assistants, tireless men who [have] been bustling back and forth between ships shortly after the voyage started, anxiously checking propellant tanks, tubing, rocket motors, turbopumps and all other vital equipment. Excessive heat could cause dangerous hairline cracks in the rocket motors; unexpectedly large meteors could smash through the thin bumpers surrounding the propellant tanks; fittings could come loose. The engineers have to be careful.

We are still slowing down. At the start of the fourth day, our speed has dropped to 800 miles an hour, only slightly more than the speed of a conventional jet fighter. Ahead, the harsh surface features of the moon are clearly outlined. Behind, the blue-green ball of the earth appears to be barely a yard in diameter.

Our fleet of unpowered rocket ships is now passing the neutral point between the gravitational fields of earth and the moon. Our momentum has dripped off to almost nothing—yet we're about to pick up speed. For now we must begin falling toward the moon, about 23,600 miles away. With no atmosphere to slow us we'll smash into the moon at 6,000 miles an hour unless we do something about it.

Rotating the Moon Ship

This is what we do: aboard each ship, near its center of gravity, is a positioning device consisting of three fly-wheels set at right angles to one another and operated by electric motors. One of the wheel heads is in the same direction as our flight path—in other words; along the **longitudinal** axis of the vehicle, like the rear wheels of a car. Another parallels the **latitudinal** axis like the steering wheel of an ocean vessel. The third lies along the horizontal axis like the rear steering wheel of a hook and ladder truck. If we start any one of the

Gyroscopes: Wheels or disks mounted to spin rapidly about an axis.

Longitudinal: Running lengthwise.

Latitudinal: Distance from side to side; width.

wheels spinning, it causes our rocket ship to turn slowly in the other direction (pilots know this "torque" effect; as increased power causes a plane's propeller to spin more rapidly in one direction, the pilot has to fight his controls to keep the plane rolling in the other direction).

The captain of our space ship orders the longitudinal flywheel set in motion. Slowly our craft begins to cartwheel; when it has turned a revolution, it stops. We are going toward the moon tail-end-first, a position which will enable us to brake our fall with our rocket motors when the right time comes.

*Tension increases aboard the three ships. The landing is tricky— so tricky that it will be done entirely by automatic pilot to diminish the possibility of human error. Our scientists compute the rate of descent, the spot at which we expect to strike; the speed and direction of the moon (it's traveling at 2,280 miles an hour at right angles to our path). These and other essential statistics are fed into a tape. The tape, based on the same principle as the **player-piano roll** and the **automatic business-card machine**, will control the automatic pilot. (Actually, a number of tapes intended to provide for all the eventualities will be fixed up along before the flight, but last minute-checks are necessary to see which tape to use and to see whether a manual correction of our course is required before the autopilot takes over.)*

Now we lower part of our landing gear—four spiderlike legs, hinged to the square rocket assembly, which have been folded against the framework.

As we near the end of our trip, the gravity of the moon, which is still to one side of us, begins to pull us off our elliptical course, and we turn the ship to conform to this change of direction. At an altitude of 550 miles the rocket motors begin firing; we feel the shock of their blasts inside the personnel sphere and suddenly our weight returns. Objects which have not been secured beforehand tumble to the floor. The force of the rocket motors is such that we have about one third our normal earth weight.

The final 10 minutes are especially tense. The tape-guided automatic pilots are now in full control. We fall more and more slowly, floating over the landing area like descending helicopters as we approach, the fifth leg of our landing gear—a big telescoping shock absorber which has been housed in the center of the rocket assembly is lowered through the fiery blast of the motors. The long green rocket flames begin to slash against the baked lunar surface. Swirling clouds of brown-gray dust are thrown out sideways; they settle immediately instead of hanging in air, as they would on the earth.

Player-piano roll: The replaceable paper cylinder, attached to a mechanism that plays a piano automatically, that tells the piano what notes to play.

Automatic business-card machine: A machine with a keyboard used to punch holes in cards to represent information to be fed into a computer.

The broad round shoe of the telescopic landing leg digs into the soft volcanic ground. If it strikes too hard an electronic mechanism inside it immediately calls on the rocket motors for more power to cushion the blow. For a few seconds, we balance on the single leg[,] then the four outrigger legs slide out to help support the weight of the ship, and are locked into position. The whirring of machinery dies away. There is absolute silence. We have reached the moon.

Now we shall explore it.

What happened next . . .

The *Collier's* series was immensely popular. Von Braun continued his work with the U.S. military. Between April 1950 and February 1956 he and his team developed the Redstone rocket. Von Braun wanted to launch a satellite (a man-made object that orbits space) before the former Soviet Union, but military officials continually denied his requests. After the Soviets launched the *Sputnik 1* satellite in 1957 (see First Satellite entry), von Braun immediately received authorization from the U.S. government to develop and launch a satellite. Utilizing the technology of the Redstone rocket, von Braun and his team, in cooperation with the Jet Propulsion Laboratory of the California Institute of Technology, developed the *Explorer 1* satellite. *Explorer 1* was launched on January 31, 1958.

Later in 1958, the United States formed the National Aeronautics and Space Administration (NASA). In 1960 von Braun was appointed director of the George C. Marshall Space Flight Center, a NASA agency at Huntsville, Alabama. Von Braun was instrumental in the launching of the Saturn rockets and of *Apollo 8,* the first spacecraft to travel to the Moon.

Von Braun retired from NASA in 1972 to take a post in a private engineering firm. He became an advocate for space travel and wrote a number of articles and books promoting the benefits of a well-funded and publicly supported space agency. Historians agree, however, that nothing did more to energize the American public and excite them about space travel than the articles he had published in *Collier's* magazine.

Wernher von Braun, with a Saturn rocket on the launch pad at Kennedy Space Center. *(NASA)*

Von Braun died of cancer at a hospital in Alexandria, Virginia, on June 16, 1977.

Did you know . . .

- Von Braun's first article in the *Collier's* series was about a manned space station, which required the use of rockets. Only fifteen years after writing this article, he helped design the *Saturn 5* rocket, which was instrumental in the success of *Apollo 8.*

- In the late 1990s the U.S. government released documents showing that, prior to the Soviet launch of *Sputnik 1,* President Dwight D. Eisenhower (1890–1969; served 1953–61) had deliberately delayed the launch of a U.S. satellite. He wanted to use *Sputnik 1* as an excuse for gaining public support for deploying a spy satellite against the Soviets. Eisenhower's ploy was successful, but von Braun had been unaware of the plan.

- Part of von Braun's book on Mars, originally titled *Das Marsproject,* appeared as the last installment of the *Collier's* series. The entire book was published in German in 1952 and translated into English in 1953. Von Braun envisioned the Mars expedition requiring three "landing boats" and seven cargo or transport ships.

Consider the following . . .

- Von Braun's articles helped impress upon the American people the importance of space travel. Do you think space exploration is important today?

- NASA, in cooperation with Russian cosmonauts and scientists, has conducted research on Mars, although no human being has yet traveled to the red planet. Do you think a human being will ever walk on Mars? If you walked on Mars, what types of things would you look for?

For More Information

Books

Hunt, Linda. *Secret Agenda: The United States Government, Nazi Scientists, and Project Paperclip, 1945 to 1990.* New York: St. Martin's Press, 1991.

Von Braun, Wernher. "Man on the Moon: The Journey." In *Exploring the Unknown: Selected Documents in the History of the U.S. Civil Space Program, Volume I: Organizing for Exploration.* Edited by John M. Logsdon. Washington, DC: National Aeronautics and Space Administration, 1995.

Ward, Bob. *Mr. Space: The Life of Wernher von Braun.* Washington, DC: Smithsonian Press, 2004.

Periodicals

Cowan, Robert C. "Declassified Papers Show U.S. Won Space Race After All." *Christian Science Monitor* (October 23, 1999): p. 15.

"Previously Unpublished von Braun Drawings." *Ad Astra* (July/August 2000): pp. 46–47.

Von Braun, Wernher. "Man on the Moon—The Journey." *Collier's* (October 18, 1952): pp. 52–60.

Von Braun, Wernher, with Cornelius Ryan. "Baby Space Station." *Collier's* (June 27, 1953): pp. 33–40.

Von Braun, Wernher, with Cornelius Ryan. "Can We Get to Mars?" *Collier's* (April 30, 1954): pp. 22–28.

Web Sites

Graham, John F. "A Biography of Wernher von Braun." *Marshall Space Flight Center, NASA.* http://liftoff.msfc.nasa.gov/academy/history/VonBraun/VonBraun.html (accessed on July 19, 2004).

"Wernher von Braun." *Spartacus Educational.* http://www.spartacus.schoolnet.co.uk/USAbraun.htm (accessed on July 19, 2004).

First Satellite

"Announcement of the First Satellite"
Originally published in *Pravda,* October 5, 1957; also available at *NASA*
(Web site)

On October 4, 1957, the former Soviet Union launched the space satellite *Sputnik 1,* beating the United States to become the first nation to send an artificial body into Earth orbit. The Soviets' success sparked America into action, and the "space race" reached a fevered pitch. Two Soviet men, Konstantin Tsiolkovsky (1857–1935; pronounced KAHN-stan-teen tsee-ohl-KAHV-skee) and Sergei Korolev (1907–1966; pronounced SEHR-gay KOR-o-lev), were instrumental in enabling the Soviets to launch *Sputnik 1.*

Although *Sputnik 1* was launched in 1957, the satellite had been many decades in the making. In fact, the origins of the satellite can be traced back to the nineteenth century, when Tsiolkovsky, a self-educated scientist, pioneered the field of aeronautics (study of flight). His work provided the essential formulas and research necessary for later successful flight efforts. He began his experiments in the 1870s, examining every aspect of space flight. He thought about designs for spacecrafts and launch plans, and he built a mechanism that could measure the effects that accelerated gravity has on the human body. Tsiolkovsky also produced revolutionary work concerning aerodynamics (the study of the motion of air and gaseous fluids), the shape of aircraft wings, and internal combustion engines.

By 1896 Tsiolkovsky had developed all the formulas necessary to plot the trajectory, or flight path, of a spacecraft. The following year he designed and built the first Russian wind tunnel, which propelled air over various types of aircraft and tested his theories. Then he wrote a well-received paper, "Air Pressure on Surfaces Introduced into an Artificial Air Flow," which earned him a research grant from the Russian Academy of Sciences. This paper puts forth a formula known as the basic rocket equation (mathematical formulas that describe how to build and launch a rocket.) Throughout the remainder of his career, which lasted until 1935, Tsiolkovsky pioneered work in the field of aeronautics and astronautics (the study of the construction and operation of vehicles for space travel) that is now regarded as the basis upon which all rocket science—and subsequently the development of the first satellite—is built.

Sputnik 1, **the first satellite.** *(AP/Wide World Photos)*

Rocket engineer Korolev was a sharp contrast to Tsiolkovsky. Credited with developing the staged rocket (a rocket that ignites at specified stages in order to propel an object long distances into space), he was born a generation later and benefited from the best schooling and training. He designed his first glider (an aircraft similar to an airplane but without an engine) at the age of seventeen, later earning a spot at the Kiev Polytechnic Institute and then at the Moscow Higher Technical University. He continued working on gliders until 1931, when his interest in rocketry led him to found the Group for Investigation of Reactive Motion (GIRD). At the same time, the American scientist Robert H. Goddard (1882–1945; see entry) was conducting research on rocket-propelled aircraft. Although Korolev did not know it, Goddard had already flown the first liquid-propelled rockets. Shortly after founding the agency, Korolev succeeded in accomplishing the same feat with the GIRD-9 and GIRD-10 rockets. For two years he and his partner conducted tests before the military placed GIRD under the supervision of the Reaction Propulsion Scientific Institute (RNII). During this time Korolev worked on his gliders and rockets, building the RP-318, the first rocket-propelled manned aircraft. Korolev's partner, Soviet engineer Valentin Petrovich Glushko (1908–1989), designed the ORM-65 rocket engine that propelled the craft.

In 1938, prior to the launch of the aircraft, Glushko was thrown into prison by Soviet dictator Joseph Stalin (1879–1953). Fearing for his life, Glushko denounced Korolev as an enemy of the state. Korolev was sentenced to ten years of hard labor. Stalin recognized the importance of aeronautics and began a program known as "sharashakas" to exploit prison laborers for work in scientific experiments. An aircraft designer who was also imprisoned and part of this program, Sergei Tupolev (1906–1966), stepped in on Korolev's behalf and requested that the government allow Korolev to assist in experiments. In September 1940 Korolev, his health destroyed by the brutal labor camp, was transferred back to Moscow (capital city of Russia and of the former Soviet Union) to work for the TSKB-39 sharashaka. He was able to continue his work on rockets only in the evening, after his work for the government was completed. The rocket he spent a year designing and building, the RP-318, was flown on February 28, 1940. Korolev was not present for the launch.

For the next twenty years Korolev worked on ballistic missile projects. (A ballistic missile propels itself upward for the first half of its flight but then falls freely downward toward its target.) He was also involved in the Soviet attempt to build a version of the British V-2 rocket. In the early 1950s Korolev began working with German scientists who were attempting to build the first intercontinental (capable of traveling between continents) booster rocket to be used as a ballistic missile. Without the knowledge of the German scientists, Korolev used some of their theories and began to develop a rocket of his own. Later known as the R-7, his rocket was capable of traveling farther than the rocket being designed by the Germans. After years of setbacks and problems, the R-7 was launched successfully on August 21, 1957. Less than two months later the Soviets launched *Sputnik 1*, the first artificial satellite to be sent into orbit. *Sputnik 1* was a small, spherical (globe-shaped) object 58 centimeters (22.8 inches) in diameter, which weighed just over 86 pounds (39 kilograms). Equipped with two transmitters, it was able to send signals back to scientific stations situated all over the Soviet Union. With the launch of *Sputnik 1*, the Soviets made the first significant impact in the field of astronautics.

Things to remember while reading "Announcement of the First Satellite":

- By sending an object into space and successfully putting it into orbit, Soviet scientists felt that manned spaceflight was the next logical step. This view was shared by American and German scientists. The success of *Sputnik 1* allowed scientists all over the world to cease regarding interplanetary travel as a dream and start thinking about it as an eventual reality.

- The successful launch of *Sputnik 1* was a great shock to the United States. The Soviets heralded it as a victory and as proof that Communist nations could compete with democratic countries. In many ways, the space race was as much about proving the supremacy of a certain political ideology as it was about getting a man to the Moon. American president Dwight D. Eisenhower (1890–1969; served 1953–61) immediately signed an act forming the National Aeronautics and Space Administration (NASA) to begin work on launching a manned spacecraft.

- Many Americans feared that the launch of *Sputnik 1* had initiated a new era in hostile relations with the Soviets. Afraid that the Soviet Union would be able to launch spy satellites and ballistic missiles, the American public was highly supportive of the NASA space program.

"Announcement of the First Satellite"

*On October 4, 1957, the Soviet Union launched the first Earth-orbiting **satellite** to support the scientific research effort undertaken*

Satellite: An object orbiting Earth, the Moon, or another celestial body.

by several nations during the 1957–58 **International Geophysical Year.** The Soviets called the satellite "Sputnik," or "fellow traveler," and reported the achievement in a **tersely** worded press release issued by the official news agency, Tass. The report was printed in the October 5 issue of Pravda. The United States had also been working on a scientific satellite program, Project Vanguard, but had not yet launched a satellite.

For several years scientific research and experimental design work have been conducted in the Soviet Union on the creation of artificial satellites of the earth.

As already reported in the press, the first launching of the satellites in the USSR [Union of Soviet Socialist Republics; the Soviet Union] were planned for realization in accordance with the scientific research program of the International Geophysical Year.

*As a result of very intensive work by scientific research institutes and design **bureaus** the first artificial satellite in the world has been created. On October 4, 1957, this first satellite was successfully launched in the USSR. According to **preliminary** data, the carrier rocket has imparted to the satellite the required orbital **velocity** of about 8000 meters per second. At the present time the satellite is describing **elliptical trajectories** around the earth, and its flight can be observed in the rays of the rising and setting sun with the aid of very simple **optical** instruments (binoculars, telescopes, etc.).*

*According to calculations which now are being supplemented by direct observations, the satellite will travel at altitudes up to 900 kilometers above the surface of the earth; the time for a complete revolution of the satellite will be one hour and thirty-five minutes; the angle of **inclination** of its orbit to the **equatorial** plane is 65 degrees. On October 5 the satellite will pass over the Moscow area twice—at 1:46 A.M. and at 6:42 A.M. Moscow time. Reports about the subsequent movement of the first artificial satellite launched in the USSR on October 4 will be issued regularly by broadcasting stations.*

*The satellite has a spherical shape 58 centimeters [22.8 inches] in diameter and weighs 83.6 kilograms. It is equipped with two radio transmitters continuously **emitting** signals at **frequencies** of 20.005 and 40.002 megacycles per second (wave lengths of about 15 and 7.5 meters, respectively). The power of the transmitters ensures reliable reception of the signals by a broad range of radio amateurs. The signals have the form of **telegraph** pulses of about 0.3 second's duration with a pause of the same duration. The signal of one frequency is sent during the pause in the signal of the other frequency.*

International Geophysical Year: An eighteen-month period (July 1957–December 1958) of maximum sunspot activity, designated for cooperative study of the Sun-Earth environment by scientists of sixty-seven nations.

Tersely: Shortly or abruptly.

Bureaus: Specialized administrative units.

Preliminary: Introductory; first.

Velocity: Quickness of motion; speed.

Elliptical trajectories: Oval or curved flight paths made in space.

Optical: Visual.

Inclination: Slope; deviation from the true vertical or horizontal.

Equatorial: Located at the equator.

Emitting: Releasing.

Frequencies: Number of complete variations per second of energy in the form of waves.

Telegraph: Apparatus or process for communication at a distance by electronic transmission over wire.

Scientific stations located at various points in the Soviet Union are tracking the satellite and determining the elements of its trajectory. Since the **density** of the **rarified** upper layers of the atmosphere is not accurately known, there are no data at present for the precise determination of the satellite's lifetime and of the point of its entry into the dense layers of the atmosphere. Calculations have shown that owing to the tremendous velocity of the satellite, at the end of its existence it will burn up on reaching the dense layers of the atmosphere at an altitude of several tens of kilometers.

As early as the end of the nineteenth century the possibility of realizing cosmic flights by means of rockets was first scientifically **substantiated** in Russia by the works of the outstanding Russian scientist K[onstatin] E. Tsiolkovskii [Tsiolkovsky].

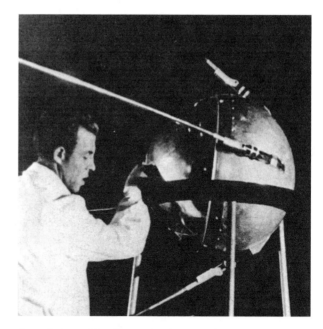

Sputnik 1 **satellite shown in the assembly shop as a Soviet technician puts finishing touches on it.** *(NASA)*

The successful launching of the first man-made earth satellite makes a most important contribution to the treasure-house of world science and culture. The scientific experiment accomplished at such a great height is of tremendous importance for learning the properties of cosmic space and for studying the earth as a planet of our solar system.

During the International Geophysical Year the Soviet Union proposes launching several more artificial earth satellites. These subsequent satellites will be larger and heavier and they will be used to carry out programs of scientific research.

Artificial earth satellites will pave the way to interplanetary travel and, apparently our contemporaries will witness how the freed and **conscientious** labor of the people of the new **socialist** society makes the most daring dreams of mankind a reality.

What happened next . . .

The Soviets launched *Sputnik 2* on October 5. The capsule not only carried a heavier payload, or cargo, than *Sputnik 1,*

Density: Thickness or solidity, having more mass per unit volume.

Rarified: Very high.

Substantiated: Verified by proof or evidence.

Conscientious: Careful.

Socialist: System or condition of society in which the means of production are owned and controlled by the state.

but it also transported the first passenger into space: a dog named Laika. Korolev immediately began to pressure the Soviet government to focus on a manned spaceflight. Although reluctant, the government agreed and made Korolev the head of the effort to design the spacecraft. Korolev was not given complete freedom, however. He was required to design the spacecraft with specifications that allowed the government to fulfill its intentions to use spacecraft for spying purposes. He designed the Vostok manned space program, which sent the first human being, cosmonaut (astronaut) Yuri Gagarin (1934–1968), into orbit on April 12, 1961.

Korolev continued to work for the Soviet government, particularly in the development of ballistic missiles. This program contributed to the escalating arms race between the Soviet Union and the United States. Modifications of his Vostok rocket designs allowed the Soviets to build and launch the Soyuz, the world's first reusable spacecraft, which is now called a space shuttle. (Still in operation in 2004, the Soyuz is the longest-serving spacecraft in the world. A space shuttle is a vehicle that transports people and cargo between Earth and space.) Korolev died unexpectedly in 1966 from complications following cancer surgery. Two weeks later, the *Luna 9* probe he had designed landed on the Moon and sent back the first photographs ever taken from the surface. Political squabbling and lack of government funds prevented the Soviet Union from developing a manned Moon exploration program. Thus the United States was the first nation to land humans on the Moon. On July 20, 1969, astronaut Neil Armstrong (1930–) stepped out of the *Apollo 11* spacecraft onto the lunar surface. Within fifteen minutes he was followed by fellow astronaut Buzz Aldrin (1930–) (see Michael Collins and Edwin E. Aldrin Jr. entry).

In the meantime, Russian scientists had been focusing their efforts on developing a space station called the Salyut. (Often termed a "hotel" or "house" in the sky, a space station is a craft that permanently orbits Earth and serves as a base for trips into outer space.) The Salyut was successfully launched in April 1971. The following October, Soyuz transported three cosmonauts to the Salyut, becoming the first craft to orbit Earth with a multimember crew. The cosmonauts also performed the first spacewalk.

After taking the Salyut out of service, the Soviet Union launched the *Mir* space station. It remained in orbit for more than fifteen years, until 2001, although it was officially vacated in 1999. During that time the space station was almost continually occupied. A total of one hundred cosmonauts and astronauts from other nations conducted nearly 16,500 experiments during those years, primarily on how humans adapt to long-term space flight. Civilians also visited *Mir*, among them a Japanese journalist and a British candy maker. When the Soviet Union fell in 1991, Russia (formerly the largest Soviet state) began maintaining friendly relations with the United States. The two countries began working together on space ventures, including missions to *Mir*. By 1999 seven NASA astronauts had stayed aboard *Mir*. When the space station was taken out of orbit in 2001, most of the craft burned up over the Pacific Ocean. The remaining remnants crashed into the Pacific in 2004.

Did you know . . .

- Recently declassified government documents reveal that President Eisenhower purposefully delayed American efforts to send a satellite into orbit. Eisenhower argued that by allowing the Soviets to launch a satellite first, the United States would have the legal right to launch subsequent spy satellites. He felt that the Soviets being the first to launch a satellite would have little or no effect on American morale. Eisenhower was wrong. Many wonder how the face of the space race would have changed had Eisenhower allowed the American and German scientists working for the National Advisory Committee on Aeronautics (NACA; the forerunner to NASA) to launch their satellite in January 1957.

- Before working for the Soviet space agency, Korolev was sentenced to ten years of hard labor in the Kolyma gold mines. This was essentially a death sentence. Had Sergei Tupolev not intervened on his behalf, Korolev would have died in prison.

- Korolev's *Luna 9* lander marks the last time the Soviet Union achieved a significant accomplishment in space first. Historians feel that had Korolev lived, he might have enabled the Soviet space program to send a man to the Moon before the United States.

Consider the following . . .

- When the Soviets launched *Sputnik 1,* many Americans felt as though the national pride of the United States had been hurt. If another nation, such as China or Russia, is able to send the first manned spacecraft to Mars, do you think Americans would be upset? Would you? Why or why not?

- Ask your teacher to explain the tensions between the United States and the Soviet Union in 1957. If you had been the U.S. president and you knew that American scientists could send a satellite into orbit, would you have allowed them? Or do you think that President Eisenhower's decision was a good one? For instance, do you think the president was correct in wanting to wait until the United States could launch spy satellites? Why or why not?

For More Information

Books

Dickson, Paul. *Sputnik: The Shock of the Century.* Berkeley, CA: Berkeley Trade, 2003.

Harford, James. *Korolev: How One Man Masterminded the Soviet Drive to Beat America to the Moon.* New York: Wiley, 1997.

Periodicals

Frazier, Allison. "They Gave Us Space: Space Pioneers of the 20th Century." *Ad Astra* (January/February 2000): pp. 25–26.

Gautier, Daniel James. "Sergei Pavlovich Korolev." *Ad Astra* (July/August 1991): p. 27.

Web Sites

"'Announcement of the First Satellite.' from *Pravda,* October 5, 1957." *NASA.* http://www.hq.nasa.gov/office/pao/History/sputnik/14.html (accessed on August 2, 2004).

"The Early Space Stations (1969–1985)." *RussianSpaceWeb.com.* http://www.russianspaceweb.com/spacecraft_manned_salyut.html (accessed on August 2, 2004).

Lethbridge, Cliff. "Konstantin Eduardovitch Tsiolkovsky." *Spaceline.* http://www.spaceline.org/history/21.html (accessed on August 2, 2004).

"*Mir.*" *RussianSpaceWeb.* http://www.russianspaceweb.com/mir_chronology.html (accessed on August 2, 2004).

"Sergei Korolev—*Sputnik* Biographies." *NASA.* http://www.hq.nasa.gov/office/pao/History/sputnik/korolev.html (accessed on August 2, 2004).

"Soyuz Spacecraft." *RussianSpaceWeb.* http://www.russianspaceweb.com/soyuz.html (accessed on August 2, 2004).

"*Sputnik* and the Dawn of the Space Age." www.hq.nasa.gov/office/pao/History/sputnik/ (accessed on August 2, 2004).

John F. Kennedy

*Excerpt from Special Message to the Congress on Urgent
National Needs*
Presented on May 25, 1961

On May 25, 1961, President John F. Kennedy (1917–1963; served 1961–63) addressed a joint session of the U.S. Congress and declared that the United States would be the first nation to put a man on the Moon. He vowed that this goal would be reached by the end of the decade. Kennedy's announcement came at a crucial time in U.S. history. The United States and the former Soviet Union were engaged in a period of hostile relations known as the Cold War (1945–91). They were competing for military superiority as well as dominance in space. Nearly four years earlier, on October 5, 1957, Americans had been stunned to learn that the former Soviet Union had launched the *Sputnik 1* satellite (a man-made device that orbits Earth; see First Satellite entry). The Soviets had thus become the first country to put a craft into orbit successfully. American morale was shaken: Many citizens looked at the Soviet Union as a backward nation incapable of competing with the United States. Kennedy realized the importance of rallying the nation behind a cause, and he made that cause winning the race to the Moon.

Kennedy had other reasons to worry about public morale. Three weeks earlier, on May 5, astronaut Alan Shepard (1923–1998) became the first American in space. He piloted a Mercury spacecraft 115 miles above Earth's surface and 302 miles across the Atlantic Ocean. Americans were ecstatic, but the celebration was short lived. Soon afterward came news that the Soviets had sent Russian cosmonaut Yuri Gagarin (1934–1938) into space the previous month—once again beating the Americans in the space race. Moreover, Gagarin had made a nearly complete orbit of Earth, whereas Shepard had made only a brief flight. In addition, the U.S. government had recently failed in an attempt to overthrow Cuban Communist dictator Fidel Castro (1926–) in what became known as the Bay of Pigs invasion. The event was an international disaster. More than ever, Kennedy needed a cause the American people could believe in, one that would win the respect of the world.

President John F. Kennedy addressing a joint session of Congress on May 25, 1961. Kennedy announced that the United States would be the first nation to put a man on the Moon. *(NASA)*

In his address, titled Special Message to the Congress on Urgent National Needs, Kennedy boldly outlined America's newest priority: "First, I believe that this nation should commit itself to achieving the goal, before the decade is out, of landing a man on the moon and returning him safely to the Earth. No single space project in this period will be more impressive to mankind, or more important for the long-range exploration of space; and none will be so difficult or expensive to accomplish." This statement became a rallying cry for the American people. Never before had science and space exploration been made a top national priority. With one speech, Kennedy was able to achieve his goal of restoring America's morale.

Things to remember while reading an excerpt from President Kennedy's Special Message to the Congress on Urgent National Needs:

- Kennedy states that the "urgent time schedule" and massive national resources needed to meet the goal of sending a man to the Moon would be a new experience for the United States. In fact, during World War II (1939–45), a tight time schedule and a massive amount of resources were necessary for the development of the atomic bomb. This top-secret program was known as the "Manhattan Project." Kennedy was aware of how the project was accomplished. He wanted to instill the same sense of importance and immediacy publicly in the American people that had been done privately during World War II.

- Many historians believe that Kennedy's speech was so inspiring because he made it seem like the whole of the United States was going to the Moon: "It will not be one man going to the moon—if we make this judgment affirmatively," he said, "it will be an entire nation. For all of us must work to put him there."

- Kennedy asked Congress for a considerable amount of money for space exploration. Never before had an American leader asked that so many funds be dedicated to one program during a time of peace.

Excerpt from President Kennedy's Special Message to the Congress on Urgent National Needs

*[I]f we are to win the battle that is now going on around the world between freedom and **tyranny**, the dramatic achievements in space which occurred in recent weeks should have made clear to us all, as did the Sputnik in 1957, the impact of this adventure on the minds of men everywhere, who are attempting to make a determination of which road they should take. Since early in my term, our efforts in*

Tyranny: Oppressive power.

space have been under review. With the advice of the Vice President, who is Chairman of the National Space Council, we have examined where we are strong and where we are not, where we may succeed and where we may not. Now it is time to take longer strides—time for a great new American **enterprise**—time for this nation to take a clearly leading role in space achievement, which in many ways may hold the key to our future on Earth.

I believe we possess all the resources and talents necessary. But the facts of the matter are that we have never made the national decisions or **marshalled** the national resources required for such leadership. We have never specified long-range goals on an urgent time schedule, or managed our resources and our time so as to insure their fulfillment.

Recognizing the head start obtained by the Soviets with their large rocket engines, which gives them many months of lead time, and recognizing the likelihood that they will exploit this lead for some time to come in still more impressive successes, we nevertheless are required to make new efforts on our own. For while we cannot guarantee that we shall one day be first, we can guarantee that any failure to make this effort will make us last. We take an additional risk by making it in full view of the world, but as shown by the feat of astronaut [Alan] Shepard, this very risk enhances our stature when we are successful. But this is not merely a race. Space is open to us now; and our eagerness to share its meaning is not governed by the efforts of others. We go into space because whatever mankind must undertake, free men must fully share.

I therefore ask the Congress, above and beyond the increases I have earlier requested for space activities, to provide the funds which are needed to meet the following national goals:

First, I believe that this nation should commit itself to achieving the goal, before this decade is out, of landing a man on the moon and returning him safely to the Earth. No single space project in this period will be more impressive to mankind, or more important for the long-range exploration of space; and none will be so difficult or expensive to accomplish. We propose to accelerate the development of the appropriate lunar space craft. We propose to develop alternate liquid and solid fuel boosters, much larger than any now being developed, until certain which is superior. We propose additional funds for other engine development and for unmanned explorations—explorations which are particularly important for one purpose which this nation will never overlook: the survival of the man who first makes

Enterprise: Project that is especially difficult, complicated, or risky.

Marshalled: Brought together or united.

A U.S. astronaut on the surface of the Moon salutes the American flag. *(NASA)*

this daring flight. But in a very real sense, it will not be one man going to the moon—if we make this judgment affirmatively, it will be an entire nation. For all of us must work to put him there.

*Secondly, an additional twenty-three million dollars, together with seven million dollars already available, will accelerate development of the **Rover nuclear rocket.** This gives promise of some day providing a means for even more exciting and ambitious exploration of space, perhaps beyond the moon, perhaps to the very end of the solar system itself.*

Third, an additional fifty million dollars will make the most of our present leadership, by accelerating the use of space satellites for worldwide communications.

Fourth, an additional seventy-five million dollars—of which fifty-three million dollars is for the Weather Bureau—will help give us at

Rover nuclear rocket: A rocket powered by a nuclear reactor. Project Rover, a U.S. program created during the mid-1960s, was an effort to build a nuclear reactor, a cheaper reliable alternative to chemical rocket engines, to power a rocket in space.

the earliest possible time a satellite system for world-wide weather observation.

Let it be clear—and this is a judgment which the Members of the Congress must finally make—let it be clear that I am asking the Congress and the country to accept a firm commitment to a new course of action, a course which will last for many years and carry very heavy costs: five hundred thirty-one million dollars in fiscal '62—an estimated seven to nine billion dollars additional over the next five years. If we are to go only half way, or reduce our sights in the face of difficulty, in my judgment it would be better not to go at all.

Now this is a choice which this country must make, and I am confident that under the leadership of the Space Committees of the Congress, and the Appropriating Committees, that you will consider the matter carefully.

It is a most important decision that we make as a nation. But all of you have lived through the last four years and have seen the significance of space and the adventures in space, and no one can predict with certainty what the ultimate meaning will be of mastery of space.

I believe we should go to the moon. But I think every citizen of this country as well as the Members of the Congress should consider the matter carefully in making their judgment, to which we have given attention over many weeks and months, because it is a heavy burden, and there is no sense in agreeing or desiring that the United States take an affirmative position in outer space, unless we are prepared to do the work and bear the burdens to make it successful. If we are not, we should decide today and this year.

This decision demands a major national commitment of scientific and technical manpower, material and facilities, and the possibility of their diversion from other important activities where they are already thinly spread. It means a degree of dedication, organization and discipline which have not always characterized our research and development efforts. It means we cannot afford undue work stoppages, inflated costs of material or talent, wasteful interagency rivalries, or a high turnover of key personnel.

New objectives and new money cannot solve these problems. They could in fact, aggravate them further—unless every scientist, every engineer, every serviceman, every technician, contractor, and civil servant gives his personal pledge that this nation will move forward, with the full speed of freedom, in the exciting adventure of space.

What happened next . . .

Citizens responded immediately to Kennedy's vision. Thousands of young people dreamed of becoming astronauts or rocket scientists, and college enrollments skyrocketed. Most of the students studied science, and as people entered scientific professions the United States became an increasingly technological society. On September 12, 1962, Kennedy gave another speech, at Rice University, concerning the journey to the Moon, once again voicing his dedication to the space program (see box on page 58).

With the financial support of the government, the National Aeronautics and Space Administration (NASA) embarked on an unprecedented period of research and development. Project Mercury, which had been begun in 1958, developed the basic technology necessary to send humans into space. These flights were short, however; soon after Kennedy's address to Congress, NASA set a goal of making longer flights. On February 20, 1962, astronaut John Glenn orbited Earth in a Mercury space capsule, proving longer trips were possible (see John Glenn, with Nick Taylor entry). In 1964, NASA began Project Gemini. This program trained astronauts how to return to Earth from space, how to link different space vehicles, and, through the use of special chambers, provided "experience" in walking in weightless environments. Gemini was also responsible for launching several satellites that provided vital information about the Moon's surface and environment, allowing scientists to decide where and how to land a spacecraft.

Project Apollo began tragically in 1967, when the *Apollo 1* spacecraft exploded on the launch pad, killing all three astronauts aboard. Manned Apollo flights were suspended for over a year. Then, on July 24, 1969, millions of people around the world watched on television as *Apollo 11* (see Michael Collins and Edwin E. Aldrin entry) successfully landed U.S. astronauts Neil Armstrong (1930–) and Buzz Aldrin (1930–) on the Moon and delivered them safely home. Unfortunately, President Kennedy, who had vowed that the nation would experience

Apollo mission's _Saturn 5_ rocket lifts off at Cape Kennedy, Florida.
(© Bettmann/Corbis)

this day, was not alive to witness the result of his vision. He was assassinated in Dallas, Texas, on November 22, 1963.

Did you know . . .

- After the successful Moon landing of _Apollo 17_ in 1972, no other spacecraft has landed on the Moon. Project Apollo was discontinued after this flight, and NASA con-

Kennedy's Speech at Rice University

On September 12, 1962, President Kennedy visited Rice University in Houston, Texas, and addressed the student body. College enrollment had already begun to increase when Kennedy delivered his address, and his remarks reflect the importance the nation had begun to put on science. He outlined the advancements already made by NASA and once again emphasized that the United States would put a man on the Moon before the end of the decade. He asked the students at Rice to play a part in this endeavor. The following is an excerpt from his speech.

But if I were to say, my fellow citizens, that we shall send to the moon, 240,000 miles away from the control station in Houston, a giant rocket more than 300 feet tall, the length of this football field, made of new metal alloys, some of which have not yet been invented, capable of standing heat and stresses several times more than have ever been experienced, fitted together with precision better than the finest watch, carrying all the equipment needed for propulsion, guidance, control, communications, food and survival, on an untried mission, to an unknown celestial body, and then return it safely to Earth, reentering the atmosphere at speeds of over 25,000 miles per hour, causing heat about half that of the temperature of the sun—almost as hot as it is here today—and do all this, and do it right, and do it first before this decade is out— then we must be bold. . . . It may be done while some of you are still here at school at this college and university. It will be done during the term of office of some of the people who sit here on this platform. But it will be done. And it will be done before the end of this decade. . . . Many years ago the great British explorer George Mallory [1886– 1924], who was to die on Mt. Everest, was asked why did he want to climb it. He said, 'Because it is there.' Well, space is there, and we're going to climb it, and the moon and the planets are there, and new hopes for knowledge and peace are there.

centrated its efforts on space shuttle missions (see Space Shuttle entry).

- The early space race between the United States and the Soviet Union was heated and competitive. Today, Russia (which became a separate country after the fall of the Soviet Union in 1991) and the United States cooperate in space shuttle missions, most notably flights to the *Mir* (see Patrick Meyer entry) space station and the International Space Station.

- In January 2004 President George W. Bush (1946–; served 2001–) made a speech in which he announced that the United States would resume missions to the Moon in the near future (see George W. Bush entry).

Consider the following . . .

- President Kennedy committed the United States to sending a man to the Moon because of the nation's intensely competitive "space race" with the former Soviet Union. After the fall of the Soviet Union, the United States and Russia began cooperating on a number of space missions. Do you think this was a positive development? Why or why not?

- Do you think it was a mistake for the United States to discontinue missions to the Moon after *Apollo 17*?

- In 2004 President George W. Bush announced that the United States would someday send humans to Mars. Some people have compared this goal to President Kennedy's vow to put a man on the Moon. Do you agree? Do you believe that someday Americans will be walking on the surface of Mars?

For More Information

Books

Cole, Michael D. *Apollo 11: First Moon Landing.* Springfield, NJ: Enslow, 1995.

Dallek, Robert. *An Unfinished Life: John F. Kennedy, 1917–1963.* Boston: Little, Brown and Company, 2003.

Web Sites

Kennedy, John F. Moon Speech—Rice Stadium, September 12, 1962. *Johnson Space Center, NASA.* http://vesuvius.jsc.nasa.gov/er/seh/ricetalk.htm (accessed on July 19, 2004).

Kennedy, John F. Special Message to the Congress on Urgent National Needs, May 25, 1961. *John F. Kennedy Library and Museum.* http://www.cs.umb.edu/jfklibrary/j052561.htm (accessed on July 22, 2004).

Shepler, John. "President Kennedy's Moon Landing." *JohnShepler.com.* http://www.johnshepler.com/articles/kennedy.html (accessed on July 19, 2004).

Other Sources

"The Speeches of John F. Kennedy." In *The Speeches Collection Volume 1.* New York: MPI Home Video, 2002 (DVD).

Tom Wolfe

Excerpts from **The Right Stuff**
Published in 1979; reprinted in 1980

On July 29, 1958, President Dwight D. Eisenhower (1890–1969; served 1953–61) signed the National Aeronautics and Space Act, officially creating the National Aeronautics and Space Administration (NASA). By October 1 NASA had set up its offices and begun plans to achieve its goal of sending astronauts into outer space; this endeavor was called Project Mercury. After an exhaustive search, seven men became America's first astronauts, known to the world as the Mercury 7. Beginning in January 1961 and ending in May 1963, Project Mercury resulted in six successful space missions that allowed NASA to begin work on sending a man to the Moon.

On October 4, 1957, the former Soviet Union became the first nation to send a craft into space when it launched the satellite *Sputnik 1* (see First Satellite entry). The United States responded in the summer of 1958 by replacing the National Advisory Committee for Aeronautics (NACA) with NASA, an agency committed to achieving the goal of manned spaceflight. On December 17, 1958, exactly fifty-five years after Orville (1871–1948) and Wilbur (1867–1912) Wright became the first men to build and fly an airplane, Project Mercury was

Project Mercury astronauts, whose selection was announced April 9, 1959: (front row, left to right) Walter Schirra Jr., Donald Slayton, John Glenn, and M. Scott Carpenter; (back row) Alan Shepard, Gus Grissom, and L. Gordon Cooper. *(NASA)*

announced to the public. An immediate search for astronauts began.

NASA established strict guidelines for astronaut candidates. Applicants had to be under the age of forty, in excellent physical shape, and less than 5 feet 11 inches tall (1.5 meters 27.9 centimeters). They were also required to have logged over 1,500 flight hours as a test pilot. More than five hundred people applied. Through vigorous testing, NASA reduced the pool of applicants to thirty-two. After subjecting the men to a battery of difficult and exhausting tests, on April 9, 1959, NASA announced its selection of the Mercury 7: M. Scott Carpenter (1925–), L. Gordon Cooper Jr. (1927–), John Glenn Jr. (1921–),

Virgil I."Gus" Grissom (1926–1967); Walter Schirra Jr. (1923–), Alan Shepard Jr. (1923–1998), and Donald K. "Deke" Slayton (1924–1993). The men became instant heroes.

For the engineers working on Project Mercury, their challenge was designing and building a craft that could protect a human being from the extreme hot and cold temperatures that would be experienced during space travel. They needed a craft that could both handle the pressures of vacuum (emptiness of space) and radiation and protect the astronaut from the temperature change upon reentry. It was an awesome task. The engineers responded by building a cone-shaped craft 6.8 feet (2.07 meters) long and 6.2 feet (1.89 meters) in diameter that had a 19.2-foot (5.85 meter) escape tower attached on top; the escape tower was equipped with a solid-propellant engine that would be engaged in case of an emergency. The entire craft was approximately 26 feet (7.92 meters) tall and weighed about 17,500 pounds (7,945 kilograms). Depending on the mission, the craft was launched using different rocket technology. For the suborbital flights (flights that did not involve the craft orbiting the entire globe), the capsule was launched using Redstone rockets. In the orbital flights, Atlas-D launch vehicles were used. There were eighteen thrusters (engines that develop thrust, or driving force, by releasing a jet of fluid or stream of particles) on the craft, all of which were operated by the astronaut to control the ship's attitude (the way the ship points). To exit the orbit, three retro-rockets (back up rocket engines used in slowing down) fired to send the craft back to Earth.

Astronaut safety was the engineers' primary concern. Their design ensured that, in the event of a mishap, the solid-propellant engine would fire the capsule away from the rocket and out of harm's way. A parachute would then engage and the capsule would fall safely into the ocean. The craft contained extremely tight quarters, with only enough room for the pilot, who sat in a specially designed couch that faced a control panel with 55 switches, 120 controls, 30 fuses, and 35 mechanical levers. The capsule that contained the astronaut had a blunt (not pointed) end, allowing it to enter the atmosphere at the proper angle. It was covered with a special shield that would protect it from the over 3,000°F (1,648.9°C) heat that would be generated upon reentry. Once the capsule was back in Earth's atmosphere, the shield would detach and a balloon would inflate to help soften the landing. Parachutes would open at the proper altitude to assist in slowing the craft down.

Before a human being was put in the capsule, seven suborbital and four orbital flights were conducted. In January 1961, a chimpanzee named Ham (1956–1983) was placed into a suborbital flight that reached nearly 157 miles (253 kilometers) in altitude. There were unexpected events during the flight; a leaky valve greatly reduced the cabin pressure, and when Ham splashed down in the ocean—130 miles (209 kilometers) off target—the capsule began to take on water. Ham was rescued and the mission was considered a success. NASA decided a human being could survive space flight.

On May 5, 1961, Alan Shepard Jr. became the first American in space. He piloted the *Friendship 7* to an altitude of 116 miles (186.6 kilometers) and a speed of 5,146 miles (8,280 kilometers) per hour as an American public glued to their television sets watched his launch and successful landing. The flight lasted only 15 minutes and 22 seconds but proved that a human being could survive in space with relative comfort. A similar flight piloted by Gus Grissom was launched in July 1961. Grissom's *Liberty Bell 7* flight mirrored Shepard's until splashdown, when the emergency escape hatch blew off unexpectedly. Grissom was rescued by a helicopter, though not before his spacesuit was completely waterlogged. The capsule took on water and sunk to the bottom of the sea, where it remained until it was located and retrieved in 1999.

Project Mercury's greatest moment came on February 20, 1962, when John Glenn (see entry) piloted *Friendship 7* into a successful orbit of Earth. Three times Glenn circumnavigated (went around) the globe, becoming the first astronaut to do so. Although there was fear that the capsule's heat shield was faulty, Glenn returned safely to Earth, where he was praised as a national hero. The American people saw the importance of spaceflight and rallied around NASA's efforts to continue their important work. Two more flights followed. In May Scott Carpenter flew the *Aurora 7* without incident. In October Walter Schirra piloted *Sigma 7* to a record six orbits in a mission lasting 9 hours and 13 minutes. Project Mercury was an unqualified success.

The final flight took place in May 1963. It was the longest flight ever attempted by NASA. Lasting 34 hours and 19 minutes, pilot Gordon Cooper flew the *Faith 7* around Earth twenty-two and one-half times. NASA was so pleased with the results from the *Faith 7* mission that the final flight was canceled. Encouraged by the success of Project Mercury, President John F. Kennedy (1917–1963; served 1961–63) announced the government's plan to send a man to the Moon. Had it not been for Project Mercury, the Apollo and Gemini programs would never have been possible.

Tom Wolfe, author of *The Right Stuff*. *(AP/Wide World Photos)*

Things to remember while reading excerpts from *The Right Stuff:*

- Author Tom Wolfe (1931–) has always been fascinated by astronauts. It takes a great deal of skill, intelligence, courage, and fearlessness to go into space. For the men known as the Mercury 7, it took a great deal of trust on their part that humans were capable of building a craft they could pilot safely. Wolfe's book *The Right Stuff* discusses the lives and accomplishments of the men who pioneered space travel.

- In the beginning stages of Project Mercury, the astronauts had no manual control over flying the space capsule. All the candidates were trained test pilots, with thousands of miles of flight experience. Many of the men who were being approached by NASA, however, did not want to be part of the mission because their piloting skills were not required.

- Although the following excerpts focus on the astronauts, it took the combined efforts of thousands of scientists, medical doctors, and military personnel to make Project Mercury successful.

Excerpts from The Right Stuff

This book grew out of some ordinary curiosity. What is it, I wondered, that makes a man willing to sit up on top of an enormous Roman candle, such as a Redstone, Atlas, Titan, or Saturn rocket, and wait for someone to light the fuse? I decided on the simplest approach as possible. I would ask a few astronauts and find out. So I asked a few in December of 1972 when they gathered at Cape Canaveral to watch the last mission to the moon, Apollo 17. I discovered quickly enough that none of them, no matter how talkative otherwise, was about to answer that question or even linger for more than a few seconds on the subject at the heart of it, which is to say, courage. . . .

But I did sense that the answer was not to be found in any set of traits specific to the task of flying into space. The great majority of the astronauts who had flown the rockets had come from the ranks of test pilots. All but a few had been military test pilots, and even those few, such as Neil Armstrong, had been trained in the military. And it was this that led me to a rich and fabulous terrain that, in a literary sense, had remained as dark as the far side of the moon for more than half a century: military flying and the modern American officer corps. . . .

*A young man might go into military flight training believing that he was entering some sort of technical school in which he was simply going to acquire a certain set of skills. Instead, he found himself all at once enclosed in a **fraternity**. And in this fraternity, even though it was military, men were not rated by their outward ranks as ensigns, lieutenants, commanders, or whatever. No, herein the world was divided into those who had it and those who did not. This quality, this it, was never named, however, nor was it talked about in any way.*

*As to just what this **ineffable** quality was . . . well, it obviously involved bravery. But it was not bravery in the simple sense of being willing to risk your life. The idea seemed to be that any fool could do that, if that was all that was required, just as any fool could throw away his life in the process. No, the idea here (in the all-enclosing fraternity) seemed to be that a man should have the ability to go up in a **hurtling** piece of machinery and put his hide on the line and then have the **moxie**, the reflexes, the experience, the coolness, to*

Fraternity: A group of people, usually men, associated or formally organized for a common purpose, interest, or pleasure.

Ineffable: Indescribable.

Hurtling: Rapidly moving.

Moxie: Courage, determination.

*pull it back in the last yawning moment—and then to go up again the next day, and the next day, and every next day, even if the series should prove **infinite**—and, ultimately, in its best expression, do so in a cause that means something to thousands, to a people, to a nation, to humanity, to God. Nor was there a test to show whether or not a pilot had this righteous quality. There was, instead, a seemingly infinite series of tests. A career in flying was like climbing one of the ancient **Babylonian** pyramids made up of a dizzy progression of steps and ledges, a ziggurat, a pyramid extraordinarily high and steep; and the idea was to prove at every foot of the way up that pyramid that you were one of the elected and anointed ones who had the right stuff and could move higher and higher and even—ultimately, God willing, one day—that you might be able to join that special few at the very top, the elite who had the capacity to bring tears to men's eyes, the very Brotherhood of the Right Stuff itself.*

*None of this was to be mentioned, and yet it was acted out in a way that a young man could not fail to understand. When a new flight (i.e., a class) of trainees arrived at Pensacola [Florida], they were brought into an auditorium for a little lecture. An officer would tell them: "Take a look at the man on either side of you." Quite a few actually swivelled their heads this way and that, in the interest of appearing **diligent**. Then the officer would say: "One of the three of you is not going to make it!"—meaning, not getting his wings. That was the opening theme, the **motif** of primary training. We already know that one-third of you do not have the right stuff—it only remains to find out who. . . .*

*The rocket pilots at Edwards [Air Force Base] simply could not understand what sort of madness possessed everybody. They watched in **consternation** as a war effort mentality took over. Catch up! On all fronts! That was the **imperative**. They could scarcely believe the outcome of a meeting held in Los Angeles in March of 1958. This was an emergency meeting (what emergency?) of government, military, and aircraft industry leaders to discuss the possibility of getting a man into space before the Russians. Suddenly there was no longer time for orderly progress. To put an X-15b or an X-20 into orbit, with an Edwards rocket pilot aboard, would require rockets that were still three or four years away from delivery. So a so-called quick and dirty approach was seized upon. Using available rockets such as the Redstone (70,000 pounds of thrust) and the just-developed Atlas (376,000 pounds), they would try to launch not a flying ship but a pod, a container, a capsule, with a man in it. The man would not be a pilot; he would be a human cannonball. He would not be able*

Infinite: Never-ending.

Babylonian: Referring to the ancient city of Babylon, now in ruins, on the Euphrates River, about 55 miles south of Baghdad, Iraq.

Diligent: Hard-working, industrious.

Motif: Repeated theme or idea.

Consternation: Amazement or dismay that hinders or throws into confusion.

Imperative: Command, order.

Redstone rocket containing the *Mercury* capsule. *(NASA)*

to alter the course of the capsule in the slightest. The capsule would go up like a cannonball and come down like a cannonball, splashing into the ocean, with a parachute to slow it down and spare the life of the human specimen inside. The job was assigned to NACA, the National Advisory Committee for Aeronautics, which was converted into NASA, the National Aeronautics and Space Administration. The project was called Project Mercury.

The capsule approach was the brainchild of a highly regarded Air Force research physicist, Brigadier General Don Flickinger [1907–1997]. The Air Force named it the MISS project, for "man in space soonest." The man in the MISS capsule would be an aeromedical test subject and little more. In fact, in the first flights, as Flickinger envisioned it, the capsule would contain a chimpanzee. Mercury was a slightly modified version of MISS, so naturally enough Flickinger became one of the five men in charge of selecting Project Mercury's astronauts, as they would be called. The fact that NASA would soon be choosing men to go into space had not been made public, but **Scott Crossfield** was aware of it. Shortly after the Sputnik I launching, Crossfield, Flickinger, and seven others had been named to an emergency committee on "human factors and training" for space flight. Crossfield had also worked closely with Flickinger when he was testing pressure suits at Wright-Patterson Air Force Base in preparation for the X-15 project. Now Crossfield approached Flickinger and told him he was interested in becoming an astronaut. Flickinger liked Crossfield and admired him. And he told him: "Scotty, don't even bother applying, because you'll only be turned down. You're too independent." Crossfield was the most prominent of the rocket pilots, now that [Chuck] Yeager [1923–] was no longer at Edwards, and he had as well developed an ego as any of Edwards' fabled jocks, and he was one of the most brilliant of all the pilots when it came to engineering. Flickinger seemed to be telling him Project Mercury wasn't suited for the righteous brothers of yore, the veterans of those high desert rat-shack broomstick days where there were no chiefs and no Indians and the pilots huddled in the hangar with the engineers and then went out and took the beast up and lit the candle and reached for the stars and rode his chimney and landed it on the lake bed and made it to **Pancho's** in time for beer call. When Flickinger explained to him that the first flight of the Mercury system would be made by a chimpanzee . . . well, Crossfield wasn't even particularly interested any more. Nor were most of the other pilots who were in line to fly the X-15. A monkey's gonna make the first flight. That was what you started hearing. Astronaut meant "star

Scott Crossfield: Test pilot A. Scott Crossfield (1921–).

Pancho's: A hangout for the test pilots, owned by female stunt pilot and civilian test pilot Florence Lowe "Pancho" Barnes (1901–1975).

voyager," but in fact the poor devil would be a guinea pig for the study of the effects of weightlessness on the body and the central nervous system. As the **brethren** knew, NASA's original civil-service job specifications for Mercury astronaut[s] did not even require that the star voyager be a pilot of any description whatsoever. Just about any young male college graduate with experience in a physically dangerous pursuit would do, so long as he was under five feet eleven and could fit into the Mercury capsule. The announcement calling for volunteers did mention test pilots being among the types of men who might qualify, but it also mentioned submarine crew members, parachute jumpers, arctic explorers, mountain climbers, deep sea divers, even scuba divers, combat veterans, and, for that matter, mere veterans of combat training, and men who had served as test subjects for acceleration and atmospheric pressure tests, such as the Air Force and Navy had been running. The astronaut would not be expected to do anything; he only had to be able to take it.

NASA was ready to issue the call when the President himself, [Dwight D.] Eisenhower, stepped in. He foresaw **bedlam**. Every **lunatic** in the U.S.A. would volunteer for this thing. Every **dingaling** in the U.S. Congress would be **touting** his favorite son. It would be chaos. The selection process might take months, and the inevitable business of security clearances would take a few more. Late in December Eisenhower directed that NASA select the astronauts from among the 540 military test pilots already on duty, even though they were rather overqualified for the job. The main thing was that their records were immediately available, they already had security clearance, and they could be ordered to Washington at a moment's notice. The specifications were that they be under five feet eleven and no older than thirty-nine and that they be graduates of test-pilot schools, with at least 1,500 hours of flying time and experience in

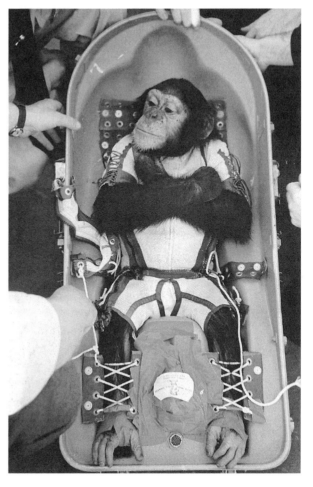

Ham, a chimpanzee, was placed on a suborbital flight to test the safety of the capsule that would eventually contain a Mercury astronaut. *(AP/Wide World Photos)*

Brethren: Group of unconventional test pilots, including Scott Crossfield.

Bedlam: Extreme confusion or noisy uproar.

Lunatic: Insane person.

Dingaling: Scatterbrained or stupid person.

Touting: Publicizing or promoting.

jets, and that they have bachelor's degrees "or the equivalent." One hundred and ten of the pilots fit the profile. There were men on the NASA selection committee who wondered if the pool was big enough. They figured that they would be lucky if one test pilot in ten volunteered. Even that wouldn't quite be enough, because they were looking for twelve astronaut candidates. They only needed six for the flights themselves, but they assumed that at least half the candidates would drop out because of the frustration of training to become passive guinea pigs in an automated capsule.

After all, they already knew how the leading test pilots at Edwards felt. North American [airplane manufacturers] had just rolled out the first X-15 in the fall of 1958, and Crossfield and his colleagues, Joe Walker [1921–1966] and Iven Kincheloe [1928–1958], had become absorbed in the assignment. Joe Walker was NASA's prime pilot for the project, and Kincheloe was [a] prime pilot for the Air Force. Kincheloe had set the world altitude record of 126,000 feet in the X-2, and the Air Force envisioned him as the new Yeager . . . and then some. Kincheloe was a combat hero and test pilot out of some dream, blond, handsome, powerful, bright, supremely ambitious and yet popular with all who worked with him, including other pilots. There was absolutely no ceiling on his future at the Air Force. Then one perfectly sunny day he was making a routine takeoff in an F-104 and the panel lit up red and he had that one second *in which to decide* whether or not to punch out at an altitude of about fifty feet . . . a choice complicated by the fact that the F-104's seat ejected straight down, out of the belly . . . and so he decided to roll the ship over and eject upside down, but he went out sideways and was killed. His backup, Major Robert White [1924–], took his place in the X-15 project. Joe Walker's backup was a former Navy fighter pilot named Neil Armstrong [1930–]. Crossfield, White, Walker, Armstrong—they no longer even had time to think about Project Mercury. Project Mercury did not mean the end of the X-15 program. Not at all. The testing of the X-15 would proceed, in order to develop a true spacecraft, a ship that a pilot could fly into space and fly back down through the atmosphere for a landing. Much was made of the fact that the X-15 would "land with dignity" rather than splash down in the water like the proposed Mercury capsule. Press interest in the X-15 had become tremendous, because it was the country's sole existing "spaceship." Reporters had started writing about Kincheloe as "Mr. Space," since he was the one who held the altitude record. After his death they hung the title on Crossfield. It was a bother . . . but a fellow could learn to live with it. . . . In any case, Project Mercury, the hu-

*man cannonball approach, looked like a **Larry Lightbulb scheme**, and it gave off the **funk** of panic. Any pilot who went into it would no longer be a pilot. He would be like a laboratory animal wired up from skull to rectum with medical sensors. The rocket pilots had fought this medical crap every foot of the way. Scott Crossfield had reluctantly allowed them to wire him for heartbeat and respiration in rocket flights but had refused to let them insert the rectal thermometer. The pilots who signed up to crawl into the Mercury capsule—the* capsule, *everybody noted, not the* ship—*would be called "astronauts." But, in fact, they would be lab rabbits with wires up the tail and everywhere else. Nobody in his right mind would hang his hide out over the edge for ten or fifteen years and ascend the pyramid and finally reach the dome of the world, Edwards . . . only to end up like that: a lab rabbit curled up motionless in a* capsule *with his little heart pitter-patter and a **wire up the kazoo**.*

*Some of the most righteous of the brethren weren't even eligible for the preliminary screening for Project Mercury. Yeager was young enough—still only thirty-five—but had never attended college. Crossfield and Joe Walker were civilians. Not that any of them gave a damn . . . at the time. The commanding officer at Edwards passed the word around that he wanted his top boys, the test pilots in Fighter Ops, to avoid Project Mercury because it would be a ridiculous waste of talent; they would just become **"Spam in a can."** This phrase "Spam in a can" became very popular at Edwards as the nickname for Project Mercury.*

Larry Lightbulb scheme: Offensive term used to refer to experiments thought up by scientists without regard to the effect on human test subjects.

Funk: Atmosphere.

Wire up the kazoo: A medical sensor inserted rectally.

Spam in a can: Slang phrase meaning useless. (Spam was an unpopular canned meat product.)

What happened next . . .

NASA began work in earnest to send a man to the Moon. In 1964 the agency initiated Project Gemini, which provided astronauts with experience in returning to Earth from space as well as practice in successfully linking space vehicles and "walking" in space. Gemini also involved the launching of a series of unmanned satellites, which would gain information about the Moon and its surface to determine whether humans could survive there. Gemini was the transition between Mercury's short flights and Project Apollo, a program to train astronauts for landing and survival on the surface of the Moon. The program's first mission, *Apollo 1,* ended tragically on January 27, 1967, when three astronauts died in a launch pad fire in their module. The *Apollo 1* commander was Gus Grissom, one of the Mercury 7, and his crew members were Edward White (1930–1967) and Roger Chaffee (1935–1967). The cause of the fire was determined to be an electrical short circuit near Grissom's seat. As a result of the accident the program was temporarily delayed while safety precautions were reviewed. The next five *Apollo* missions were unmanned flights that tested the safety of the equipment. The first manned flight, *Apollo 7,* was launched in October 1968. Ten months later, on July 20, 1969, *Apollo 11* successfully took astronauts Neil Armstrong (1930–), Buzz Aldrin (1930–), and Michael Collins (1930–) to the Moon. During the mission Armstrong became the first human to walk on the Moon, followed fifteen minutes later by Aldrin (see Buzz Aldrin and Michael Collins entry). The last Apollo mission was *Apollo 17,* which visited the Moon in December 1972.

After *Apollo 17* the United States did not undertake any other moon flights. Interest in further moon exploration steadily decreased in the early 1970s, so NASA concentrated its efforts on the Large Space Telescope (LST) project. Initiated in 1969, the LST was an observatory (a structure housing a telescope, a device that observes celestial objects) that would continuously orbit Earth. An immediate result of the LST project was a plan for a space shuttle, a reusable vehicle that would launch the LST into orbit. The U.S. space shuttle program officially began in 1972 (see Space Shuttle entry).

Did you know . . .

- Wolfe's book *The Right Stuff* was made into a successful movie with the same title in 1983.

- John Glenn returned to space thirty-six years later, aboard the space shuttle *Discovery.*

- Gordon Cooper was the first astronaut to release a satellite into space. He released a six-inch sphere with a beacon attached to test his visual ability to track objects in space.

- Donald K. "Deke" Slayton was the only member of the Mercury 7 who did not get to fly under Project Mercury. Scheduled to be on the last flight, his turn was canceled due to the success of Cooper's mission.

- Women also wanted to be astronauts. A group of thirteen women went through various phases of astronaut training before being denied the right to train for Project Mercury. The women, who called themselves the "Mercury 13," (see Martha Ackmann entry) fought for their right to go to space by appealing to both President Lyndon Johnson (1908–1973; served 1963–69) and the U.S. Congress. Their pleas fell on deaf ears, and none of them were allowed to fly.

Consider the following . . .

- The Mercury 7 astronauts were space pioneers. Do you think that you would have been brave enough to go into space in 1962? How about now? Do you think it is safer to go to space now than it was in 1962? Why or why not?

- NASA now has an ultimate goal of sending a manned mission to Mars. Do you think this is an important mission, or have we learned all we need to know from space exploration? Why or why not?

For More Information

Books

Carpenter, Scott, and Kris Stoever. *For Spacious Skies: The Uncommon Journey of a Mercury Astronaut*. New York: Penguin, 2004.

Glenn, John H. *Letters to John Glenn: With Comments by J. H. Glenn, Jr.* New York: World Book Encyclopedia Science Service, 1964.

Kranz, Gene. *Failure Is Not an Option: Mercury to* Apollo 13 *and Beyond*. New York: Simon & Schuster, 2000.

Spangenburg, Ray, Diane Moser, and Kit Moser. *Project Mercury*. New York: Scholastic, 2000.

Wolfe, Tom. *The Right Stuff*. New York: Farrar, Straus and Giroux, 1979; Reprinted, New York: Bantam, 1980.

Web Sites

"Mercury." *Kennedy Space Center, NASA*. www-pao.ksc.nasa.gov/kscpao/history/mercury/mercury.htm (accessed on August 4, 2004).

"Space History: Project Mercury." *The Ultimate Space Place*. www.thespaceplace.com/history/mercury2.html (accessed on August 4, 2004).

Other Sources

The Right Stuff. Warner Home Video, 1983 (DVD).

Martha Ackmann

Excerpts from **The Mercury 13: The Untold Story of Thirteen American Women and the Dream of Space Flight**
Published in 2003

In 1959 seven astronauts were introduced to the United States as the future of space travel. Known as the Mercury 7, the men became instant heroes, and they went on to make significant contributions to the U.S. space program. At the time Americans did not know that thirteen women had also qualified for spaceflights, undergoing the same rigorous testing and preparations as their male counterparts. Although none of these women—now called the Mercury 13—ever had the opportunity to travel into space, their pioneering spirit paved the way for future women astronauts. Had the Mercury 13 not proved to those in power that women could succeed in the field of aeronautics, Sally Ride (1951–), the first American woman to travel in space, may never have left the ground.

In 1958 the United States established the National Aeronautics and Space Administration (NASA), which integrated U.S. space research agencies and started an astronaut training program. The formation of NASA was a direct response to *Sputnik 1,* an artificial satellite (a man-made device that orbits Earth) that the former Soviet Union had launched the previous year (see First Satellite entry). This event sent shock waves through American society, because at the time the United States and the Soviet Union were engaged in a political stand-off known as the Cold War (1945–91). Not only were the two superpowers involved in an arms race for military superiority but they were also competing for dominance in space. *Sputnik 1* was a sign that the Soviet Union was winning the space race.

Determined to move ahead of the Soviets, NASA developed a manned space flight program with the goal of sending the first person into Earth orbit. According to the plan, the program would progress in three stages: Project Mercury, Project Gemini, and Project Apollo. Project Mercury developed the basic technology for manned space flight and investigated a human's ability to survive and perform in space. Project Gemini provided astronauts with experience in returning to Earth from space as well as in successfully linking space vehicles and "walking" in space. Integrating the information and experience gained from Mercury and Gemini, Project Apollo would land a person safely on the Moon.

NASA aggressively promoted Project Mercury, seeking a pool of applicants from whom a few would be selected to train as the first U.S. astronauts. NASA administrator T. Keith Glennan (1905–1995) convinced President Dwight D. Eisenhower (1890–1969; served 1953–61) that military jet test pilots would be the most qualified astronauts, so experience as a military pilot became the primary requirement. In April 1959, after applicants had been screened and tested, Glennan presented seven astronaut candidates—all males and all military test pilots—to the American public. Called the "Mercury 7," they were M. Scott Carpenter (1925–), L. Gordon Cooper Jr. (1927–), John Glenn (1921–), Virgil I. "Gus" Grissom (1926–1967), Walter Schirra Jr. (1923–), Alan Shepard Jr. (1923–1998), and Donald K. "Deke" Slayton (1924–1993).

At the time it was difficult for women to break out of the traditional roles assigned to them. Therefore, when the United States entered into the space race, women were largely overlooked as potential astronauts. Yet two American men, Dr. Robert Lovelace (1929–) and Air Force Brigadier General Donald Flickinger (1907–1997), thought the future of space travel might lie in the hands of women. Lovelace had designed the intense medical tests required for astronaut candidates, and Flickinger was a central figure in the development of the American space program. Both wondered whether women, if given the opportunity, could handle the rigorous demands of space travel. But Lovelace and Flickinger were in the distinct minority. Knowing that NASA would never allow women to even be *tested* as potential astronauts, the doctor and the general decided to conduct the tests in secret. In *The Mercury 13: The Untold Story of Thirteen American Women and the Dream of Space Flight* author Martha Ackmann tells the story of their testing program, which played an important role in the history of American space exploration.

Lovelace and Flickinger chose one woman to undergo the same seventy-five tests that had been given to the male astronauts. The tests evaluated heart rate, lung capacity, loneliness level, pain level, noise tolerance, sensory deprivation, and spinning, tilting, and dropping into water tanks to measure resistance to vertigo (dizziness). In February 1960, Jerrie Cobb (1931–), the first female pilot of an Aero Commander plane, reported to the Lovelace Clinic in Albuquerque, New Mexico, to face the challenge. Regarded as an excellent pilot, Cobb had logged over ten thousand flight hours—twice as many as Mercury 7 astronaut John Glenn, who became the first American to orbit Earth. Cobb's reputation was deserved: She did very well in the first series of tests, known as phase one, so well in fact that she was immediately sent to the Naval School of Aviation in Pensacola, Florida, to begin phase-two testing. NASA reluctantly agreed to allow Cobb to enter this stage of astronaut training.

Excited about Cobb's test results and progress, Lovelace contacted his friend Jackie Cochran (c. 1906–1980), a famous female pilot, who agreed to provide the funding necessary for additional women to take the tests. Initially, all applicants were required to be under the age of thirty-five, be in good physical condition, have a college degree, to hold pilot's licenses (of commercial rating or better), and have over two thousand hours of flight time. Twenty-five women were selected, and twelve had passed the tests by the summer of 1961. They swore themselves to secrecy, since the American public was lukewarm, at best, regarding female astronauts. The women were: Rhea Allison Woltman (1928–), Jane "Janey"

Seven crew members of Mercury 13 (from left): Gene Nora Jessen, Mary Wallace "Wally" Funk, Jerrie Cobb, Jerri Truhill, Sarah Ratley, Myrtle "K" Cagle, and Bernice "B" Steadman. *(NASA)*

Briggs Hart (1920–), Mary Wallace "Wally" Funk (1938–), Jean Hixson (1921–1962), Myrtle "K" Cagle (1922–), Irene Leverton (1924–), Sarah Lee Gorelick Ratley (1931–), twin sisters Jan (1924–) and Marion Dietrich (1924–1974), Gene Nora Stumbough Jessen (1934–), Bernice "B" Steadman (1923–), and Jerry Sloan Truhill (1928–).

All the women completed phase-one testing. Cobb, Funk, and Woltman passed phase two, and Cobb and Funk completed phase three, which means that they achieved equal status with their male counterparts, the Mercury 7. Without warning or official explanation, NASA suspended the testing program in July 1961, even though the Mercury 13 had achieved excellent results on the tests and had at times performed even better than their male counterparts. Lovelace had presented evidence that women were less likely to suffer heart attacks and suffered fewer effects from cold, heat, loneliness, noise, and pain. Furthermore, because most women weigh less than men, it was much less expensive to send them into space, because less rocket power was required to put the ship into orbit.

Things to remember while reading excerpts from *The Mercury 13: The Untold Story of Thirteen American Women and the Dream of Space Flight:*

- The Mercury 13 were unable to get any answers from NASA about the abrupt decision to cancel the testing program. Frustrated by the stonewalling, Janey Hart and Jerrie Cobb made an appointment to meet with Vice President Lyndon B. Johnson (1908–1973) and ask him to intervene on their behalf. Johnson had been a major force in establishing the space agency, so his word would carry considerable weight. This was the first time Hart and Cobb had ever met. They had originally proposed that all the members of the Mercury 13 convene to discuss strategy and objectives, but that plan did not work out. Consequently, when Hart and Cobb prepared to talk with Johnson, they did so without any input from the other members.

- The United States had received reliable intelligence that the Soviet Union was considering sending a female astronaut into space. The members of the Mercury 13 were hopeful that this fact could be used to their advantage and that the vice president would understand the importance of beating the Soviets to the punch.

- In the early 1960s, women were still regarded as incapable of handling the same tasks and pressures as men. The unwillingness of NASA to consider scientific evidence reflects this attitude. Instead of refuting the womens' points with scientific research, the opponents of the program relied upon unsound information and false myths.

Excerpts from The Mercury 13: The Untold Story of Thirteen American Women and the Dream of Space Flight

*In April 1959, the American public got its first look at the seven young men who would propel the country into the manned space race. "The nation's Mercury astronauts," Keith Glennan announced with great fanfare, as the NASA press conference erupted in applause and photographers rushed to the front of the room for closeups. Malcolm Scott Carpenter; Leroy G. Cooper; John H. Glenn, Jr.; Virgil I. "Gus" Grissom; Walter M. Schirra, Jr.; Alan B. Shepard, Jr.; and Donald K. "Deke" Slayton—they were as all-American as a **John Philip Sousa march**, smiling, crew cut, stand-and-salute soldiers from small towns across the country. Between the ages of thirty-two and thirty-seven, they were the shining embodiments of their middle-class, white, Protestant backgrounds. Reporters immediately wanted to know everything about them: why did they want to go into space; what did their wives think of their dangerous work; how did their religious beliefs square with the idea of spaceflight; who would be the first one to be launched? Also seated on the **dais** that day were two other men, just as eager to talk about the Mercury program as the seven astronauts. Dr. W. Randolph Lovelace II, chairman of NASA's Life Science Committee, and Brigadier General Donald Flickinger of the Air Force helped design the medical testing procedures for the astronaut candidates that took place at the Lovelace Foundation in Albuquerque and at the Wright Air Development Center's (WADC) Aeromedical Laboratory at Wright-Patterson Air Force Base in Dayton. They played a central role in selecting the Mercury 7. The fifty-one-year-old Lovelace, an engaging and well-respected man, knew his astronaut tests had been formidable. "I just hope they never give me a physical examination," he joked, glancing at the astronauts with a wink. "It's been a rough, long period that they have been through. I can tell you that you pick highly intelligent, highly motivated and intelligent men, and everyone is that type of person. . . . I can tell you that I am very, very thrilled that we have had a part in the program."*

What Dr. Lovelace did not say at that moment was that he and Flickinger were interested in testing women for potential spaceflight and had a hunch that females might offer some advantages over men as astronauts. They wondered if women's lower body weight,

John Philip Sousa march: Spirited piece of music written by American composer John Philip Sousa (1854–1932), famous for his marches.

Dais: Raised platform.

for example, would make them better human cargo for American rockets, which were having a difficult time lifting heavier **payloads**. Every pound in the spacecraft necessitated more booster power. Greater human weight also required a greater oxygen supply and more food. If the weight of the space capsule could be reduced even slightly by using a lighter astronaut, the ability to boost the capsule would be less of a concern. Lovelace and Flickinger were also curious to determine whether women could measure up to the same demanding standard that the Mercury astronauts established. Were women physically weaker, less **resilient**, less capable of dealing with isolation, stress, and danger? Lovelace and Flickinger were reluctant to accept general assumptions about women's inferiority and wanted to scientifically evaluate women and compare their data to the men's. As scientists intimately connected to the international community, they also knew that the Soviets were already discussing the possibility of women astronauts. Some rumors coming out of Moscow suggested that Russia might even launch a woman in their first orbital spaceflight, and everyone believed the first human mission was **imminent**. At the very least, Lovelace and Flickinger wanted to test one woman on the same medical trials the seven Mercury astronauts just had completed under their supervision at Wright-Patterson and the Lovelace Foundation. If a single woman test subject did well, perhaps others would also. They just needed to find the right volunteer. For them, an exceptional woman pilot would make the ideal candidate. . . .

Air Force Brigadier General Donald Flickinger hoped to move quickly in testing Jerrie Cobb. Since he had been responsible for designing spaceflight simulation evaluation for all seven Project Mercury astronauts at Wright-Patterson Air Force Base in Dayton, Flickinger wanted to test Cobb on the same drills and compare her scores to the ones the men had posted the previous spring. While the first phase of astronaut tests administered by the Lovelace Foundation focused on a candidate's physical aptitude for spaceflight, the second phase, conducted shortly afterward at Wright-Patterson, measured how a potential astronaut might respond to the unique stresses of outer space. Under Flickinger's direction, the staff at the Wright-Patterson Air Development Center's Aeromedical Laboratory provided an extensive battery of psychological exams, including a sensory isolation test calculated to gauge how an astronaut reacted to the simulated silence and stillness of space. Tests at Wright-Patterson also measured the astronauts's ability to function in weightlessness and under the heavy gravitational forces of the **centrifuge**.

Payloads: Loads carried by an aircraft or spacecraft consisting of things (such as passengers or instruments) necessary to the purpose of the flight.

Resilient: Able to recover or adjust quickly.

Imminent: About to take place.

Centrifuge: Machine used to simulate gravitational effects.

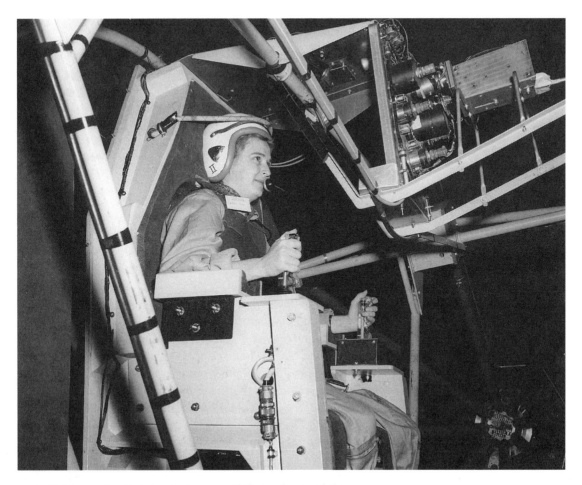

Jerrie Cobb was the first female to pass all three phases of the Mercury Astronaut Program but was not allowed to become an astronaut due to NASA regulations. *(NASA)*

Don Flickinger had first approached NASA with the idea of testing women for their viability as astronauts in the late 1950s. NASA was not interested. The space agency believed women were physically incapable of handling the demands of space. "You must remember," Flickinger's friend Dr. Stanley Mohler [1927–] explained, "the aviation journals in the late 1950s were full of articles claiming that when women menstruate, their brain changes, they become distracted and can't think clearly. They're more likely to crash." Flickinger did not pay attention to those myths. Rather than dropping the proposal or continuing to **lobby** NASA, Flickinger, along with Randy Lovelace, decided to test a woman candidate as part of their own

Lobby: Petition; try to gain support.

*independent experiment, not under the official **auspices** of NASA. If their results proved that a woman scored well on the same tests that the Project Mercury astronauts underwent, and using the same equipment, Flickinger again would approach NASA with the data. In testing first and presenting data later, Flickinger was hoping for an end run around NASA. Scientific data that **refuted** prevailing social attitudes had to be acknowledged, Flickinger and Lovelace believed. How could NASA ignore the possibility of female astronauts if data collected by two members of its Special Committee on Life Sciences proved that women were physically capable?. . .*

*Colonel John Stapp [1910–1999] chief of the Wright-Patterson Aeromedical Laboratory, had long made up his mind about women as astronauts. Females were considerably less equipped to withstand the emotional stresses that accompany spaceflight, he argued. "Economically, the cost of putting a woman in space is **prohibitive**," he said, "strictly a luxury item we can ill afford." Although the physicians Nichols [Ruth Nichols (1901–1960), one of the first women tested] spoke to admitted their ignorance of the workings of the female body, Stapp offered a quantifiable assessment about women's physical abilities, albeit without citing any specific test results. Women, he said, were physiologically 85 percent as efficient as men of the same weight, size, and age. He was not sure if women were able to maintain effort and motivation in extremely stressful situations and he doubted that women would be able to be objective and offer sound judgment when they were tired or nervous. Women, he said, needed to be protected against exposure to dangerous work. "To expose women needlessly," he said, "to the known as well as the incalculable dangers of pioneer spaceflight would be like employing women as riveters, truck drivers, steel workers, or coal miners. . . ."*

*While admitting ignorance about the capacity of the female body for spaceflight, the Air Force was not curious to learn anything new. Rejecting any experiment that offered insight into women's physiology was not a matter of disinterest alone. Discovering that women were stronger and more physically capable than assumed might challenge the military's assertion of male strength, bravery, and superiority. As long as military men were viewed as possessing unique physical qualities that permitted them to accomplish dangerous missions, they held a **monopoly** as jet test pilots and as astronauts on spaceflights. Wright-Patterson officers simply preferred not to know what women pilots could do rather than face the possibility of "adverse publicity" that might accompany new scientific understanding about women. They certainly did not want to know that a fifty-eight-*

Auspices: Support or protection.

Refuted: Proved wrong.

Prohibitive: Too expensive; excessive.

Monopoly: Exclusive control.

Women in the twenty-first century have a more active presence in the U.S. space program. This female astronaut installs thermal blankets on the International Space Station. *(Johnson Space Center, NASA)*

year-old woman could hold her own in space tests designed for virile young soldiers. . . .

The Vice President [Lyndon Johnson] agreed to meet with the women [Janey Hart and Jerrie Cobb] at 11 A.M. in his office across from the Senate chambers. A master of political real estate, Johnson maintained his Senate leadership after he assumed the vice presidency. Journalists around Capitol Hill referred to the elaborate chambers of Office P-38 as the "Taj Mahal"; it was an impressive room with views of the Supreme Court, a large crystal chandelier, and ornate **frescoes** on the ceiling. Johnson rushed to the meeting after attending a bill-signing ceremony at the White House with President [John F.] Kennedy [1917–1963; served 1961–63]. The Vice President had just an hour to meet with the women, grab something to eat, and prepare to open the Senate at noon. As Johnson walked out to greet them in his reception area, Cobb and Hart gathered up their pocket books and extended their hands in greeting.

Cobb focused immediately on the scientific benefits that could be gained by sending a woman into space. She presented Johnson with the same points she had been making for nearly two years: women weighed less, ate less, consumed less oxygen than men. Therefore, women would need less booster power to propel them into space. Recent studies, she explained, proved that women showed an amazing ability to withstand isolation and inactivity. She reviewed the tests in the isolation tank she had completed with Dr. [Jay] Shurley [1917–] in Oklahoma City and indicated that Wally Funk and Rhea Hurrle [Rhea Allison Woltman] had performed equally as well. New research, she continued, revealed that women could withstand more heat, noise, and vibration than men. With such results, Cobb argued, how could the United States government discontinue testing of women astronaut candidates?

Hart then added her points. Space should not be blocked off as an environment for men only, she said. It was an antiquated idea to suggest that women only wanted to stay at home, tied to the kitchen. Women wanted to explore the universe and push themselves to the far reaches of their ability, just as men did. Besides, opening this door to women was part of a larger national effort toward equity and fairness for all Americans. As Johnson knew, President Kennedy himself has announced on the very day that John Glenn had orbited the earth that he was establishing a Commission of the Status of Women. In an executive order posted at all government agencies, the President made it clear that "women are entitled to equality of opportunity for employment in Government and in industry. But a mere statement supporting equality of opportunity must be implemented by affirmative steps to see that the doors are really open for training, selection, advancement and equal pay." Eventually women would explore outer space, Hart argued. Why not begin at the earliest moment we can?

Frescoes: Paintings done on a plaster wall.

Johnson leaned back in his chair. Above him on the ceiling were four **allegorical** frescoes depicting human ambition. All four figures were women, dressed in impressive robes and staring down at him. Johnson folded his hands and leaned his large shoulders against the back of his leather chair. Jackie Cochran had turned him in favor of women fliers a long time ago, he began. In fact, Cochran had once saved Johnson's political neck, an aide later recalled. In the final days of his 1948 Senate primary race, Johnson had collapsed in pain from a kidney stone, high fever, and dangerous infection. He could not afford to take time off for surgery—the days lost on the campaign trail would be politically fatal. When Jackie Cochran heard about his plight, she recalled that an esteemed urologist from Great Britain was visiting the Mayo Clinic. Cochran called one of Johnson's campaign managers and informed him she would appear at the hospital emergency entrance at 1:30 and fly Johnson to Minnesota in her Lockheed Electra. She did. Johnson was relieved of his pain without surgery and was back on the campaign trail in two weeks. Johnson did not forget personal favors like that.

Many minority groups were asking for attention from NASA, the Vice President continued. They wanted to be astronauts, too. If the United States allowed women into space, then blacks, Mexicans, Chinese, and other minorities would want to fly too. Cobb sat, listening politely, looking prim in her tailored dress, with three strands of pearls around her neck. What's wrong with minorities serving as astronauts if they are qualified, she asked? Johnson did not answer. Cobb continued. If the Vice President were proposing that only citizens who were in the majority should be launched into space, then women should be considered. Women are certainly not in the minority, she thought, in terms of numbers, money, votes, and tax dollars. Leaning toward them women with a pained expression on his face, Lyndon Johnson looked directly at Cobb and Hart and gave them his final thought. As much as he would like to help the cause of women astronauts, it was really an issue for [NASA administrator] James Webb [1906–1992] and those at NASA. It hurt him to say it because he was eager to help, but the question just was not up to him to address. Johnson called an end to the meeting and started talking on his private telephone.

Janey Hart was angry. She knew Johnson was "putting on a performance that made it look as though it was painful to tell us." Clearly Johnson was not going to lend a hand to their cause, even though a word from the Vice President to James Webb would make an enormous difference. What Hart did not understand was why.

Allegorical: Pertaining to an abstract idea represented symbolically in a work of art by a human figure.

Hart and Cobb left Johnson's chambers and met with a crowd of reporters outside in the Capitol hallway. Hart stood with her arms tightly folded across her chest, her pocketbook stuffed into the crook of her arm. Her goal at this point seemed to be to mind her manners and hold her anger in check. Cobb leaned near the wall, her face set rigidly in a practiced smile. "I'm hoping that something will come out of these meetings," she said as reporters scribbled into their notebooks. Later, newspaper reporters declared that two would-be "astronettes" had pleaded their case in Washington. The Vice President—using the current jargon from Cape Canaveral—had said the women were "A-OK" but the decision was not his to make.

Cobb and Hart never saw the letter to James Webb that Liz Carpenter had drafted for the Vice President's signature. Johnson decided not to show it to them because he had no intention of signing it. He did not want to ask James Webb to look into the question of women astronauts. Perhaps Johnson thought starting a woman's program would jeopardize the whole works, Carpenter later said. Taking out his pen, Johnson drew Carpenter's draft across the large desk and scribbled forcefully across the bottom of the page. In his distinctive hand, Johnson announced the verdict that Hart, Cobb, and the press never knew: "Let's Stop This Now!"

What happened next . . .

Supporters of the Mercury 13 protested NASA's decision and pressured the U.S. Congress to hold hearings on discrimination against women in the space program. In July 1962, a Congressional subcommittee met to discuss the reinstatement of the training program. The representatives of NASA claimed that the women were ineligible to become astronauts because they had not gone through the military jet-pilot training program at Edwards Air Force base in California. None of the women had completed this program because women were not eligible for jet-pilot training, a ban that remained in effect until 1973. The truth was that male military officers, both in the armed forces and at NASA, did not want women to fly in space: Such a development would reflect negatively on the traditional image of airmen as strong, brave risk-takers. With no one willing to help the women, Mercury 13 disbanded with-

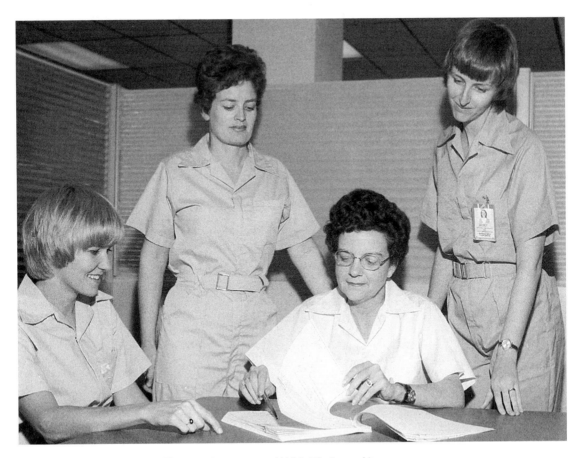

An all-female crew of scientific experimenters at NASA. Their working conditions simulate, as nearly as possible, conditions that exist in space. *(NASA)*

out a single member being given the chance to serve as an astronaut. They returned to active private lives, remaining in the aviation field as commercial pilots, flight instructors, owners of aviation-related businesses, air-race competitors, and flying hobbyists.

Did you know . . .
- In 1963, a year after the Mercury 13 disbanded, the Soviet Union sent female cosmonaut Valentina Tereshkova (1937–) into space. The United States did not send a woman into space until twenty years later, when Sally Ride became the first female American to travel in space.

- In 1995 ten of the Mercury 13 members, some meeting for the first time, gathered at Cape Canaveral, Florida. They were there to witness the launch of Eileen Collins (1956–), the first American woman pilot astronaut to travel in space. Before entering the space shuttle *Discovery*, Collins paid tribute to the Mercury 13 pioneers, saying, "They gave us [women astronauts] a history."

- Although most of the Mercury 13 were disappointed about NASA's decision to cancel the testing program, they did not make any further efforts to pursue a career in space-flight. Cobb and Funk were the exceptions: Hoping to fly in space one day, both stayed physically fit and were still flying airplanes as they approached the age of seventy. In 1998, when John Glenn took his second flight at age seventy-six, Cobb and her supporters started a movement to pressure NASA to give her a mission in space. Once again, NASA ignored her. In 2001 Funk signed a contract with a civilian space launch company, Interorbital Systems, to take a suborbital flight. Her trip had been delayed several times by 2004, but she remained optimistic about finally traveling in space.

Consider the following . . .

- If Vice President Johnson had intervened on the behalf of the Mercury 13, do you think any of them would have been allowed to travel to space? Why or why not?

- Glenn returned to space at the age of seventy-six. Do you think NASA should extend an invitation to Cobb, who is still an active pilot at the age of eighty-five?

For More Information

Books

Ackmann, Martha. *The Mercury 13: The Untold Story of Thirteen American Women and the Dream of Space Flight.* New York: Random House, 2003.

Cobb, Jerrie. *Jerrie Cobb, Solo Pilot.* Sun City, FL: Jerrie Cobb Foundation, 1997.

Nolen, Stephanie. *Promised the Moon: The Untold Story of the First Women in the Space Race.* New York: Four Walls Eight Windows, 2003.

Periodicals

"'Mercury 13' Project Helped Pave Way for Female Astronauts." *Government CustomWire* (April 8, 2004).

"Star Struck." *Weekly Reader—Senior* (April 2, 2004): pp. 2–3.

"Stars in Their Eyes." *People* (July 7, 2003): pp. 111–14.

Web Sites

Burbank, Sam. "Mercury 13's Wally Funk Fights for Her Place in Space." *NationalGeographic.com.* http://news.nationalgeographic.com/news/2003/07/0709_030709_tvspacewoman.html (accessed on July 19, 2004).

DeFrange, Ann. "State-Born Aviatrix Yearns for Space. 2nd Astronaut Bid Supported." *The Sunday Oklahoman* (May 17, 1998): pp. 1–2; http://freepages.genealogy.rootsweb.com/~swokla/family/jerricobb.html (accessed on July 19, 2004).

Funk, Wally. *The Mercury 13 Story.* www.ninety-nines.org/mercury.html (accessed on July 19, 2004).

"Mercury 13—The Women of the Mercury Era." http://www.mercury13.com/ (accessed on July 19, 2004).

John Glenn, with Nick Taylor

Excerpts from **John Glenn: A Memoir**
Published in 1999

John Herschel Glenn Jr. (1921–) has accomplished more in one lifetime than many people could achieve in three. First a combat pilot in World War II (1939–45) and the Korean War (1950–53), Glenn was named one of the Mercury 7, the original group of men chosen to be American astronauts, in 1959. On February 20, 1962, Glenn became a national hero when he successfully orbited Earth three times in the space capsule *Friendship 7* before returning safely. Thirty-six years later—after successful careers as a businessman and a U.S. senator—Glenn returned to space aboard the shuttle *Discovery,* at the age of seventy-seven, becoming the oldest astronaut to fly a mission.

After completing training as a fighter-bomber pilot, Glenn married his high school sweetheart, Annie, and flew missions in World War II and the Korean War. Glenn then became a test pilot, and after two years of training and experience, was commissioned to oversee the development of new fighter planes. Under Project Bullet, Glenn flew the F8U Crusader across the United States, making the first transcontinental supersonic flight in three hours and twenty-three minutes.

In 1958 the government announced its plans to begin a space program with the aim of orbiting a human being around Earth. Glenn, captivated by the idea of being able to fly out of Earth's atmosphere, began a rigorous training program to become one of the first men selected. In April 1959, Glenn became a member of the Mercury 7, the elite group of men chosen to be America's first astronauts. National Aeronautics and Space Administration (NASA) flew two suborbital (within Earth orbit) missions, for which Glenn was a backup pilot, before announcing plans to launch Mercury-*Atlas 6,* the first manned spacecraft to fly an orbital mission. Glenn was chosen as the pilot.

John Glenn. *(AP/Wide World Photos)*

Glenn accomplished his mission on February 20, 1962, when he successfully orbited Earth. Unknown to the American public as they anxiously awaited Glenn's safe return, a flight sensor had indicated a problem with the space capsule's protective heat shield. There was no way for Glenn to fix the problem in flight, and if the heat shield slipped, the capsule would disintegrate upon attempting to reenter Earth's atmosphere. NASA mission control informed Glenn of the problem, advising him to change the reentry plan. Glenn took command of the capsule himself and piloted safely back to Earth, where he was celebrated as a national hero.

Glenn retired from the military in 1965 after being promoted to a full colonel. He then became a successful businessman until 1977, when he was elected a U.S. senator from Ohio. Glenn served in the Senate until 1997, when he retired to pursue other interests, such as returning to space. Glenn approached NASA and proposed that he conduct a test on the effects of weightlessness on older people. After convincing NASA of his own physical and mental fitness, Glenn joined the crew of the space shuttle *Discovery*. On October 29, 1998,

First American in Space

On May 5, 1961, Alan Shepard (1923–1998) became the first American in space. He piloted the Mercury space capsule 115 miles (185 kilometers) above Earth's surface and 302 miles (486 kilometers) across the Atlantic Ocean. Although the trip lasted for only about fifteen minutes, his journey was almost technically perfect, paving the way for many more flights by U.S. astronauts. In 1963 Shepard was diagnosed as having Méière's syndrome, a disease of the inner ear. NASA removed him from active flight duty and reassigned him to the NASA center in Houston, Texas, where he became chief of the astronaut office.

In 1968 Shepard underwent a successful operation in which a small drain tube was implanted in his inner ear. He then applied for readmission to active duty, and the following year NASA chose him to command the *Apollo 14* flight to the Moon. On January 31, 1971, *Apollo 14* blasted off from Cape Kennedy, nearly ten years after Shepard's first space flight. Five days later Shepard and

fellow astronaut Edgar Mitchell (1930–) landed on the Moon's surface. From their lunar module, the two astronauts stepped out into the Fra Mauro Highlands, as the world watched on television. (The Fra Mauro Highlands is a widespread hilly geological area covering large portions of the lunar surface, with an eighty-kilometer-diameter crater, the Fra Mauro crater, located within it. The Fra Mauro crater and surrounding formation take their names from a 15th century Italian monk and mapmaker.)

The astronauts had brought a lunar cart with them, and during two trips outside the lunar module they conducted experiments and gathered rock specimens. On one excursion Shepard hit a golf ball across the Moon's surface. In addition, the astronauts left behind a small scientific station that would continue to send messages to scientists on Earth. The story of the flight was immortalized in a book by author Tom Wolfe (see entry) and in a movie, both titled *The Right Stuff.*

Glenn became the oldest person, at the age of seventy-seven, to fly in space. The nine-day flight was a complete success, and the shuttle returned safely to Earth's surface. Glenn retired fully from public life in 1999.

Things to remember while reading excerpts from *John Glenn: A Memoir:*

- The excerpts are from Glenn's autobiography, which he wrote after retiring in 1999. The first excerpt discusses

Glenn's recollections of flying *Friendship 7* in 1962. The second excerpt concerns his time aboard *Discovery* in 1998.

- During his first flight, Glenn had only a small window on one side of the capsule, which severely limited his vision. For his second flight, Glenn was afforded a much grander view because of the large number of windows on the *Discovery*. There was also a great difference in size between the two crafts. *Friendship 7* was large enough to hold only Glenn; *Discovery* was large enough to hold a team of scientists.

- In the first excerpt Glenn writes, "That was Al Shepard on the capsule communicator's microphone at mission control. . . ." He is referring to Alan Shepard, who was the first American to fly in space (see box on page 92).

- Glenn mentions Annie, his wife, and Dave and Lyn, his children, in the second passage.

Excerpts from John Glenn: A Memoir

*Liftoff was slow. The Atlas's 367,000 pounds of thrust were barely enough to overcome its 125-ton weight. I wasn't really off until the forty-two-inch **umbilical cord** that took electrical connections to the base of the rocket pulled loose. That was my last connection with Earth. It took the two boosters and the **sustainer** engine three seconds of fire and thunder to lift the thing that far. From where I sat the rise seemed **ponderous** and stately, as if the rocket were an elephant trying to become a ballerina. Then the mission elapsed-time clock on the cockpit panel ticked into life and I could report, "The clock is operating. We're under way."*

I could hardly believe it. Finally!

*The rocket rolled and headed slightly north of east. At thirteen seconds I felt a little shudder. "A little bumpy along about here," I reported. The **G forces** started to build up. The engines burned fuel at an enormous rate, one ton a second, more in the first minute than a jet airliner flying coast to coast, as the fuel was consumed the rocket grew lighter and rose faster. At forty-eight seconds I began to feel the*

Umbilical cord: A tethering or supply line (as for an astronaut outside a spacecraft or a diver underwater).

Sustainer: System that keeps up or prolongs.

Ponderous: Unwieldy or clumsy.

G forces: Units of force on a body that is equal to thirty-two feet per second.

John Glenn in a silver Mercury space suit during pre-training activities.
(NASA)

Aerodynamic: Motion of air
and gaseous fluids.

*vibration associated with high Q, the worst seconds of **aerodynamic** stress, when the capsule was pushing through air resistance amounting to almost a thousand pounds per square foot. The shaking got worse, then smoothed out at 1:12, and I felt the relief of knowing I* was through max Q, the part of the launch where the rocket was most likely to blow.

At 2:09 the booster engines cut off and fell away. I was forty miles high and forty-five miles from the Cape. The rocket pitched forward for the few seconds it took for the escape tower's **jettison** rocket to fire, taking the half-ton tower away from the capsule. The G forces fell to just over one. The Atlas pitched up again and, driven by the sustainer engine and the two smaller **vernier** engines, which made course corrections, resumed its acceleration toward a top speed of 17,545 miles per hour in the ever thinning air. Another instant of relief.

Pilots gear their moments of greatest attention to the times when flight conditions change. When you get through them, you're glad for a fraction of a second, and then you think about the next thing you have to do.

The Gs built again, pushing me back into the couch. The sky looked dark outside the window. Following the flight plan, I repeated the fuel, oxygen, cabin pressure, and battery readings from the dials in front of me in the tiny cabin. The arc of the flight was taking me out over Bermuda. "Cape is go and I am a go. Capsule is in good shape," I reported.

"Roger, twenty seconds to SECO." That was Al Shepard on the capsule communicator's microphone at mission control, warning me that the next crucial moment—sustainer engine cutoff—was seconds away.

Five minutes into the flight, if all went well, I would achieve orbital speed, hit zero G, and, if the angle of **ascent** was right, be inserted into orbit at a height of about a hundred miles. The sustainer and vernier engines would cut off, the capsule-to-rocket clamp would release, and the **posigrade rockets** would fire to separate Friendship 7 from the Atlas.

It happened as programmed. The weight and fuel tolerances were so tight that the engines had less than three seconds' worth of fuel remaining when I hit that keyhole in the sky. Suddenly I was no longer pushed back against the seat but had a momentary sensation of tumbling forward.

"Zero G and I feel fine," I said exultantly. "Capsule is turning around." Through the window, I could see the curve of the Earth and its thin film of atmosphere. "Oh," I exclaimed, "that view is tremendous!". . .

Jettison: Voluntary release of cargo during flight to lighten a ship's load.

Vernier: Any of two or more small supplemental rocket engines or gas nozzles on a missile or a rocket vehicle for making the fine adjustments in the speed or course of controlling the position of the craft.

Ascent: Rising or mounting upward.

Posigrade rockets: Supplementary rockets that are fired in the direction of the spacecraft's motion to separate the sections.

John Glenn, with Nick Taylor   95

Glenn returns to space

The space shuttle is the most complex machine ever made. It has two million parts, and a million of them move. Its wiring laid end to end would stretch 230 miles, and it has six hundred circuit breakers. The orbiter itself has three eighty-thousand-horsepower engines that each develop 393,800 pounds of **thrust.** They are fed by the huge rust-orange tank to which the orbiter and the boosters cling during launch, and the two-solid-fuel rocket boosters each develop 3.3 million pounds of thrust. The weight at liftoff is about 4.5 million pounds, and total thrust at liftoff is over 7 million pounds.

It was up there ready to go, and the liquid oxygen that **oxidizes** the liquid hydrogen fuel venting out the top in wisps of vapor adds to the sense of drama. It's a huge machine containing an almost **unfathomable** amount of power. That's the point when it hits you. It's for real—you're going up.

The elevator took us up. It was a beautiful day, and I paused to glance around at the Cape and the space complex that had changed so much since the time of Project Mercury. As I looked south to the Canaveral light house, the Atlas and Titan launch **gantries** that are the remaining occupants of Heavy Row were reminders of the early days. Pad 14, where Friendship 7 and the rest of the Project Mercury Atlas flights had launched, was still there, but its gantry had been dismantled long ago. The blockhouse is a museum. It was hard to imagine that virtually the entire history of space travel had occurred between my first ride and my second. Somebody had pointed out that more time had passed between Friendship 7 and this Discovery mission that had passed between Lindbergh's solo transatlantic flight and Friendship 7. It didn't seem that long to me, but that is the way lives pass when you look back on them: in a blink of an eye.

I don't think anyone was scared. **Apprehensive?** Yes. I felt the same constructive apprehension I'd felt as a forty-year-old, keyed up and ready to go. Everybody knows something could go wrong, but you just put that behind you and go do what you've been trained to do. . . .

About six seconds from zero, the booster's main engines lit. I felt the shuddering and the **resonance** as they built toward full thrust. The shuttle bent as if it was starting to bow, then straightened. The push of the orbiter's engines is straight up, but the center of gravity of the whole launch assembly, including the solid rocket booster engines and the external tank, is a point a few feet into the

Thrust: Driving force.

Oxidizes: Mixes with oxygen.

Unfathomable: Impossible to comprehend.

Gantries: Frame structures raised on side supports so as to span over or around something.

Apprehensive: Anxious.

Resonance: Vibration of large amplitude in a mechanical or electrical system.

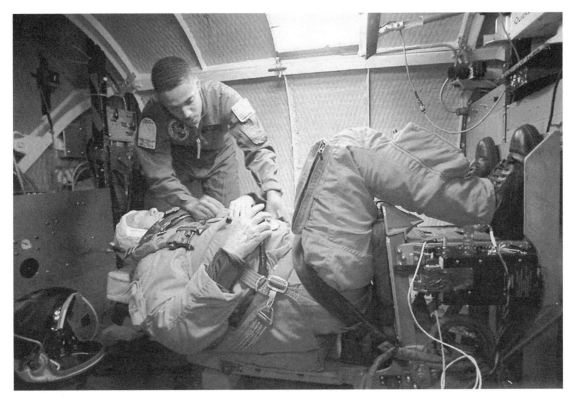

John Glenn preparing for his second mission in space on the space shuttle *Discovery.* *(Johnson Space Center, NASA)*

tank, so the assembly, held down by eight massive bolts, flexes in that direction.

As it came back to vertical, the solid walls lit. We were going someplace. The shaking and the shuddering and the roar told us that. In rapid sequence the solids built up power, the explosive hold-down bolts were fired, and over seven million pounds of thrust pushed us up at 1.6 Gs.

I hit the timer on my knees and the one on my wristwatch. The wristwatch gave the mission elapsed time starting from our launch, and would also count the days. The timeline for all our activities, including research experiments, required us to know the day as well as the hour and minute from launch.

The vehicle was moving at a hundred miles an hour by the time it cleared the launch tower. It was accelerating far more rapidly than the Atlas, and its shaking and vibration were much more pronounced.

Max Q, and the worst shaking and shuddering, came about sixty seconds after launch. The main engines **throttled** *back automatically to keep the vehicle within its structural limits. Then came the voice from the ground, "Go at throttle up," which meant we were through the area of maximum aerodynamic pressure and the main engines had returned to full throttle.*

The solid-fuel boosters run for two minutes and six seconds. Everyone looks forward to the moment they burn out and detach. They're the one thing in the launch vehicle you have absolutely no control over. You can't throttle them back, you can't shut them off, and you can't detach them. There are no emergency procedures if anything goes wrong. You just hope everything keeps working right. I had told Annie and Dave and Lyn, who still worried, that when the solids were gone we were home free.

They burned out. I felt a sudden loss of thrust, then heard a bang like a rifle shot as the explosive bolts holding them to the external tank fired and detached them. They would cartwheel down until their parachutes deployed to bring them down for retrieval and reuse.

With the solids gone, the ride eased out. The orbiter's main engines run smoothly, and you ride into orbit accelerating as the fuel in the external tank is burned, making the vehicle lighter. You hit three Gs just before you reach orbit.

Then another bang, more muffled than the first, signaled that the spent external tank was jetissoned. It would burn up reentering the atmosphere over the Indian Ocean. After that, we were operating on the fuel that was stored within the orbiter itself for the final sprint to orbital **velocity.** . . .

The importance of the cameras that waited at the ready on the Velcro patches beside most of the shuttle's windows came to the fore with Hurricane Mitch. It had made landfall in Honduras on the day before our launch, and hung over Honduras and Nicaragua for several days, dumping twenty-five inches of rain, causing mudslides that swept away entire villages, and killing over seven thousand people. A few days into our flight, mission control called for photographs of the devastated areas.

One of the laptops on the flight deck was set up to track Discovery on its orbits around the world. By following the track on the screen, you could anticipate when you were approaching an area that needed to be photographed. You couldn't wait until you recognized Honduras, for instance, because at 17,500 miles an hour—five miles

Throttled: Varied the thrust; decreased the flow of fuel to an engine.

Velocity: Quickness of motion; speed.

per second—the photo angles you wanted would have slid by already. We got the shots we wanted.

In some cases, the higher orbit of Discovery *meant more spectacular views than I had seen in* Friendship 7. *Coming over the Florida Keys at one point in the mission, for example, I looked out toward the north and was startled that I could see Lake Erie. In fact, I could look beyond straight into Canada. The entire East Coast was visible— the hook of Cape Cod, Long Island, Cape Hatteras, down to the clear coral sands of the Bahamas and the Caribbean, south to Cuba, and beyond.*

A night of thunderstorms over South Africa produced a view of a field of lightning flashes that must have stretched over eight hundred or a thousand miles, the flashes looking like bubbles of light breaking by the hundreds on the surface of a boiling pot.

All the while, our views of Earth were stolen from the time we gave the eighty-three experiments on board. Each crew member kept on his or her timeline, and as we neared the end of the mission all of the experiments were working and successful. This remained our primary mission, and we were confident that we were making real contributions to science.

What happened next . . .

Upon returning to Earth, Glenn underwent a series of tests to determine the effects of weightlessness on the elderly. Over five years after his flight, Glenn maintained that he experienced no adverse effects from space travel. Glenn had no plans to return to space.

Did you know . . .

- Although he attended a number of universities, Glenn did not earn his bachelor's degree until 1962. After he returned from space, he completed a degree in mathematics from Muskingum College.

- In 1962, after returning from space, Glenn addressed a joint session of Congress, an honor usually reserved for the president and world leaders. His speech is regarded as one of the most important ever delivered on behalf of the space program.

- Glenn lost his first two bids for the U.S. Senate before winning a seat in 1974.

- In the 1984 presidential election, Glenn ran for the Democratic Party nomination. Although he was warmly greeted by crowds and was a popular candidate, he dropped out of the race after it became clear that former Vice President Walter F. Mondale (1928–) was going to win the nomination.

- Glenn's second flight was the inspiration for *Space Cowboys* (2000), a high-tech space adventure film about aging former astronauts who try to prevent a satellite from slamming into Earth. *Space Cowboys* was made in cooperation with NASA.

Consider the following . . .

- Glenn returned to space at the age of seventy-seven. Do you think there should be an age limit for astronauts? Why or why not?

- When NASA announced its national search for astronauts, one of the requirements was that the candidate hold a bachelor's degree. Glenn had completed over two years of course work, but still needed more credits to earn his diploma. However, Glenn's experience as a pilot earned him a spot as an astronaut in the Mercury Project. Do you think it is important to have a degree in order to be an astronaut, or should experience be more important? Why or why not?

For More Information

Books

Glenn, John H. *Letters to John Glenn: With Comments by J. H. Glenn, Jr.* New York: World Book Encyclopedia Science Service, 1964.

Glenn, John, with Nick Taylor. *John Glenn: A Memoir.* New York: Bantam, 1999.

Montgomery, Scott, and Timothy R. Gaffney. *Back in Orbit.* Atlanta, GA: Longstreet, 1998.

Pierce, Philip N., and Karl Schuon. *John H. Glenn: Astronaut.* New York: Franklin Watts, 1962.

Wolfe, Tom. *The Right Stuff.* New York: Farrar, Straus, and Giroux, 1979; Reprinted, New York: Bantam, 1980.

Periodicals

Newcott, William R. "John Glenn: Man with a Mission." *National Geographic* (June 1999): pp. 60–81.

"Space Cowboys." *Astronomy* (September 2000): p. 107.

"Victory Lap." *Time* (November 9, 1998): p. 64.

Web Sites

"Astronaut Bio: John H. Glenn." *Johnson Space Center, NASA.* http://www.grc.nasa.gov/WWW/PAO/html/glennbio.htm (accessed on August 9, 2004).

Bowman, Lee. "Aging in Space." *Simply Family.* http://www.simplyfamily.com/display.cfm?articleID=000207_John_Glenn.cfm (accessed on August 9, 2004).

The John Glenn Institute for Public Service and Public Policy at Ohio State University. www.glenninstitute.org (accessed on August 9, 2004).

Michael Collins and Edwin E. "Buzz" Aldrin Jr.

Excerpts from "The Eagle Has Landed," in Apollo Expeditions to the Moon

Published in 1975; available at NASA (Web site)

On July 16, 1969, the spacecraft *Apollo 11* took off from Cape Kennedy (now Cape Canaveral) in Florida, sending three American astronauts into space. Three days later, two of the astronauts, Neil Armstrong (1930–) and Edwin E. "Buzz" Aldrin Jr. (1930–), became the first men to walk on the surface of the moon. Project Apollo—which had been born out of the Mercury Project that successfully sent manned capsules into orbit—proved to be one of the most successful endeavors in the history of the National Aeronautics and Space Administration (NASA).

In 1958, shortly after the Soviet Union sent the satellite *Sputnik 1* into orbit, President Dwight D. Eisenhower (1890–1969; served 1953–61) signed the National Aeronautics and Space Act, which established NASA. The ultimate goal of the new agency was to send a manned spacecraft to the Moon; however, NASA first had to prove it could send a human into space and return the person safely. Project Mercury was begun in 1958. Perhaps its greatest success came on February 20, 1962, when astronaut John Glenn Jr. (1921–) successfully orbited Earth three times in the space capsule *Friendship 7*. In

1964, bolstered by positive results from Project Mercury, NASA began Project Gemini and Project Apollo. Project Gemini provided astronauts with experience in returning to Earth from space as well as practice in successfully linking space vehicles and "walking" in space. Working in tandem with Gemini, Project Apollo (named for the Greek god of the Sun) focused on the design, development, and testing of spacecraft and related technology that would place a human on the Moon.

Project Apollo was a massive undertaking. Under the auspices of NASA, German-born rocket scientist Werhner von Braun (1912–1977) and his colleagues developed the three-stage *Saturn V* rocket to launch the spacecraft. (Von Braun and his team had developed the V-2 rocket for Nazi Germany during World War II and had immigrated to the United States in 1945, at the end of the war.) The Saturn operated in stages, a concept that was originated by Russian engineer Konstantin Tsiolkovsky (1857–1935; pronounced KAHN-stan-tyeen tsee-ohl-KAHV-skee) and tested by American physicist Robert H. Goddard (see entry). Russian rocket engineer Sergei Korolev (1907–1966) is credited with developing the staged rocket, which ignites at specified stages in order to propel an object long distances into space (see First Satellite entry). The rocket's first two stages propelled the spacecraft out of Earth's gravity into space and then dropped off. The third stage put the spacecraft into Earth orbit. The rocket then refired to send the spacecraft at a speed of 25,000 miles (40,225 kilometers) per hour toward the Moon, with the third stage dropping off along the way.

The Apollo spacecraft itself consisted of the command module, where the astronauts were stationed; the service module, which contained electrical power and fuel; and the lunar module, which, after entering the Moon's orbit, could separate from the rest of the spacecraft and carry the astronauts to the surface of the Moon. The lunar module, which stood 23 feet (7 meters) high and weighed 15 tons (13.6 metric tons), rested first on spiderlike legs used for landing and then on a launch platform for departure from the Moon's surface. The lunar module lacked heat shields and operated only in the vacuum of space. After launching itself from the Moon's surface, the lunar module would go into lunar orbit and dock with the command module, which would then readjust its course to head back to Earth. The service module powered the spacecraft on the return trip, falling away to reentry into Earth's atmosphere.

Men who wanted to be astronauts were put through a difficult eighteen-month training regimen, requiring them to participate in strenuous physical exercises, to attend classes, and to practice in-flight exercises. Although there were a number of qualified candidates, three men were chosen to pilot *Apollo/Saturn 204*: Virgil "Gus" Grissom (1926–1967), Edward White (1930–1967), and Roger Chaffee (1935–1967) trained for a mission to pilot the rocket around Earth. On January 27, 1967, the *Apollo/Saturn 204* rocket caught fire on its launchpad and the crew were trapped inside. The hatch handle would not open, and all three men perished. Project Apollo was off to a terrible start and, as a result of the astronauts' deaths, the program was temporarily delayed. Safety precautions resulted from a lengthy investigation. The next five Apollo missions were unmanned flights to test the safety of the new equipment.

The Apollo program rebounded with the successful flights of *Apollo 7* through *Apollo 10*. It was decided that *Apollo 11* would attempt a Moon landing. Three astronauts were chosen: Aldrin, Armstrong, and Michael Collins (1930–). Aldrin was the only one of the three who was not a test pilot, but he had earned a doctorate in orbital mechanics from the Massachusetts Institute of Technology (MIT). He had been the pilot of *Gemini 12*, during which time he set a new record for walking in space, proving that astronauts could work outside an orbiting vehicle to make repairs. Armstrong became the first civilian (nonmilitary) astronaut in NASA. He had an impressive history of testing rocket planes, such as the X-15, for the National Advisory Committee for Aeronautics (NACA), the forerunner of NASA. Armstrong's background made him a perfect fit for Project Apollo. He had been the command pilot for *Gemini 8*, launched on March 16, 1966, before being named to the *Apollo 11* crew. Collins was a graduate of the U.S. Military Academy at West Point and had joined NASA as an astronaut in 1963. In 1966 he was the pilot of *Gemini 10*, becoming the third American to walk in space. The *Apollo 11* crew therefore had a great deal of experience between them, and they seemed the perfect choices to perform a seemingly impossible mission.

On July 16, 1969, Aldrin, Armstrong, and Collins boarded *Apollo 11* and blasted off from Cape Kennedy (now Cape

Apollo 11 astronauts (from left): Neil Armstrong, Michael Collins, and Buzz Aldrin. *(© Reuters/Corbis)*

Canaveral) in Florida. The *Apollo 11* spacecraft consisted of three stages, or separate components—the *Saturn 5* booster rocket, attached to the *Columbia* command module and the *Eagle* lunar landing module. The *Saturn 5* booster rocket propelled the craft into space. All three astronauts rode in the *Columbia* command module on the trip to and from the Moon. The *Eagle* lunar landing module would land Armstrong and Aldrin on the Moon.

On July 19, *Saturn 5* propelled the craft into lunar orbit and circled the Moon twice. The next day Aldrin and Armstrong transferred to the *Eagle*. After about five hours of tests, the *Eagle* and the *Columbia* separated successfully and the *Eagle* entered its own orbit. Within two hours Aldrin and Armstrong

Apollo 11 **blasts off from Cape Kennedy (now Cape Canaveral) in Florida.** *(NASA)*

began the 300-mile descent toward the Moon. At that point a yellow caution light came on in the *Eagle,* signaling that the computer system had became overloaded. Under continuous instructions from the mission control center in Houston, Texas, the *Eagle* made a gradual touchdown.

Seven hours after touchdown, at 10:56 P.M. Eastern Standard Time (EST), Armstrong climbed down a nine-step ladder and became the first human to set foot on the Moon. Aldrin joined him fifteen minutes later. Aldrin and Armstrong quickly adjusted to the lighter gravity, finding they could walk easily on the lunar surface. They spent nearly twenty-one hours on the Moon.

During their stay Armstrong and Aldrin installed a television camera, conducted scientific experiments, took photographs, and collected rock and soil samples. They left an American flag, a mission patch, and medals commemorating American and Russian space explorers who had died in the line of duty. They also set up a plaque that read: "Here men from the planet Earth first set foot upon the Moon. We came in peace for all mankind." The astronauts' moon walk was televised live on Earth, and President Richard M. Nixon (1913–1994; served 1969–74) made a telephone call to the astronauts from the White House. After returning to the *Eagle,* they rested for eight hours. Then they launched off the surface of the Moon and, two hours later, docked with the *Columbia.* After unloading their equipment onto *Columbia* they abandoned the *Eagle.* The *Columbia* set out for Earth on its thirty-first orbit of the Moon. Sixty hours later, at 12:50 P.M. EST on July 24, the spacecraft splashed down in the sea some 950 miles (1,529 kilometers) southwest of Hawaii, only 2.7 miles (4.34 kilometers) from its destination point. The three astronauts were hailed as national heroes.

Things to remember while reading excerpts from "The Eagle Has Landed," in *Apollo Expeditions to the Moon:*

- In the excerpted passages, Armstrong, Aldrin, and Collins recall their memories of the historic landing.

- The astronauts' journey was being watched on television by most Americans and by people in nations all around the world. No matter where one was from, the idea that human beings could walk on the Moon and return to talk about it was an incredible achievement.

- The lunar module seated only two people. Collins was an expert at navigation, and he remained behind in the

"Tranquility" craft to help communicate with Aldrin and Armstrong and guide the lunar module to a safe landing.

Excerpts from "The Eagle Has Landed," in Apollo Expeditions to the Moon

THE MOST AWESOME SPHERE

*COLLINS: Day 4 has a decidedly different feel to it. Instead of nine hours' sleep, I get seven—and fitful ones at that. Despite our concentrated effort to conserve our energy on the way to the Moon, the pressure is overtaking us (or me at least), and I feel that all of us are aware that the honeymoon is over and we are about to lay our little pink bodies on the line. Our first shock comes as we stop our spinning motion and swing ourselves around so as to bring the Moon into view. We have not been able to see the Moon for nearly a day now, and the change is electrifying. The Moon I have known all my life, that **two-dimensional** small yellow disk in the sky, has gone away somewhere, to be replaced by the most awesome sphere I have ever seen. To begin with it is huge, completely filling our window. Second, it is **three-dimensional**. The belly of it bulges out toward us in such a pronounced fashion that I almost feel I can reach out and touch it. To add to the dramatic effect, we can see the stars again. We are in the shadow of the Moon now, and the **elusive** stars have reappeared.*

*As we ease around on the left side of the Moon, I marvel again at the **precision** of our path. We have missed hitting the Moon by a **paltry** 300 **nautical miles**, at a distance of nearly a quarter of a million miles from Earth, and don't forget that the Moon is a moving target and that we are racing through the sky just ahead of its leading edge. When we launched the other day the Moon was nowhere near where it is now; it was some 40 degrees of, or nearly 200,000 miles, behind where it is now, and yet those big computers in the basement in Houston didn't even whimper but belched out super-accurate predictions.*

As we pass behind the Moon, we have just over eight minutes to go before the burn. We are super-careful now, checking and rechecking each step several times. When the moment finally arrives,

Two-dimensional: Having two dimensions; lacking depth.

Three-dimensional: Giving the illusion of depth or varying distances.

Elusive: Hard to pin down.

Precision: Exactness.

Paltry: Meager or measly.

Nautical mile: Length of distance used for sea and air navigation.

Apollo 11 **module floating over the Moon.** *(NASA)*

the big engine instantly springs into action and reassuringly plasters us back in our seats. The acceleration is only a fraction of one G but it feels good nonetheless. For six minutes we sit there peering intent as hawks at our instrument panel, scanning the important dials and gauges, making sure that the proper thing is being done to us. When the engine shuts down, we discuss the matter with our computer and I read out the results: "Minus one, plus one, plus one." The accuracy of the overall system is phenomenal: out of a total of nearly three thousand feet per second, we have **velocity** errors in our body **axis coordinate** system of only a tenth of one foot per second in each of the three directions. That is one accurate burn, and even Neil acknowledges the fact.

Velocity: Quickness of motion; speed.

Axis: Straight line about which a body or geometric figure rotates.

Coordinate: Set of numbers used in specifying the location of a point on a line, on a surface, or in space.

ALDRIN: The second burn to place us in closer circular orbit of the Moon, the orbit from which Neil and I would separate from the Columbia *and continue on to the Moon, was critically important. It had to be made in exactly the right place and for exactly the correct length of time. If we overburned for as little as two seconds we'd be on an impact course for the other side of the Moon. Through a complicated and detailed system of checks and balances, both in Houston and in lunar orbit, plus star checks and detailed platform* **alignments***, two hours after our first lunar orbit we made our second burn, in an atmosphere of nervous and intense concentration. It, too, worked perfectly. . . .*

A YELLOW CAUTION LIGHT

At six thousand feet above the lunar surface a yellow caution light came on and we encountered one of the few potentially serious problems in the entire flight, a problem which might have caused us to **abort***, had it not been for a man on the ground who really knew his job. . . .*

ALDRIN: *Back in Houston, not to mention on board the Eagle, hearts shot up into throats while we waited to learn what would happen. We received two of the caution lights when Steve Bales [c.1942–] the flight controller responsible for the LM [lunar module] computer activity, told us to proceed, through Charlie Duke [1935–] the capsule communicator. We received three or four more warnings but kept on going. When Mike, Neil, and I were presented with Medals of Freedom by President Nixon, Steve also received one. He certainly deserved it, because without him we might not have landed.*

ARMSTRONG: *In the final phases of the descent after a number of program alarms, we looked at the landing area and found a very large* **crater***. This is the area we decided we would not go into; we extended the downward range. The exhaust dust was kicked up by the engine and this caused some concern in that it* **degraded** *our ability to determine not only our altitude in the final phases but also our* **translational** *velocities over the ground. It's quite important not to stub your toe during the final phases of touchdown.*

Eagle: 540 feet, down at 30 (feet per second) . . . 4 forward . . . 4 forward . . . drifting to the right a little . . . O.K. . . .

Houston: 30 seconds (fuel remaining).

Eagle: Contact Light! O.K., engine stop . . . descent engine command override off . . .

Houston: We copy you down, Eagle.

Alignments: Positions or arrangements.

Abort: Terminate prematurely.

Crater: A bowl-shaped depression around a volcano or on the Moon.

Degraded: Reduced to standards far below the normal level.

Translational: Transformation of coordinates in which the new axes are parallel to the old ones.

Eagle: Houston, Tranquility Base here. The Eagle has landed.

Houston: Roger, Tranquility. We copy you on the ground. You've got a bunch of guys about to turn blue. We're breathing again. Thanks a lot. . . .

ARMSTRONG: *Once [we] settled on the surface, the dust settled immediately and we had an excellent view of the area surrounding the LM. We saw a crater surface, **pockmarked** with craters up to 10, 20, 30 feet, and many smaller craters down to a diameter of 1 foot tall and, of course, the surface was very fine-grained. There were a surprising number of rocks of all sizes.*

A number of experts had, prior to the flight, predicted that a good bit of difficulty might be encountered by people due to the variety of strange atmospheric and gravitational characteristics. This didn't prove to be the case and after landing we felt very comfortable in the lunar gravity. It was, in fact, in our view preferable to both weight-lessness and to the Earth's gravity.

When we actually descended the ladder it was found to be very much like the lunar-gravity simulations we had performed here on Earth. No difficulty was encountered in descending the ladder. The last step was about 3½ feet from the surface, and we were some-what concerned that we might have difficulty reentering the LM at the end of our activity period. So we practiced that before bringing the camera down.

ALDRIN: *We opened the hatch and Neil, with me as his naviga-tor, began backing out of the tiny opening. It seemed like a small eternity before I heard Neil say, "That's one small step for man . . . one giant leap for mankind." In less than fifteen minutes I was back-ing awkwardly out of the hatch and onto the surface to join Neil, who, in the tradition of all tourists, had his camera ready to photo-graph my arrival.*

*I felt **buoyant** and full of **goose pimples** when I stepped down on the surface. I immediately looked down at my feet and became **intrigued** with the peculiar properties of the lunar dust. If one kicks sand on a beach, it scatters in numerous directions with some grains traveling father than others. On the Moon the dust travels exactly and precisely as it goes in various directions, and every grain of it lands nearly the same distance away. . . .*

COAXING THE FLAG TO STAND

[ALDRIN:] *During a pause in experiments, Neil suggested that we proceed with the flag. It took both of us to set it up and it was*

Pockmarked: Marked with depressions or pits.

Buoyant: Cheerful.

Goose pimples: Tiny bumps that develop around body hair as a reaction to excitement or fear.

Intrigued: Interested, curious.

*nearly a disaster. Public relations obviously needs practice just as everything else does. A small **telescoping** arm was attached to the flagpole to keep the flag extended and **perpendicular**. As hard as we tried, the telescope wouldn't fully extend. Thus the flag which should have been flat, had its own **unique** permanent wave. Then to our **dismay** the staff of the pole wouldn't go far enough into the lunar surface to support itself in an upright position. After much struggling we finally coaxed it to remain upright, but in a most **precarious** position. I dreaded the possibility of the American flag collapsing into the lunar dust in front of the television camera.*

What happened next . . .

Armstrong, Aldrin, and Collins returned safely to Earth and were heralded around the world as heroes. The Apollo program continued, although it never accomplishing anything to rival the first Moon landing. However, NASA's finest hour occurred when *Apollo 13,* launched in 1970, experienced major difficulties in flight. The oxygen supply was greatly reduced, carbon dioxide was seeping into the command module, and one side of the craft was virtually destroyed. The three astronauts aboard the spacecraft—James A. Lovell (1928–), John L. Swigert Jr. (1931–1982), and Fred W. Haise Jr. (1933–)—were guided home by the ingenious work of NASA scientists on the ground. The last Apollo mission was *Apollo 17,* which visited the Moon in December 1972.

After *Apollo 17* the United States did not undertake any other moon flights. Interest in further moon exploration steadily waned in the early 1970s, so NASA concentrated its efforts on the Large Space Telescope (LST) project. Initiated in 1969, the LST was an observatory (a structure housing a telescope, a device that observes celestial objects) that would continuously orbit Earth. An immediate result of the LST project was a plan for a space shuttle, a reusable vehicle that would launch the LST into orbit. The U.S. space shuttle program officially began in 1972, and over the next three decades five shuttles were built and operated by NASA. In 2004 President George W. Bush (1946–; served 2001–; see entry) made a

Apollo 11 splashed down in the Pacific Ocean southwest of Hawaii after completing its lunar landing mission. Astronauts Michael Collins, Buzz Aldrin, and Neil Armstrong await pickup by a helicopter from a nearby U.S. recovery ship. *(© Bettmann/Corbis)*

speech in which he announced a major revitalization of NASA, which included a return to the Moon.

Did you know . . .

- As the astronauts flew away from the Moon in the *Eagle*, Aldrin looked over and saw the American flag fall down. As there is no wind on the Moon, the flag most likely remains on the surface.

- Armstrong's statement, "That's one small step for man, one giant leap for mankind," is one of the most famous quotes in American history.

- Armstrong left the lunar module first, taking the crew's only camera with him. Armstrong kept the camera most of the time, so a majority of the pictures taken on the Moon feature Aldrin. Aldrin is quoted as saying he regrets this fact, but he and Armstrong had never rehearsed who would take pictures when.

Consider the following. . .

- Armstrong was the first human being ever to set foot on the Moon. While he and Aldrin were on the surface, they played like children, seeing how far they could jump and collecting the most unusual rocks they could find. If you were the first person on the Moon what would you most likely do?

- When *Apollo 11* broadcast from the Moon, millions of people watched at home on their television sets. Yet, only a year later, when the *Apollo 13* mission was broadcast from outer space, no major television network carried the event live. Network executives argued that by this time the American public regarded a flight to the Moon to be "routine." Do you think that after the first Moon landing NASA should have given traveling to the Moon higher public priority? Why or why not? Should NASA still be making regular trips there?

- If you had a chance to go to the Moon, would you go? If you could do one thing on the Moon—such as hit a baseball, throw a Frisbee, or conduct an experiment—what would you do? Explain your ideas.

For More Information

Books

Armstrong, Neil, Michael Collins, and Edwin Aldrin. *The First Lunar Landing: 20th Anniversary.* Washington, DC: National Aeronautics and Space Administration, 1989.

Chaikin, Andrew. *A Man on the Moon.* New York: Time-Life, 1969.

Collins, Michael and Edwin E. Aldrin Jr. "The Eagle Has Landed." In *Apollo Expeditions to the Moon.* Edited by Edgar M. Cortright. Washington, DC: National Aeronautics and Space Administration, 1975; http://www.hq.nasa.gov/office/pao/History/SP-350/cover.html (accessed on August 9, 2004).

Kranz, Gene. *Failure Is Not an Option: Mercury to* Apollo 13 *and Beyond.* New York: Simon & Schuster, 2000.

Periodicals

Folger, Tim, Sarah Richardson, and Carl Zimmer. "Remembering Apollo." *Discover* (July 1994), p. 38.

Web Sites

"Apollo 11: 30th Anniversary." *NASA.* http://www.hq.nasa.gov/office/pao/History/ap11ann/introduction.htm (accessed on August 9, 2004).

"Apollo 13." Goddard Space Flight Center, NASA. http://nssdc.gsfc.nasa.gov/planetary/lunar/apollo13info.html (accessed on August 9, 2004).

"Buzz Aldrin." *Johnson Space Center, NASA.* http://www.jsc.nasa.gov/Bios/htmlbios/aldrin-b.html (accessed on August 9, 2004).

Lloyd, Robin. *"Apollo 11.* Experiment Still Returning Results." *CNN.* July 21, 1999. http://www.cnn.com/TECH/space/9907/21/apollo.experiment/ (accessed on August 9, 2004).

"Neil Armstrong." *Johnson Space Center, NASA.* http://www.jsc.nasa.gov/Bios/htmlbios/armstrong-na.html (accessed on August 9, 2004).

Phillips, Tony. "What Neil & Buzz Left on the Moon." *Science@NASA.* http://science.nasa.gov/headlines/y2004/21jul_llr.htm (accessed on August 9, 2004).

Space Shuttle

James C. Fletcher
"NASA Document III-31: The Space Shuttle"
Published in November 22, 1971; reprinted from *Exploring the Unknown: Selected Documents in the History of the U.S. Civil Space Program. Volume I: Organizing for Exploration,* **published in 1995**

Remarks on the Space Shuttle Program
Richard M. Nixon
Presented on January 5, 1972

The U.S. space program began in 1958 with the establishment of the National Aeronautics and Space Administration (NASA). This initiative was the direct result of a space race between the United States and the former Soviet Union at a time when the two superpowers were involved in a period of hostile relations known as the Cold War (1945–91). A year earlier the Soviets had sent *Sputnik 1,* the first artificial satellite, into orbit. Americans were shocked by the event, fearing that the United States was losing the Cold War. NASA responded by launching Project Mercury for the training of astronauts. The seven members of the first astronaut corps were called the Mercury 7 (see Tom Wolfe entry). In May 1961 Mercury astronaut Alan Shepard (1923–1998) became the first American in space. Yet the United States was still lagging behind the Soviet Union in the space race: A month before Shepard made his brief flight over the Atlantic Ocean, Soviet cosmonaut Yuri Gagarin (1934–1968) became the first human to travel in space by making a nearly complete orbit of Earth.

On May 25, 1961, less than three weeks after Shepard's flight, President John F. Kennedy (1917–1963; served 1961–63) confronted the Soviet challenge in a speech before a joint session of Congress. He committed the United States to putting a man on the Moon within the next ten years (see John F. Kennedy entry). NASA immediately accelerated Project Apollo and its Moon mission program, and within eight years the agency had achieved Kennedy's goal. In 1969 the spacecraft *Apollo 11* successfully landed astronauts Neil Armstrong (1930–) and Edwin "Buzz" Aldrin (1930–) on the Moon (see Michael Collins and Edwin E. Aldrin entry). The moon landing was a victory for the United States in the space race. The Soviet Union had never developed a moon exploration program because of political power struggles and lack of government funding.

In the meantime, however, the Soviet Union had moved ahead in another important area. By the early 1960s the Soviets had already launched the Salyut space station and were operating Soyuz space shuttles. (A space station is an orbiting craft in which humans can live for extended periods of time. A space shuttle is a reusable craft that transports people and cargo between Earth and space.) When *Apollo 11* landed on the Moon the United States had preliminary research on a space station and a space shuttle, but there were no official programs. The situation changed in the early 1970s, with the end of Project Apollo. In 1972 *Apollo 17* made the final moon landing. The American public and the U.S. government had lost interest in moon exploration, so NASA had turned its attention to unmanned spaceflight projects such as the Large Space Telescope (LST). Initiated in 1969, the LST was an observatory (a structure housing a telescope, a device that observes celestial objects) that would continuously orbit Earth. NASA officials also realized that they could not abandon the manned spaceflight program. An immediate result of the LST

James C. Fletcher, NASA administrator during the development of the space shuttle program.
(© Bettmann/Corbis)

project was a plan for a space shuttle that would release the LST into orbit. (The LST eventually became the Hubble Space Telescope, which was launched in 1990.)

On November 22, 1971, at the height of discussions about building a space shuttle, NASA administrator James C. Fletcher (1919–1991) presented a paper to the White House. The paper was titled "The Space Shuttle" but officially designated "NASA Document III–31."

Things to remember while reading "NASA Document III-31: The Space Shuttle":

- Fletcher was told to offer a "best-case scenario" to make the shuttle program appealing to the United States government. Fletcher breaks his arguments down into four major areas, primarily emphasizing the importance of the United States staying ahead of the Soviet Union in the space race.

- Like President Nixon, Fletcher believes that the shuttle will usher in an age of space travel in which complicated missions will become routine and frequent.

- Fletcher notes that "Americans went on to set foot on the Moon, while the Russians have continued to expand their capabilities in near-Earth space." Since the early 1960s the Russians had been developing the Soyuz, a reusable manned spacecraft. In 1971 a three-seat Soyuz vehicle delivered two crews to the Russian space station *Salyut*, the world's first space station. This was an important event in the space race between the United States and the Soviet Union.

"NASA Document III-31: The Space Shuttle"

This paper outlines NASA's case for proceeding with the space shuttle. The principal points are as follows:

1. The U.S. cannot forego manned space flight.
2. The space shuttle is the only meaningful new manned space program that can be accomplished on a modest budget.
3. The space shuttle is a necessary next step for the practical use of space. It will help

    —space science,
    —civilian space applications,
    —military space applications, and
    —the U.S. position in international competition and cooperation in space.

4. The cost and complexity of today's shuttle is one-half of what it was six months ago.
5. Starting the shuttle now will have significant positive effect on **aerospace** employment. Not starting would be a serious blow to both the morale and health of the Aerospace Industry.

The U.S. Cannot Forego Manned Space Flight

Man has worked hard to achieve—and has indeed achieved—the freedom of mobility on land, the freedom of sailing on his oceans, and the freedom of flying in the atmosphere.

And now, within the last dozen years, man has discovered that he can also have the freedom of space. Russians and Americans, at almost the same time, first took **tentative** small steps beyond the earth's atmosphere, and soon learned to operate, to maneuver, and to **rendezvous** and dock in near-earth space. Americans went on to set foot on the moon, while the Russians have continued to expand their capabilities in near-earth space.

Man has learned to fly in space, and man will continue to fly in space. And, given this fact, the United States cannot afford to forego its responsibility—to itself and to the free world—to have a part in manned space flight. Space is not all remote. Men in near-earth orbit can be less than 100 miles from any point on earth—no farther from the U.S. than Cuba. For the U.S. not to be in space, while others do have men in space, is unthinkable, and a position which Americans cannot accept.

Why the Space Shuttle?

There are three reasons why the space shuttle is the right next step in manned space flight and the U.S. space program:

First, the shuttle is the only meaningful space program which can be accomplished on a modest budget. Somewhat less expensive

Aerospace: Science that deals with Earth's atmosphere and the space beyond, including travel in, and creation and manufacture of vehicles used in aerospace.

Tentative: Uncertain.

Rendezvous: Meet up with.

"space acrobatics" can be imagined but would accomplish little and be dead-ended. Additional Apollo or Skylab flights would be very costly, especially as left-over Apollo components run out, and would give diminishing returns. Meaningful alternatives, such as a space laboratory or a revisit to the moon to establish semi-permanent bases are much *more expensive, and a visit to Mars, although exciting and interesting, is completely beyond our means at the present time.*

Second, the space shuttle is needed to make space operations less complex and costly. Today we have to mount an enormous effort every time we launch a manned vehicle, or even a large unmanned mission. The reusable space shuttle gives us a way to avoid this. This airplane-like spacecraft will make a launch into orbit an almost routine event—at a cost $1/10th$ of today's cost of space operations. How is this possible? Simply by not throwing everything away after we have used it just once—just as we don't throw away an airplane after its first trip from Washington to Los Angeles.

The shuttle even looks like an airplane, but it has rocket engines instead of jet engines. It is launched vertically, flies into orbit under its own power, stays there as long as it is needed, then glides back into the atmosphere and lands on a runway, ready for its next use. And it will do this so economically that, if necessary, it can provide transportation to and from space each week, at an annual operating cost that is equivalent to only 15 percent of today's total NASA budget, or about the total cost of a single Apollo flight. Space operations would indeed become routine.

Third, the space shuttle is needed to do useful things. The long term need is clear. In the 1980's and beyond, the low cost to orbit the shuttle gives is essential for all the dramatic and practical future programs we can conceive. One example is a space station. Such a system would allow many men to spend long periods engaged in scientific, military, or even commercial activities in a more or less permanent station which could be visited cheaply and frequently and **refurbished,** *by means of a shuttle. Another interesting example is revisits to the moon to establish bases there; the shuttle would take the systems needed to orbit for the assembly.*

But what will the shuttle do before then? Why are routine operations so important? There is no single answer to these questions as there are many areas—in science, in civilian application, and in military applications—where we can see now that the shuttle is needed; and there will be many more by the time routine shuttle service is available.

Refurbished: Resupplied.

A space shuttle is similar to an airplane, but it has rocket engines instead of jet engines and launches vertically into the sky rather than horizontally along the ground. *(NASA)*

Take, for example, space science. *Today it takes two to five years to get a new experiment ready for space flight, simply because operations in space are so costly that extreme care is taken to make everything just right. And because it takes so long, many investigations that should be carried out—to get fundamental knowledge about the sun, the stars, the universe, and, therefore, about ourselves on earth—are just not undertaken. At the same time, we have already demonstrated, by taking scientists and their instruments up in a Convair 990 airplane, that space science can be done in a much more straight-forward way with a much smaller investment in time and money, and with an ability to react quickly to new discoveries, because airplane operations are* routine. *This is what the shuttle will do for space science.*

Or take civilian space applications. *Today new experiments in space communications, or in earth resources, are difficult and expensive for the same reasons as discussed under science. But with routine space operations instruments could quickly be adjusted until the* **optimum** *combination is found for any given application—a process that today involves several satellites, several years of time, and great expense.*

One can also imagine new applications that would only be feasible with the routine operation of the space shuttle. For example, it may prove possible (with an economical space transportation system, such as the shuttle) to place into orbit huge fields of solar batteries—and then beam the collected energy down to earth. This would be a truly pollution-free power source that does not require the earth's **latent** *energy sources. Or perhaps one could develop a global environment monitoring system, international in scope, that could help control the mess man has made of our environment. These are just two examples of what might be done with* routine *space shuttle operations.*

What about military space applications? *It is true that our military planning has not yet defined a specific need for man in space for military purposes. But will this always be the case? Have the Russians made the same decision? If not, the shuttle will be there to provide, quickly and routinely, for military operations in space, whatever they may be. It will give us a quick reaction time and the ability to fly* **ad hoc** *military missions whenever they are necessary. In any event, even without new* military needs, *the shuttle will provide the transportation for today's rocket-launched military spacecraft at substantially reduced cost.*

Optimum: Most favorable.

Latent: Capable of becoming active though not now visible; hidden.

Ad hoc: Unplanned, improvised.

Finally, the shuttle helps our international *position—both our competitive position with the Soviets and our prospects of cooperation with them and with other nations.*

Without the shuttle when our present manned space program ends in 1973 we will surrender center stage in space to the only other nation that has the determination and capability to occupy it. The United States and the whole free world would then face a decade or more in which Soviet supremacy in space would be unchallenged. With the shuttle, the United States will have a clear space superiority over the rest of the world because of the low cost to orbit and the **inherent** *flexibility and quick reaction capability of a reusable system. The rest of the world—the free world at least—would depend on the United States for launch of most of their payloads.*

On the side of cooperation, the shuttle would encourage far greater international participation in space flight. Scientists—as well as astronauts—of many nations could be taken along, with their own experiments, because shuttle operations will be routine. We are already discussing compatible docking systems with the Soviets, so that their spacecraft and ours can join in space. Perhaps ultimately men of all nations will work together in space—in joint environmental monitoring, international **disarmament** *inspections, or perhaps even in* **joint commercial enterprises**—*and through these activities help humanity work together better on its planet earth. Is there a more hopeful way?*

The Cost of the Shuttle Has Been Cut in Half

Six months ago NASA's plan for the shuttle was one involving heavy investment—$10 billion before the first manned orbital flight—in order to achieve a very low subsequent cost per flight—less than $5 million. But since then the design has been refined, and a trade-off has been made between investment cost and operational cost per flight. The result: a shuttle that can be developed for an investment of $4.5–$5 billion over a period of six years that will still only cost around $10 million or less per flight. (This means 30 flights per year at an annual cost for space transportation of 10 percent of today's NASA total budget, or one flight per week for 15 percent.)

This reduction in investment cost was partly the result of a trade-off just mentioned, and partly due to a series of technical changes. The orbiter has been drastically reduced in size—from a length of 206 feet down to 110 feet. But the payload carrying capacity has not been reduced: it is still 40,000 pounds in polar orbit, or 65,000

Inherent: Part of the basic nature of a person or thing; essential.

Disarmament: Laying aside arms or weapons.

Joint commercial enterprises: A business project or undertaking done by two parties for the purpose of making a profit.

Compensate: Make up, be
equal to.

*pounds in an easterly orbit, in a payload compartment that measures
15 x 60 feet.*

*The reduction in investment cost is highly significant. It means
that the peak funding requirements, in any one year, can be kept
down to a level that, even in a highly constrained NASA budget, will
still allow for major advances in space science and applications, as
well as in aeronautics.*

The Shuttle and the Aerospace Industry

*The shuttle is a technological challenge requiring the kind of ca-
pability that exists today in the aerospace industry. An accelerated
start on the shuttle would lead to a direct employment of 8,800 by
the end of 1972, and 24,000 by the end of 1973. This cannot **compensate** for the 270,000 laid off by NASA cutbacks since the peak of
the Apollo program but would take up the slack of further layoffs from
Skylab and the remainder of the Apollo programs.*

Conclusions

*Given the fact that manned space flight is part of our lives, and
that the U.S. must take part in it, it is essential to reduce drastically
the complexity and cost of manned space operations. Only the space
shuttle will do this. It will provide both* routine *and* quick reaction
*space operations for space science and for civilian and military ap-
plications. The shuttle will do this at an investment cost that fits well
within the highly constrained NASA budget. It will have low operating costs, and allow 30 to 50 space flights per year at a transportation cost equivalent to 10–15 percent of today's total NASA budget.*

The shuttle program is launched

The U.S. space shuttle program officially began in 1972,
when President Richard M. Nixon (1913–1994; served 1969–74)
announced NASA's plans to develop a multiuse spacecraft. It
would perform a wider variety and greater number of missions
than the traditional one-use space rocket, and at a lower cost
to the taxpayer. On January 5, 1972, in a speech in San
Clemente, California, President Nixon informed the American
people that the United States was going to enter into the next
phase of space exploration. Having already put a man on the

President Richard Nixon (right) and James Fletcher, NASA administrator (left), discuss the proposed space shuttle vehicle in San Clemente, California, January 5, 1972. *(NASA)*

Moon, NASA wanted to build a fleet of ships that would make traveling to space a routine experience.

Things to remember while reading President Nixon's Remarks on the Space Shuttle Program:

- Presidents have a long tradition of being associated with major events in space travel. President Dwight D. Eisenhower (1890–1969; served 1953–61) signed the act that brought NASA into existence; President Kennedy made an important speech announcing the United States' intention to send a man to the Moon. President Ronald Reagan (1911–2004; served 1981–89) addressed the nation after the *Challenger* (see entry) disaster, and President George W. Bush (1946–; served 2001–; see entry) commemorated the crew of the *Columbia* explosion.

- Notice that President Nixon emphasizes that the space shuttle program will cost less than the Apollo missions and that shuttle flights will happen with greater regularity. These two factors were big selling points to the U.S. government and the American people. There was a sense that space travel could become "routine."

- President Nixon imagined that the United States would be able to establish a number of space stations, leading the world in space exploration and settlement. It soon became clear that such projects, while achievable, were decades away.

President Nixon's Remarks on the Space Shuttle Program

*I have decided today that the United States should proceed at once with the development of an entirely new type of space transportation system designed to help transform the space frontier of the 1970's into familiar territory, easily accessible for human **endeavor** in the 1980's and 90's.*

*This system will center on a space vehicle that can shuttle repeatedly from Earth to orbit and back. It will revolutionize transportation into near space, by **routinizing** it. It will take the astronomical costs out of astronautics. In short, it will go a long way toward delivering the rich benefits of practical space utilization and the valuable spinoffs from space efforts into the daily lives of Americans and all people.*

Endeavor: Effort.

Routinizing: Making routine or everyday.

The new year 1972 is a year of conclusion for America's current series of manned flights to the Moon. Much is expected from the two remaining Apollo missions—in fact, their scientific results should exceed the return from all the earlier flights together. Thus they will place a fitting **capstone** on this vastly successful undertaking. But they also bring us to an important decision point—a point of **assessing** what our space horizons are as Apollo ends, and of determining where we go from here.

In the scientific arena, the past decade of experience has taught us that spacecraft are an irreplaceable tool for learning about our near-Earth space environment, the Moon, and the planets, besides being an important aid to our studies of the Sun and stars. In utilizing space to meet needs on Earth, we have seen the tremendous potential of satellites for international communications and world-wide weather forecasting. We are gaining the capability to use satellites as tools in global monitoring and management of nature resources, in agricultural applications, and in pollution control. We can foresee their use in guiding airliners across the oceans and in bringing TV education to wide areas of the world.

However, all these possibilities, and countless others with direct and dramatic bearing on human betterment, can never be more than fractionally realized so long as every single trip from Earth to orbit remains a matter of special effort and staggering expense. This is why commitment to the Space Shuttle program is the right step for America to take, in moving out from our present beach-head in the sky to achieve a real working presence in space—because the Space Shuttle will give us routine access to space by sharply reducing costs in dollars and preparation time.

The new system will differ radically from all existing booster systems, in that most of this new system will be recovered and used again and again—up to one hundred times. The resulting economies may bring operating costs down as low as one-tenth of those present launch vehicles.

The resulting changes in modes of flight and re-entry will make the ride safer, and less demanding for the passengers, so that men and women with work to do in space can "commute" aloft, without having to spend years in training for the skills and rigors of old-style space flight. As scientists and technicians are actually able to accompany their instruments into space, limiting boundaries between our manned and unmanned space programmes will disappear. Development of new space applications will be able to proceed

Capstone: High point.

Assessing: Determining the rate or amount of.

*much faster. Repair or servicing of satellites in space will become possible, as will delivery of valuable **payloads** from orbit back to Earth.*

The general reliability and versatility which the Shuttle system offers seems likely to establish it quickly as the workhorse of our whole space effort, taking the place of all present launch vehicles except the very smallest and very largest.

NASA and many aerospace companies have carried out extensive design studies for the Shuttle. Congress has reviewed and approved this effort. Preparation is now sufficient for us to commence the actual work of construction with full confidence of success. In order to minimize technical and economic risks, the space agency will continue to take a cautious evolutionary approach in the development of this new system. Even so, by moving ahead at this time, we can have the Shuttle in manned flight by 1978, and operational a short time later.

*It is also significant that this major new national **enterprise** will engage the best efforts of thousands of highly skilled workers and hundreds of contractor firms over the next several years. The amazing 'technology explosion' that has swept this country in the years since we ventured into space should remind us that robust activity in the aerospace industry is healthy for everyone—not just in jobs and income, but in the extension of our capabilities in every direction. The continued **preeminence** of America and American industry in the aerospace field will be an important part of the Shuttle's 'payload.'*

*Views of the Earth from space have shown us how small and fragile our home planet truly is. We are learning the **imperatives** of universal brotherhood and global ecology, learning to think and act as guardians of one tiny blue and green island in the trackless oceans of the Universe. This new program will give more people more access to the liberating perspectives of space, even as it extends our ability to cope with physical challenges of Earth and broadens our opportunities for international cooperation in low-cost, multi-purpose space missions.*

*'We must sail sometimes with the wind and sometimes against it', said **Oliver Wendell Holmes**, 'but we must sail, and not drift, nor lie at anchor.' So with man's epic voyage into space—a voyage the United States of America has led and still shall lead.*

Payloads: Load carried by an aircraft or spacecraft consisting of things (such as passengers or instruments) necessary to the purpose of the flight.

Enterprise: Project that is especially difficult, complicated, or risky.

Preeminence: Superiority.

Imperatives: Orders or commands.

Oliver Wendell Holmes (1809–1894): American physician, poet, and essayist.

What happened next . . .

In cooperation with the U.S. Air Force, which had been working on a multiuse space plane program known as Dyna-soar, NASA began work on the space shuttle program. Originally, it was thought that the space shuttles would be used as transport vehicles to service a massive space station and a permanently manned lunar colony. It was also hoped that the space shuttles would be used for a manned mission to Mars. The Air Force and NASA worked together—sometimes less than pleasantly—to develop a craft that would serve both as a vehicle for work in space and for defensive purposes, such as launching spy satellites.

A number of designs were debated and considered before it was finally decided that the space craft would consist of four major parts: the orbit ship—the shuttle—which could be used over and over again; a large external fuel tank; and two reusable solid-fuel booster rockets. The external fuel tank contains liquid oxygen and liquid nitrogen that power the three main engines of the orbit ship. The tank is discarded eight and one-half minutes after takeoff and breaks up in the atmosphere upon reentry. The pieces fall into the ocean. The two solid-fuel rocket boosters contain a propellant made of ammonium perchlorate (an oxidizer) and aluminum. The boosters fall off two minutes after liftoff and also land in the ocean. However, the booster rockets are equipped with parachutes to slow their descent and allow them to land safely in the ocean, where they are recovered and prepared for use on the next mission.

At launch time the ship is set upright. It explodes from the launchpad and is sent into orbit. The shuttle's stack height (its height in launch position) is 184.2 feet (56 meters), although the orbit ship alone is 122.17 feet (37.24 meters) long. The wing span is 78.06 feet (23.7 meters) and the cabin can hold up to ten astronauts, although crews of five to seven are more common. The shuttle reaches speeds of 17,321 miles (27,869 kilometers) per hour.

NASA has built seven different shuttle types. The *Pathfinder* and *Enterprise* ships were test vehicles, never intended for space missions. The five operating shuttles were *Challenger, Columbia, Atlantis, Discovery,* and *Endeavour.* The first shuttle mission was performed by *Columbia,* which launched on April 12, 1981, commanded by a crew of two. *Challenger* was completed in July 1982, *Discovery* in November 1983, and *Atlantis* in 1985. The various shuttles have flown over 130 missions combined. The space shuttle program paved the way for modern space exploration. Originally designed to be transport ships, the various shuttles have performed a number of important missions—such as making service flights to the Hubble Space Telescope (HST) and transporting crews to the Russian *Mir* space station and the International Space Station (ISS)—and greatly increased our knowledge of the universe. The program suffered two tragedies in its thirty-year history: the explosion of the space shuttle *Challenger* on January 28, 1986; and the explosion of the space shuttle *Columbia* on February 1, 2003. In both cases, the entire crew was killed (see *Challenger* and *Columbia* Space Shuttle Disaster entries). In 2004, as a result of the *Columbia* accident, NASA administrator Sean O'Keefe (1956–) announced that future shuttle flights would be canceled until safety problems had been resolved.

Many critics consider the space shuttle program to be a failure. Originally, the shuttles were supposed to reduce the cost of space missions greatly and to increase the frequency of manned space flight. NASA soon discovered, especially after the explosion of *Challenger* that too many missions in a short period of time can result in disaster. The low cost estimate was based on an increased number of missions, so the shuttle eventually was not cost effective because a fewer number of flights were successfully completed. However, many supporters of the space shuttle program point out that the shuttle did mark a major advance in space travel by producing a space craft capable of making numerous journeys into space and, a great percentage of the time, returning safely to Earth.

Did you know . . .
- A space shuttle weighs 4.5 million pounds (2.04 kilograms) at takeoff. When the orbiter lands, it weighs 230,000 pounds (104,420 kilograms).

- The first orbiter that was completed was originally called *Constitution*. However, after a massive write-in campaign by fans of the television show *Star Trek,* the ship was renamed *Enterprise* in honor of the famous ship from the show.

- In January 2004 President George W. Bush announced that the space shuttle will be retired from service in 2010. NASA plans to replace it with the Crew Exploration Vehicle, which is expected to conduct its first manned mission by 2014.

Consider the following . . .

- Some people think that investing in NASA is a waste of taxpayer money and that the money is better used trying to improve education, health care, and other domestic issues. Do you think space exploration should be a national priority? Why or why not?

- Although the space shuttles have flown many more successful missions than those that ended in disaster, space flight is still very dangerous. Do you think that NASA and President Nixon were too optimistic about how the space shuttle program would succeed? Some people argue that there was too much pressure, either from NASA or from popular opinion, to make it seem that flying in the space shuttle was as easy as driving a car, and because of that pressure, two terrible accidents resulted. Do you think we will ever get to a point where space travel is routine? Should we even have that as a goal, given how dangerous space flight is?

- If you were to become an astronaut, where would you want to fly? Why? Can you think of any experiments you might be able to conduct that might help our understanding of the universe?

For More Information

Books

Fletcher, James C. "NASA Document III-31: The Space Shuttle." In *Exploring the Unknown: Selected Documents in the History of the U.S. Civil Space Program, Volume I: Organizing for Exploration.* Edited by John M. Logsdon. Washington, DC: National Aeronautics and Space Administration, 1995.

Taylor, Robert. *The Space Shuttle*. San Diego, CA: Lucent Books, 2002.

Torres, George. *Space Shuttle, A Quantum Leap*. Navato, CA: Presidio Press, 1986.

Web Sites

January 28: 1986: The Challenger *Disaster*. http://www.chron.com/content/interactive/special/challenger (accessed on August 10, 2004).

Nixon, Richard M. Remarks on the Space Shuttle Program. *NASA*. http://www.hq.nasa.gov/office/pao/History/stsnixon.htm (accessed on August 10, 2004).

"Space Shuttle *Columbia* and Her Crew." *NASA*. http://www.nasa.gov/columbia (accessed on August 10, 2004).

"Space Shuttle Program." *Wikipedia*. http://en.wikipedia.org/wiki/Space_shuttle (accessed on August 10, 2004).

Other Sources

The Dream Is Alive. National Air and Space Museum, Smithsonian Institution. Burbank, CA: Warner Home Video, 2001 (DVD).

Challenger

George H. W. Bush
Remarks Announcing the Winner of the Teacher in Space Project
Presented on July 19, 1985

Ronald Reagan
Address to the Nation on the Explosion of the Space Shuttle
Challenger
Presented on January 28, 1986

The midair explosion of the space shuttle *Challenger* on January 28, 1986, marked the first major in-flight disaster in the history of the U.S. space program. Seven passengers—the entire crew—lost their lives. Mourned by the nation, the loss of the crew and the shuttle resulted in an official investigation that called for far-ranging reforms in the National Aeronautics and Space Administration (NASA).

The seven-member crew of the space shuttle *Challenger*—Francis R. Scobee (1939–1986), Michael J. Smith (1945–1986), Ellison S. Onizuka (1946–1986), Ronald McNair (1946–1986), Judith A. Resnick (1949–1986), Gregory Jarvis (1944–1986), and Christa McAuliffe (1948–1986)—were used to national attention prior to the horrific tragedy of January 28. Christa McAuliffe was not a trained pilot or a scientist. She was a social studies teacher in Concord, New Hampshire, who had been selected from among eleven thousand applicants to be the first private citizen sent into space.

After an exhaustive search, McAuliffe was informed by Vice President George H. W. Bush (1924–) that she would be the first "Teacher in Space." The vice president spoke to the

Christa McAuliffe, selected by NASA to be the first "Teacher in Space." *(NASA)*

ten project finalists at 1:18 P.M. in the Roosevelt Room at the White House. He was introduced by James M. Beggs (1926–), Administrator of NASA. The winner and backup teacher were presented with small statues on behalf of NASA and the Council of Chief State School Officers. President Ronald Reagan (1911–2004), who was in Bethesda Naval Hospital recovering from surgery, was unable to attend the event.

Things to remember while reading Vice President Bush's Remarks Announcing the Winner of the Teacher in Space Project:

- McAuliffe was selected from over eleven thousand applicants and was not trained as an astronaut. Her selection was viewed by many as a sign that space travel was possible for the average person.

- Vice President Bush says that NASA searched the nation to find a teacher with "the right stuff" to make the *Challenger* flight. He is referring to *The Right Stuff,* a book by Tom Wolfe (1931–; see entry) about the Mercury 7, the first seven American men chosen to travel into space. These astronauts were national heroes.

Vice President Bush's Remarks Announcing the Winner of the Teacher in Space Project

The Vice President. We're here today to announce the first private citizen passenger in the history of space flight. The President [Ronald

Reagan] said last August that this passenger would be one of America's finest—a teacher. Well, since then, as we've heard, NASA, with the help of the heads of our State school systems, has searched the Nation for a teacher with "the right stuff." Really, there are thousands, thousands of teachers with the right stuff. And they're committed to quality in education; to teaching their students the basics—reading, writing, mathematics, science, literature, history—to teaching the foundations of our cultural heritage; to teaching the values that guide us as Americans; and to teaching that important, but difficult to obtain, quality—**clarity** of thought.

We're honoring all those teachers of merit today, and we're doing something else because the finalists here with me and the more than a hundred semifinalists will all in the months ahead serve, as Jim has said, as a link between NASA and the Nation's school system. These teachers have all received special NASA training to pass on to other teachers and to their students. And together they and NASA will be a part of an exciting partnership for quality in education.

So, let me tell you now who our teacher in space will be. And let me say I thought I was a world traveler, but this tops anything I've tried. And first, the backup teacher, who will make the flight if the winner can't: Barbara Morgan of the McCall-Donnelly Elementary School in McCall, Idaho. Barbara has been a teacher for eleven years. She first taught on the Flathead Indian Reservation in Montana. She currently teaches second grade. Congratulations. And we have a little thing for you [a small statue].

And the winner, the teacher who will be going into space: Christa McAuliffe. Where is—is that you? [Laughter] Christa teaches in Concord High School in Concord, New Hampshire. She teaches high school social studies. She's been teaching for twelve years. She plans to keep a journal of her experiences in space. She said that—and here's the quote—"Just as the pioneer travelers of the Conestoga wagon days kept personal journies [journals], I as a space traveler would do the same." Well, I'm personally looking forward to reading that journal some day.

And by the way, Christa, while you're in the program, Concord High obviously will need substitute teachers to fill in. And it's only right that we provide one of these substitutes. So, the first class you miss, your substitute will be my dear friend and the President's, Bill Bennett (1943–), the Secretary of Education.

So, congratulations to all of you. Good luck, Christa, and God bless all of you. Thank you very much for coming. And you, too, get one of these [small statues].

Clarity: Clearness.

Vice President George H.W. Bush congratulates Christa McAuliffe, a New Hampshire teacher, for being selected to fly aboard NASA's space shuttle *Challenger.* (© Bettmann/Corbis)

Ms. McAuliffe: It's not often that a teacher is at a loss for words. I know my students wouldn't think so. I've made nine wonderful friends over the last two weeks. And when that shuttle goes, there might be one body, but there's going to be ten souls that I'm taking with me.

Thank you.

The **Challenger** *explosion*

McAuliffe's joining the *Challenger* crew was not the only headline-grabbing detail. NASA had announced in early January 1986 that it planned to conduct fifteen missions in twelve months, using all four of its shuttles—*Columbia, Challenger, Atlantis,* and *Discovery.* Immediately there were problems. The first mission was postponed seven times before the first shuttle was launched on January 12. Because of severe weather, the spacecraft was forced to return to Earth late, setting NASA further behind in its ambitious schedule. Feverish work began on preparing the *Challenger* for its mission. The spacecraft had just returned from its ninth flight only two months earlier but was scheduled to return to space on January 22. The mission was considered a high priority because of the massive press attention McAuliffe had been receiving. Schoolchildren around the world were expecting live reports from space to be given by McAuliffe. As part of the mission, NASA was launching a tracking and data relay satellite (TDRS) and the high-priority Spartan-Halley comet research observatory into space. The flight was scheduled to last six days, during which time the Spartan observatory would be recovered from orbit. Because of tight schedule requirements, the Spartan could be orbited no later than January 31.

The January 22 launch date arrived but the mission was delayed. Two more delays—on January 24 and January 25—followed. Bad weather prevented a launch on January 26, pushing the mission back to the next day, Monday, January 27. After a problem with the hatch bolt was detected, the mission was once again postponed. During the night of January 27, the temperature at Cape Canaveral dropped as low as 19°F (-7.2°C). This prompted a late-night meeting of NASA managers and engineers with managers from Morton Thiokol, the government contractor that manufactured the O-rings on the booster rockets. (A booster rocket is fired to propel the spacecraft into space. The booster rocket is built in sections and then strapped onto the shuttle. The rubber O-rings are required to seal the sections together.) The Thiokol engineers were concerned that the O-rings would stiffen in the cold and cause the seal to fail. Since the O-rings had never been tested at low temperatures, the Thiokol managers overruled the engineers. They signed a statement claiming that the boosters were safe for launch at a temperature lower than 53°F (11.7°C).

Other problems arose on the morning of January 28 because a thin layer of ice had formed on the shuttle and the

The space shuttle *Challenger* exploded just minutes after takeoff, vanishing into a trail of smoke as spectators on the ground and television viewers around the world watched in dismay. *(NASA)*

launch pad. Liftoff was delayed twice because officials at the site were concerned about icicles potentially breaking off during launch and damaging insulation tiles that protected the shuttle from intense heat as it reentered Earth's atmosphere. Inspection teams examined the *Challenger* and reported no abnormalities. Countdown proceeded, and at 11:38 A.M. the *Challenger* lifted off into the blue sky. After two explosions—the first at fifty-four seconds into the launch and the second at seventy-three seconds—the space shuttle disintegrated, vanishing in a trail of smoke as a crowd on the ground and millions of television viewers throughout the world watched in disbelief. Among the spectators on the ground were McAuliffe's husband and two children and a group of her students.

President Reagan's State of the Union Address (an annual speech delivered by a U.S. president) had been scheduled for the evening of January 28. Reagan abandoned his original text, choosing instead to pay tribute to the *Challenger* crew.

Things to remember while reading President Reagan's Address to the Nation on the Explosion of the Space Shuttle *Challenger:*

- With the exception of *Apollo 1*, in which three astronauts were killed in 1967 in a ground accident, no American astronaut had lost his or her life during an in-flight mission prior to the *Challenger* explosion.

- For those who witnessed the live television broadcast of the *Challenger* explosion, the event was dramatic and shocking. Today, most people remember exactly where they were when the tragedy occurred.

President Reagan's Address to the Nation on the Explosion of the Space Shuttle Challenger

Ladies and gentlemen, I'd planned to speak to you tonight to report on the state of the Union, but the events of earlier today have led me to change those plans. Today is a day for mourning and remembering. Nancy [First Lady Nancy Reagan; 1923–] and I are pained to the core by the tragedy of the shuttle Challenger. *We know we share this pain with all of the people of our country. This is truly a national loss.*

Nineteen years ago, almost to the day, we lost three astronauts in a terrible accident on the ground. But we've never lost an astronaut in flight; we've never had a tragedy like this. And perhaps we've forgotten the courage it took for the crew of the shuttle. But they, the Challenger *Seven, were aware of the dangers, but overcame them and did their jobs brilliantly. We mourn seven heroes: Michael Smith, Dick Scobee, Judith Resnick, Ronald McNair, Ellison Onizuka, Gregory Jarvis, and Christa McAuliffe. We mourn their loss as a nation together.*

For the families of the seven, we cannot bear, as you do, the full impact of this tragedy. But we feel the loss, and we're thinking about you so very much. Your loved ones were daring and brave, and they had that special grace, that special spirit that says, "Give me a challenge, and I'll meet it with joy." They had a hunger to explore the

President Ronald Reagan addresses the public regarding the explosion of the space shuttle *Challenger* and the loss of its crew. (© *Corbis*)

universe and discover its truths. They wished to serve, and they did. They served all of us. We've grown used to wonders in this century. It's hard to dazzle us. But for twenty-five years the United States space program has been doing just that. We've grown used to the idea of space, and perhaps we forget that we've only just begun. We're still pioneers. They, the members of the *Challenger* crew, were pioneers.

And I want to say something to the schoolchildren of America who were watching the live coverage of the shuttle's take-off. I know it is hard to understand, but sometimes painful things like this happen. It's all part of the process of exploration and discovery. It's all part of taking a chance and expanding man's horizons. The future doesn't belong to the fainthearted; it belongs to the brave. The *Challenger* crew was pulling us into the future, and we'll continue to follow them.

I've always had great faith in and respect for our space program, and what happened today does nothing to diminish it. We don't hide our space program. We don't keep secrets and cover things up. We do it all up front and in public. That's the way freedom is, and we wouldn't change it for a minute. We'll continue our quest in space. There will be more shuttle flights and more shuttle crews and, yes, more volunteers, more civilians, more teachers in space. Nothing ends here; our hopes and our journeys continue. I want to add that I wish I could talk to every man and woman who works for NASA or who worked on this mission and tell them: "Your dedication and professionalism have moved and impressed us for decades. And we know of your anguish. We share it."

There's a coincidence today. On this day 390 years ago, the great [British] explorer Sir Francis Drake [c. 1540–1596] died aboard ship off the coast of Panama. In his lifetime the great frontiers were the oceans, and an historian later said, "He lived by the sea, died on it, *and was buried in it." Well, today we can say of the* **Challenger** *crew: Their dedication was, like Drake's, complete.*

The crew of the space shuttle **Challenger** *honored us by the manner in which they lived their lives. We will never forget them, nor the last time we saw them, this morning, as they prepared for their journey and waved goodbye and "slipped the* **surly** *bonds of earth" to "touch the face of God."[Quoted from American pilot John Gillespie Magee Jr.'s poem, "High Flight."]*

Surly: Arrogant, domineering.

What happened next . . .

A few days after the disaster, President Reagan eulogized (praised in a formal statement) the *Challenger* crew during a television memorial ceremony at the Johnson Space Center in Houston, Texas. On February 3, 1986, he established a presidential commission to investigate the accident, appointing former Secretary of State William P. Rogers (1913–2001) as head. Six weeks after the tragedy the shuttle's crew module was recovered from the floor of the Atlantic Ocean. The crew members were subsequently buried with full honors. There was considerable speculation about whether they had survived the initial explosion. Evidence gathered later by NASA indicated that they had survived the breakup and separation of the boosters from the shuttle. They had also begun to take emergency action inside the crew cabin. Whether all seven remained conscious through the two-minute, forty-five second fall into the ocean remains unknown. NASA investigators determined that at least two were breathing from emergency air packs they had activated.

On June 6, 1986, the Rogers Commission released a 256-page report stating that the explosion was caused by destruction of the O-rings. After checking into the history and performance of the sealing system, the commission discovered that the O-rings had failed regularly, though only partially, on previous shuttle flights. Both NASA and Thiokol were concerned about weaknesses in the seals, but they had chosen not to undertake a time-consuming redesign of the system. They regarded O-ring erosion as an "acceptable risk" because the seal had never failed completely. But when the *Challenger* flew in the dead of winter, frigid temperatures made the O-rings so brittle that they never sealed the joint. Even before the shuttle had cleared the launch tower, hot gas was already seeping through the rings. Investigators blamed NASA and Thiokol management procedures for not allowing critical information to reach the right people. The U.S. House of Representatives Committee on Science and Technology then conducted hearings on the matter. The committee determined that NASA and Thiokol had sufficient time to correct the O-ring problem, but the space agency and the manufacturer had sacrificed safety to meet flight schedules and cut costs.

The charges had a grave impact on NASA. Public confidence was shaken, and the astronaut corps was highly concerned. Astronauts had never been consulted or informed about the dangers posed by the O-ring sealing system. The Rogers Commission made nine recommendations to NASA, among them allowing astronauts and engineers a greater role in approving launches. The other recommendations included a complete redesign of the rocket booster joints, a review of astronaut escape systems, regulation of scheduling shuttle flights to assure safety, and sweeping reform of the shuttle program and management structure.

Following these decisions, several top officials left NASA. A number of experienced astronauts also resigned as a result of disillusionment with NASA and frustration over the long redesign process that delayed their chances to fly in space. An American shuttle was not launched again until September 29, 1988. NASA eventually built the *Endeavour* to replace the *Challenger,* and it flew for the first time in 1992.

Did you know . . .

- The Apollo rockets were replaced by the space shuttle designs. The last rocket, *Apollo 17,* flew in December 1972.

- The "Teacher in Space" program was discontinued after the *Challenger* explosion.

- The space shuttle *Columbia* (see *Columbia* Space Shuttle Disaster entry) broke apart over the western United States on February 1, 2003, killing all seven crew members. It was the first major space disaster since the *Challenger* explosion.

Consider the following . . .

- Private citizens have approached NASA and offered millions of dollars to accompany a trained crew on a shuttle mission. So far NASA has declined these offers. Do you think private citizens should be allowed to fly on shuttle missions? Why or why not?

- Some people want to start private companies that will fly people into space. On June 23, 2004, American test pilot Mike Melvill (1941–) successfully flew the rocket plane SpaceShipOne 62.5 miles (100 kilometers) over the Mojave Desert in California. Many members of NASA are opposed to this, saying that space travel is still highly complicated and should be left to the professionals. Do you think space travel should be limited to NASA—a government agency—or do you think private citizens, if properly trained and equipped, should be allowed to travel into space without NASA's involvement? Why or why not?

For More Information

Books

Lewis, Richard S. *Challenger: The Final Voyage.* New York: Columbia University Press, 1988.

McConnell, Malcolm. *Challenger: A Major Malfunction.* New York: Doubleday, 1987.

Periodicals

"Looking for What Went Wrong." *Time* (February 10, 1986): pp. 36–38.

"NASA Faces Wide Probe." *U.S. News and World Report* (February 17, 1986): pp. 18–19.

"Out of *Challenger*'s Ashes—Full Speed Ahead," *U.S. News and World Report* (February 10, 1986): pp. 16–19.

"Seven Who Flew for All of Us." *Time* (February 10, 1986): pp. 32–35.

"What Happened?" *Newsweek* (February 17, 1986): pp. 32–33.

Web Sites

Bush, George H. W. Remarks Announcing the Winner of the Teacher in Space Project, July 19, 1985. *Ronald Reagan Presidential Library, University of Texas.* http://www.reagan.utexas.edu/resource/speeches/1985/71985a.htm (accessed on July 19, 2004).

"Columbia." NASA. http://www.nasa.gov/columbia/home/index.html (accessed on July 19, 2004).

"Information on the STS–51L/*Challenger* Accident." *NASA.* http://www. hq.nasa.gov/office/pao/History/sts51l.html (accessed on July 19, 2004).

January 28, 1986: The Challenger *Disaster.* http://www.chron.com/ content/interactive/special/challenger (accessed on July 19, 2004).

Reagan, Ronald. Address to the Nation on the Explosion of the Space Shuttle *Challenger,* January 28, 1986. *Ronald Reagan Presidential Library, University of Texas.* http://www.reagan.utexas.edu/resources/ speeches/1986/1288b.htm (accessed on May 15, 2004).

Patrick Meyer

"Living on Mir: *An Interview with Dr. Shannon Lucid"*
Conducted in March 1998; available at *Marshall Space Flight Center,*
NASA (Web site)

By the turn of the twenty-first century, space exploration was being conducted aboard space stations. A space station has often been described as a hotel in space. Once a station is launched, it remains in orbit and is visited by crews of astronauts who travel from and to Earth aboard a space shuttle. Astronauts stay for long periods of time on a space station, which provides living accommodations and research laboratories where the astronauts conduct scientific studies and experiments. A space station is built, inhabited, and maintained through collaboration of space agencies in several countries. The most ambitious endeavor has been the International Space Station (ISS), which involved the efforts of seventeen nations when in-orbit construction began in 1998. The longest-operating space station, however, was the *Mir,* which stayed in space for nearly fifteen years, from 1986 until 2001.

The concept of a space station can be traced to the story "The Brick Moon" by the nineteenth-century American writer Edward Everett Hale (1822–1909). Originally published in *The Atlantic Monthly* magazine (1869–70), "The Brick Moon" describes how a group of former college friends build an artificial Moon made of brick. The first known mention of the term "space station" was made by the German rocket engineer Hermann Oberth (1894–1989) in 1923. He envisioned a wheel-like vehicle that would orbit Earth and provide a launching place for trips to the Moon and Mars. Three decades later the German-born American rocket engineer Wernher von Braun (1912–1977) proposed a more detailed concept of a space station in a series of articles in *Collier's* magazine. He described a giant vehicle, 250 feet in diameter, which would spin to create its own gravity as it orbited 1,000 miles (1,609 kilometers) above Earth.

The former Soviet Union launched the world's first space station, *Salyut 1,* in 1971. Six other Salyuts were sent into orbit before 1982, when the program was ended. The United States put a space station, the *Skylab,* into orbit in 1973, but it remained in space for only one year and was visited by three crews of astronauts. Soviet cosmonauts regularly traveled to the Salyuts, but they did not stay for long periods of time because the space stations did not have adequate accommodations. Improving upon the Salyut design, the Soviets built the *Mir,* the first permanent residence in space, which was launched in 1986. Nine years later Russian cosmonaut Valery Polyakov (1942–) set the record for the longest mission aboard the *Mir,* having stayed 438 days. The same year American astronaut Shannon Lucid (1943–) set the record for a non-Russian on a mission that lasted 188 days, 4 hours, and 14 seconds.

Lucid underwent extensive preparation for the *Mir* mission. After three months of intensive study of the Russian language, she began training at Star City, the cosmonaut instruction center outside Moscow, in January 1995. Every morning she woke at five o'clock to begin studying. She spent

American astronaut Shannon Lucid. (© *Ellis Richard/Corbis Sygma*)

Russian space station *Mir* flies above Earth as U.S. space shuttle *Atlantis,* carrying astronaut Shannon Lucid, approaches to dock. Lucid remained behind with Russian cosmonauts Yuri Onufrienko and Yuri Usachev for a five-month stay on *Mir.* *(AP/Wide World Photos)*

most of the day in classrooms listening to lectures on the *Mir* and Soyuz space shuttle systems—all in Russian. (The Soyuz is the longest-serving spacecraft in the world.) In the evenings Lucid continued to study the language and struggled with workbooks written in technical Russian. In February 1996, after passing the required medical and technical exams, she was certified as a *Mir* crew member by the Russian spaceflight commission.

Lucid then traveled to Baikonur, Kazakhstan, to watch the launch of the Soyuz that carried her crewmates, both named Yuri—Commander Yuri Onufrienko (1961–), a Russian air force officer, and Yuri Usachev (1957–), a Russian civilian—to the *Mir* space station. She then went back to the United States for three weeks of training with the crew of the U.S. space shuttle *Atlantis,* which would take her to *Mir.* On March 22, 1996, *Atlantis* lifted off from the Kennedy Space Center in Cape Canaveral, Florida. Three days later the shuttle docked with *Mir.*

Lucid and her fellow crew members stayed busy while living aboard *Mir.* The day began when the alarm rang at 8:00 A.M. The first activity for the crew was to put on their headphones and talk with mission control. Next they had breakfast, first adding water to their food and then eating it while floating around a table. In the afternoon they had a long lunch—again floating around the table—which usually consisted of Russian potatoes and meat casseroles. Although the crew had many responsibilities, they still had time for conversations about their own lives and experiences. They also kept in constant touch with ground control in Russia and had regular contact with Soyuz crews who delivered food and supplies. In 1998 NASA interviewer Patrick Meyer had a conversation with Lucid about her experience living aboard *Mir.*

Things to remember while reading "Living on *Mir:* An Interview with Dr. Shannon Lucid":

- Lucid mentions doing daily exercise routines. Exercise is essential while in space to counteract the effects of weightlessness. She spent two hours every day running on a treadmill, attaching herself to the machine with a bungee cord. This prevented the significant weight and muscle loss normally encountered by astronauts. When Lucid returned to Earth aboard the *Atlantis,* after staying so long in space, she was in such good physical shape that she was able to walk off the space shuttle without assistance.

- Lucid also mentions conducting experiments. The crew performed thirty-five life science and physical science experiments, such as determining how protein crystals grow in space and how quail embryos develop in zero gravity.

"Living on Mir: An Interview with Dr. Shannon Lucid"

Part 1: Practical Life on MIR

[Meyer] Q: I read in one of your previous interviews that on MIR you didn't have a shower and you had disposal clothing, so how did [you] bathe while you were on MIR?

[Lucid] A: Well you didn't like take a bath, you just had a wet rag and you wiped yourself off.

Q: Was there some special way of washing your hair?

A: It was just using the liquid shampoo—the Russians have one very similar to the stuff we use on the Shuttle—you just wet your hair with it and then wipe it out.

Q: Did you have some special way of rinsing after you had to brush your teeth or did you have some special way of brushing your teeth that is different from how we would do it on earth?

A: No, well just like on the Shuttle you just put a little bit of toothpaste on your toothbrush, get it wet, brush your teeth, and just spit into the Kleenex and throw the Kleenex away; and then just take a Kleenex and wipe off your toothbrush.

Q: I know that you had Russian cosmonauts on MIR with you— Yuri and some others that you spoke about in previous interviews. Did they shave or did they trim their beards and hair?

*A: They shaved. I feel they shaved daily because they didn't grow a beard, and they always looked shaven, you know. They had the base block so they got cleaned up in the mornings just after they woke up, and I got cleaned up in the **Spektr** so I actually never saw them shave but I assume they shaved with an electric razor. I know they had an electric razor.*

Spektr: Module on *Mir*, primarily to house experiments.

Q: How would you do something like cutting your fingernails?

A: Well actually what I did, I just cut them and cut them close to an air vent, then the loose fingernails would just pull into the filter and then I just picked them up and put them in the trash.

Q: How do you think the **hygiene** systems on the International Space Station are going to compare to what you had on MIR?

A: From what I have been able to **ascertain** and I haven't really looked into it in great detail, they will be roughly the same.

Q: When you are sleeping, and I know sleeping is a lot different in zero g than sleeping here on Earth, did you wear any special clothing when you were sleeping?

A: No, when I was asleep, I had the same clothes on that I had on during the day and on MIR we each had a sleeping bag, and so I kept mine rolled up during the day to keep it out of the way so at night I unrolled it—I actually tied it to a handrail so that I would end up in the same place the next day that I started out.

Q: So you are saying that while you were in the sleeping bag, it was **tethered**.

A: Right.

Q: When you were on MIR, did you sleep differently, in other words, did you sleep more deeply or did you have trouble sleeping?

A: No, I never had any trouble sleeping. I slept 8 hours every night that we went to bed. I always turned the lights out at midnight and I always got up with an 8 A.M. alarm—we ran on Moscow time— and so I slept 8 hours every single night.

Q: I was curious—in one of your previous interviews, you had said that you had a couple of dreams about being in space but when you were in space did you have dreams that you would consider different from dreams you would have on earth?

A: Not really. Sometimes, when I was having a dream[—]if I was dreaming in an earth situation of some sort[—]many times I was floating, so I would be in a[n] earth situation and I would be floating like I was in zero g.

Q: I know on some of the Shuttle missions, they had pillows that they strapped to their heads just so they had the comfort of home. Did you do the same thing on MIR?

A: No, I can't [imagine] why any body would want that.

Hygiene: Personal cleanliness.

Ascertain: Determine.

Tethered: Tied down.

Q: I know food in space is a lot different than it is on the ground. What do you think the differences between the types of food, I know you had Russian food when you were on MIR, would be like on Space Station? Do you think they will have similar food?

A: I think it is the same. I mean at least for the early operations the American food, the Shuttle food and the Russian food that they will be flying up is the food they will be using on MIR. I know that in the future that they will have frozen food, etc., but I think that is a long way in the future.

Q: Over the years, we work with a lot of astronauts here in the **Operations Lab**, and we know that they said some things about what the effects of zero g has on the body. Some of them have said things like they had a stuffy head, a puffy face, and they had changes in their sense of smell and taste. Did you experience any of these things and did they change over the duration?

A: No, I never had any change in taste or smell. I never have on any flight, and I've never on any of the flights and not on the MIR flight, I never had a stuffy feeling in my head. That varies from person to person but I've just been fortunate I've never had a stuffy head. Everybody gets a puffy face at first because of the fluid as it redistributes. Gradually, over the period of time that you are on a long duration flight, you'll lose that and your face just looks different. If you look at a picture of someone that's been up 5 months and compare it to when they were up there just the 3 weeks they look different—just the way that their face is filled out.

Q: The air environment is artificial on MIR, was there a difference in the air quality or was there a taste and a smell that was different on MIR than on the ground?

A: No, I never noticed any bad smell at all. There was never ever an odor problem on MIR. Air quality was really good. You know, granted once sometimes there were particles that were in the air but the filtering system took them out. So yeah I was just really really pleased with the air quality the entire time I was up there.

Q: I know in general exercise is an important thing but especially so when you are in zero gravity. Was exercise for you just a necessary chore, or was it some sort of outlet, or entertainment?

A: No, it was absolutely not entertainment, [Chuckle] absolutely not an outlet. It was something that I knew I had to do every day and every day the best thing about exercise was when I finished because I was done with it for the day.

Operations Lab: A NASA division.

Shannon Lucid exercises on a treadmill while aboard *Mir*. Exercise prevents significant weight and muscle loss that is often experienced by astronauts living in space for long periods of time. *(NASA)*

Part 2: Results

Q: I would like to transition now from these practical living aspects into the mission's purpose and some of your personal opinion[s] and feelings about it. First of all I would like to ask you where you are today in relation to your MIR mission? That is, when you were on MIR, did you have any personal research that you were involved in and that you are still working on now and do you think it's important that astronauts have their own research?

A: I didn't have any personal research—I mean all the research I was doing was the NASA experiments—but what I think is that it is very very important that the science we do on Station, that a lot of the science that the astronauts are being involved in, that the crew people be involved in, has to be interactive. By that I mean, you have to have science that you can become intellectually engaged in. I was very fortunate. I had a few experiments like that on MIR. You can-

not have just black box after black box that all you do is just flip switches on. You have to have experiments where you are really doing something like you do in a laboratory on the Earth.

Q: When you are doing research on MIR, we know that the environment on a long-duration flight is a lot different [than] say a Spacelab would be, what do you think the trade-offs are between doing a detailed planning operation like we've been doing for Spacelab and maybe setting your own schedule based on your desire for the day since you are doing something like over a long duration?

A: Well I think I had two or three, you know, really main, main, main lessons learned that I've been trying to get across, you know, to NASA, to the community and that is one of them. This was shown in Skylab and every single crew member that's come back from MIR has said: Hey, we have to remember that a long space flight is not a short space flight. You cannot run a long space flight like you do a Spacelab mission because—well, there are obviously many reasons but—for a Spacelab mission, they are 14 days/16 days, and every minute is planned, OK. That is what you have to do for that type of mission, but on a Space Station mission you cannot do that. The crew has to be [in] charge of their day, and I don't mean, by that I mean, when a person works in a laboratory here on Earth, you know what you need to get done and you plan to get it done. And actually that's the way that I worked on MIR. Now the **ground** would use a Russian form 24 which is like a timeline, but it is nothing like you think of a timeline when you think of a Spacelab mission, but, I mean it is not detailed like that. But the way I used it I said okay the ground thinks I will be working on experiments A, B, and C and then because I was on board and I knew the conditions and I knew, you know, how to work around with all the constraints the ground didn't know about, I was in charge of my schedule and how I did it. Do you understand what I'm saying?

Q: Yes, I do. [T]hat's very interesting. We, as planners, we really want to consider the differences because there are major differences.

A: Major, major differences and you know you can even stick this info in somewhere, this came out in Skylab. This isn't like something new that we learned at MIR. This is exactly what the Skylab astronauts said when they came back and you can refer the people, there is a book, I think the name of it is **House in the Sky.** Unfortunately it is out of print and I think the author's name was Cooper. It was just a little book that he published that he wrote on the Skylab mission, and it is for the general public. It is discussed at length in the

Ground: The ground control crew at Kaliningrad, Russia.

House in the Sky: The correct title is *A House in Space.* The full name of the author is Henry S. F. Cooper.

book about what Skylab taught them. That happened to Skylab, that happened on MIR, and that has to be the way that the Space Station is run. It's a different way of doing business. It's a whole new ball-game that we are in and you know I keep telling people that a Space Station flight is not a Shuttle flight and it sounds, well, like a stupid statement, but it has very profound **repercussions** that people really need to think about.

Q: We'll make sure the planners hear your statement. I was interested also in if you knew of any specific changes that had changed in the Station program based on your visit to MIR.

A: Well I do know the one that we were talking [about], you know the **Astronaut Office** gets together and they issue recommendations, and the recommendations they have that [have] come out of the Astronaut Office is that Space Station daily schedule should be more or less under control of the crew and not the ground[,] like on a Shuttle mission. It probably didn't state it quite as strongly as I did but the recommendations that have come out and also I think (and this just isn't me but) all the different crew members that have been coming back have been saying: Hey, we've got to change the way we do training. We cannot have change procedures like we do, you know for the Shuttle, which is a very necessary thing to do on Spacelab missions, and I'll just stick this in and you can stick it in, I mean like I was on SLS-2, which was a Spacelab mission, and I was very very fortunate to be able to work with the people at **Marshall** and they just did an outstanding job. I thought that the way that mission ran was just absolutely outstanding. You know with all the people and the support. But, and so, we've really learned how to do that kind of a mission, but Space Station is very different so we have to now get ready to gear up and do things differently. We cannot work on Space Station like we do on a Spacelab.

Part 3: Looking Forward

Q: Okay, I would like to talk about [a] question from a previous interview in which you discuss pioneering spirit. You [reminisce] about your childhood dream of being a pioneer like in the American West and had worried that you were born at the wrong time but then you concluded that you could grow up and explore space. I was wondering how well your real life experiences have matched those expectations of your childhood?

A: I've always been happy with events and how they came out. They generally matched my expectations.

Repercussions: Consequences.

Astronaut Office: Astronaut training facility at Kennedy Space Center in Orlando, Florida.

Marshall: George C. Marshall Space Flight Center in Huntsville, Alabama.

Q: You know pioneers have explored about everything on the planet and for many reasons: money, resources, and freedoms. But of course much of the space exploration we've done has been just for exploration sake and I know that is changing. Do you think exploration for exploration sake is a good thing?

A: I personally think that is the primary purpose, but even with a purpose, exploration is hard to sell.

Q: You also indicated in your previous interview that you were really interested in a mission to Mars. What do you think the primary goals and values and reasons and expectations for the Mars mission would be?

A: Well, then we get back to your other statement—I just think it would be neat to do it. I mean to go to see what's there.

Q: We go to schools a lot to talk to school children about the space program and today, unlike 15 years ago, we find that less children raise their hands when they are asked if they want to be an astronaut and go into space. Do you think that this pioneering spirit is still alive?

A: Oh I think so, very much.

Q: Do you think that humans will ever find (now this is your personal opinion of course) an **insurmountable** obstacle for living and working in space?

A: No, I don't think so.

Q: Given the difficulty and expense of it, do you think it's actually worth it? or do you think it's actually necessary that humans go into space?

A: Yes.

Q: In the distant future, what do you think people will think about, I mean in the far distant future, what do you think people will think about our space program?

A: Well that would be really hard to say. It depends on—I mean you can look at it from [that] perspective right now. What do the children think about just the very recent past? Like when we (in my lifetime when we went to the moon). We don't go any more. You know it's sort of like they don't understand that. I mean why did we quit. It is sort of like we are backtracking.

Q: That is hard to explain to children.

A: Yes.

Insurmountable: Impossible to overcome.

Q: Do you, given the political and economic climate we live in, do you think we will have future large scale projects like the Space Station?

A: Well there again, all you do is speculate, and I have no idea.

Q: Where do you think the agency should go? What would you like to see?

A: Oh, I would like to see us go to Mars. That's my own personal opinion.

Q: When you are 90, sitting in a comfortable chair and contemplating your life, what will you be most proud of or feel is your most important contribution?

A: When I am 90, or should we say if I am ever 90, what I will take the most pleasure in while rocking on my front porch will be the relationships that I have had in life—with my husband, children, and friends, etc.

What happened next . . .

Mir remained in orbit for more than fifteen years, until 2001, although it was officially vacated in 1999. During that time astronauts conducted nearly 16,500 experiments, primarily on how humans adapt to long-term space flight. From 1986 until 1999 the space station was almost continually occupied by a total of one hundred cosmonauts and astronauts. Among them were seven NASA astronauts, a Japanese journalist, a British candy maker, and visitors from other countries that did not have their own space programs. When Russia took *Mir* out of service in 2001, most of the spacecraft burned up over the Pacific Ocean. The remaining remnants of the space station crashed into the Pacific in 2004.

Mir became an international effort, eventually providing a model for the ISS. The ISS was nearly completed by the end of 2002, but the crash of the U.S. space shuttle *Columbia* in February 2003 forced the grounding of all U.S. shuttles (see *Columbia* Space Shuttle Disaster entry). Other nations could not continue the full-scale project without the involvement of U.S. shuttles. The future of the ISS therefore remained uncertain. In January 2004 President George W. Bush (1946–) made a speech in which he announced a major revitalization of NASA (see George W. Bush entry). One of NASA's goals was completion of the ISS by the end of the decade. In July 2004, NASA astronaut Edward Michael Fincke (1967–) and Russian cosmonaut Gennady I. Padalka (1958–) successfully conducted a spacewalk to make repairs on the ISS. Future missions were being planned in an effort to keep the ISS in orbit. In his speech, President Bush also vowed that the United States would return to the Moon and eventually send humans to Mars.

Did you know . . .

- While Lucid was living aboard *Mir* she sent letters back to Earth. In a letter dated May 19, 1996, she wrote about the arrival of the Soyuz supply shuttle *Progress,* which delivered tomatoes and onions. Lucid commented that she and her fellow crew members were so happy to have fresh vegetables that for the next few days they ate tomatoes at every meal.

- Many of the crew's experiments provided useful data for the engineers designing the ISS. The results from investigations in fluid physics, for example, helped the space station's planners build better ventilation and life-support systems. Research on combustion in microgravity (virtual absence of gravity) may also lead to improved procedures for fighting fires on the station.

- Lucid's *Mir* record was broken in 1999 by French astronaut Jean-Pierre Haigneré (1948–), who stayed on the space station for nearly 189 complete days. Haigneré was also a member of the last crew to visit *Mir.* Before returning to Earth, the crew left the space station in a standby mode, with no occupants onboard.

Consider the following . . .

- Lucid described how she performed many activities while living in space, such as keeping physically fit, eating meals, and maintaining personal hygiene. If you had a chance to interview Lucid about life on a space station, what questions would you ask her?

President Bill Clinton presents Shannon Lucid with the Congressional Space Medal of Honor at the White House in December 1996. Lucid was on Russian space station *Mir* for five months, the longest ever by an American. *(AP/Wide World Photos)*

- When Meyer asks Lucid if she thinks space exploration is worth the effort and the expense, she answers "Yes." What do you think? With all the other issues now confronting the United States and the rest of the world, do you feel that missions in space are necessary? Why or why not? Explain your position.

- Read "The Brick Moon," Edward Everett Hale's futuristic story about a space station, at http://www.voyager.edu/iss/café/articles/brickmoonrising.asp. Then do some research on the *Mir* and the ISS. Do you see any similarities between Hale's imaginary spacecraft and the actual *Mir* and ISS? Describe your findings.

For More Information

Books

Atkins, Jeannine. *The Story of Women in Space.* New York: Farrar, Straus and Giroux, 2003.

Cooper, Henry S. F. *A House in Space.* New York: Henry Holt & Company, 1976.

Periodicals

Danes, Mary K. "Space Woman on *Mir.*" *Hopscotch.* October/November 2002): p. 2.

Lucid, Shannon. "Six Months on Mir." *Scientific American* (May 1998): pp. 46–55.

Web Sites

"Astronaut Bio: Shannon Lucid." *Johnson Space Center, NASA.* http://www.jsc.nasa.gov/Bios/htmlbios/lucid.html (accessed on July 19, 2004).

Meyer, Patrick. "Living on *Mir:* An Interview with Dr. Shannon Lucid" (March 1998). *Marshall Space Flight Center, NASA.* http://liftoff.msfc.nasa.gov/academy/astronauts/livinginspace/lucid/LucidInterview.html (accessed on July 19, 2004).

"*Mir.*" *RussianSpaceWeb.* http://www.russianspaceweb.com/mir_chronology.html (accessed on July 19, 2004).

"Pink Socks and Jello: Shannon Lucid Writes a Letter Home." http://www.geocities.com/CapeCanaveral/4411/lucid.htm (accessed on July 19, 2004).

National Aeronautics and Space Administration (NASA)

Excerpts from **The Space Science Enterprise Strategic Plan: Origins, Evolution, and Destiny of the Cosmos and Life**

Originally published in 1997; reprinted from *Exploring the Unknown: Selected Documents in the History of the U.S. Civil Space Program, Volume V: Exploring the Cosmos,* published in 2001; also available at *NASA* (Web site)

On August 7, 1996, the U.S. space agency, the National Aeronautics and Space Administration, made an historic announcement: Scientists from the NASA Johnson Space Center in Houston, Texas, and from Stanford University in California had found evidence of life on the planet Mars. They made this discovery after analyzing a meteorite (the solid part of a meteor that makes it through the atmosphere to strike Earth's surface) that NASA scientists had found in Antarctica and taken to Houston in 1984. The meteorite had broken away from Mars fifteen million years ago after a comet or an asteroid struck the planet. Traveling through space for millions of years, the meteorite entered Earth's atmosphere and landed at Antarctica about thirteen thousand years ago. At first scientists thought the meteorite had come from the Moon. In 1993, after analyzing its chemical composition, they determined that it had originated on Mars.

Upon further examination, the NASA and Stanford scientists found that the meteorite contained microscopic evidence of living matter: carbonate globules (small spheres of a form of carbonic acid, a weak, unstable acid present in solutions of

This 4.5 billion-year-old meteorite rock was discovered in Antarctica in 1984. The rock is believed to have once been a part of Mars and that it was dislodged by a huge impact millions of years ago and fell to Earth about thirteen thousand years ago. *(NASA)*

carbon dioxide in water), polycyclic aromatic hydrocarbons (PAHs; a group of more than one hundred chemicals formed during the incomplete burning of organic [derived from living things] substances), magnetite globules (small, naturally magnetic spheres of the mineral iron oxide), and microscopic fossil-like structures. Carbonates are found in both living and non-living forms on Earth. But living matter is produced when a carbonate is combined with bacteria. Since the PAHs, magnetite, and fossil-like structures in the meteorite appear to have been created by ancient bacteria, scientists concluded that life may have existed on Mars. Similar evidence had been found in the 1970s, when NASA had sent Viking landers to Mars. (A lander is a spacecraft designed to land on a celestial body.) The landers carried experiments that tested the planet's soil for organic matter, but the results were inconclusive. One experiment detected no organic matter, while another found positive evidence. Scientists had been debating the issue of life on Mars ever since the Viking excursions. Yet the debate continued, even after the discovery of organic materials in the meteorite.

In conjunction with the NASA announcement in 1996, President Bill Clinton (1946–; served 1993–2000) called for continued exploration of Mars. As reported in an online *MarsNews.com* article, the president said, "I am determined that the American space program will put its full intellectual power and technological prowess behind the search for further evidence of life on Mars." The Office of Space Science (OSS), which designs and administers NASA's scientific missions, had begun working on a long-range plan, called "The Origins Initiative," earlier that year. The Origins Initiative included new space science missions as well as the continuation of existing programs.

In preparing the plan, scientists, engineers, educators, and communications specialists developed "Roadmaps" for the four areas within the OSS—Structure and Evolution of the Universe, Astronomical Search for Origins, Solar System Exploration, and Sun-Earth Connection. The National Academy of Sciences (NAS) had also compiled reports on these topics. The Roadmaps and the NAS reports were used in an NAS workshop and a symposium chaired by Vice President Al Gore (1948–). President Clinton then made a request to Congress for funding of the Origins Initiative, which would lead to the launch of about three times more space science missions from 2000 through 2004 than had been launched from 1990 through 1994. The Origins Initiative plan, officially titled *The Space Science Enterprise Strategic Plan: Origins, Evolution, and Destiny of the Cosmos and Life,* was published in November 1997.

Things to remember while reading excerpts from *The Space Science Enterprise Strategic Plan: Origins, Evolution, and Destiny of the Cosmos and Life*:

- A goal statement for the Origins Initiative appears in the opening section of *The Space Science Enterprise Strategic Plan:* "[The Origins Initiative is] aimed at following the 15-billion year chain of events from the birth of the Universe at the Big Bang; through the formation of the chemical elements, galaxies, stars, and planets; through the mixing of chemicals and energy that cradled life of Earth; to the earliest self-replicating [producing a copy of oneself] organisms and the profusion of life."

- The excerpts from *The Space Science Enterprise Strategic Plan* focus on scientific and educational objectives. The document also includes details about goals, procedures, schedules, and funding, which are not reprinted here.

- The plan includes missions for 2000 through 2004, or three to seven years in the future. At the time it was unusual for NASA to look ahead more than five years. The OSS director, Wesley Huntress (1942–), told a *Physics Today* magazine reporter that NASA was taking a new approach "so we can see where our near-term missions are leading us."

Excerpts from The Space Science Enterprise Strategic Plan: Origins, Evolution, and Destiny of the Cosmos and Life

A. Introduction: We humans are players in the greatest drama of all, the story of cosmic Origins, Evolution, and Destiny. Now, for the first time, we truly have the opportunity to seek scientific answers to questions as old as humanity itself:

- *How did the Universe begin? How did life on Earth arise?*
- *What fate awaits our planet and our species?*

We have begun to assemble answers to these grand questions using remarkable new tools on Earth and in space. But, more importantly, our understanding is growing through the intellect and imagination of men and women who look up and wonder, who devise new means of gathering information that lead to the formulation and testing of theories to explain what it all means. This is a Golden Age of discovery as exciting and significant as the time when humans turned their first telescopes to the heavens.

In the past few years, we have seen faint folds in the fabric of the Universe, the most ancient ancestors of all the galaxies, stars,

From the Big Bang to Biology

Some 15 billion years ago, matter itself came into being in the aftermath of the Big Bang, the event when space and time began. Mysterious forces sculpted the formless sea of particles, leading first to structure in the Universe and then giving birth to galaxies and stars. Some massive stars lived short lives of violent intensity and died in colossal supernova explosions. Their **death throes** scattered heavy elements produced in their interiors into **interstellar space**. Our home planet condensed from a cloud enriched with iron and **silicon**. Our lifeblood and the tools of our civilization are made of elements forged in supernovas long ago.

The early years of Earth were scenes of incredible violence as comets, **asteroids**, and eruptions **tilled** the cooling surface and built and blew away oceans and atmosphere. But within just a few hundred million years the first living organisms emerged: Life, it seems, is remarkably hardy and its origin on Earth seems to have occurred surprisingly quickly. In the nearly 4 billion years since, life on our planet has made its home in astonishingly extreme environments and diverse places, habitable so long as there is even a trace of water and usable energy.

And, so we humans, made of star-stuff, descendants of one common ancestor, cousins to all life on Earth, children of ages of evolution and adaptation—now equipped with tools of glass and metal and plastic and silicon to extend our sense beyond our ordinary grasp—are able to look out at the Universe around us and know our solar neighborhood, our intimate relationship to galaxies and stars, and our deep connection to the cosmos.

Death throes: Final moments of death.

Interstellar space: Space among the stars.

Silicon: A nonmetallic element that is the most abundant in nature after oxygen.

Asteroids: Small celestial bodies found between the orbits of Mars and Jupiter.

Tilled: Plowed.

Super-nova: The explosion of a very large star.

Biosphere: The part of the world in which life can exist.

and planets that surround us. We have used telescopes on the ground and in space to discover disks of gas and dust surrounding young stars—nurseries of potential worlds—and to discern evidence for giant planets orbiting nearby stars. We have found living creatures in extreme environments previously not thought capable of sustaining life—the dark depths of Earth's oceans and the dry valleys of the Antarctic. We have studied meteorites from Mars, one of which shows evidence of the presence of ancient water and the chemical building blocks of life, and—possibly—tiny, fossilized microbes. Our spacecraft have returned images of what may be ice floes above a liquid water ocean on Jupiter's moon Europa, and made us wonder if life may begin on moons as well as planets. We have seen a comet collide with Jupiter and studied a **super-nova** from its initial explosion to an expanding gas cloud. We have learned that Earth's climate, **biosphere**, and the workings of our entire technological civilization are profoundly

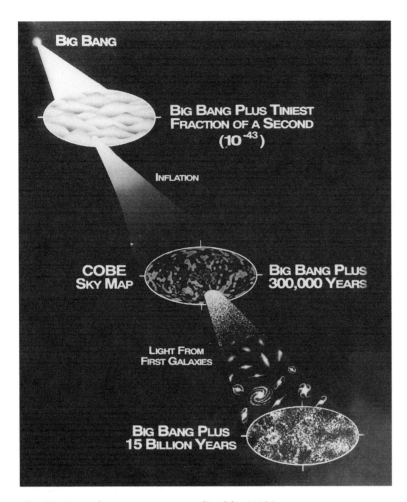

The Big Bang theory, as conceptualized by NASA. *(AP/Wide World Photos)*

influenced by the behavior of our varying Sun, a star we can study close-up. We have detected giant **black holes** *that may be as massive as a billion suns at the center of our galaxy and in other galaxies, turning centuries of theory into fact.*

We have seen bursts of **gamma rays** *from distant reaches of space and time, momentarily more powerful than a million galaxies. Our understanding of the Universe has been altered forever.*

We have learned much, but many questions remain to be answered. How could an ordered Universe emerge from a formless beginning? Is life in our solar system unique to Earth, or might there be evidence of past or present life on other moons and planets? Can we

Black holes: Hypothetical celestial objects with a gravitational field so strong that light cannot escape from it; black holes are believed to be created in the collapse of a very massive star.

Gamma rays: Photons emitted by a radioactive substance.

forecast space weather by better understanding the forces that drive our Sun? In so doing, can we better protect our astronauts and the orbiting satellites on which our global communications depend? Can we develop the scientific base of information necessary to save Earth from an incoming asteroid like the one we believe ended the epoch of the dinosaurs 65 million years ago? Will a "Big Crunch" follow the Big Bang, billions of years from now, or will our Universe expand endlessly?

In the decade ahead we have the opportunity to address many of these exciting and engaging issues, developing missions to gain new answers and enrich the story. There will be twists and turns along the way, unexpected discoveries that will show us the Universe is not quite the way we thought. And there will almost certainly be difficulties. Developing new tools to extend the frontiers of the known is always challenging. But a coherent, practical, and affordable strategy is feasible. . . . NASA's Space Science Enterprise can provide more precise answers to fundamental questions about the formation and evolution of the Universe and how the Sun influences Earth, the history of planets and satellites in our solar system, and the occurrence of life either in our tiny region of space or in the larger neighborhood of our Galaxy. . . .

B. Fundamental Questions . . . Science Objectives: Detailed Space Science planning begins with a set of Fundamental Questions. These questions—challenging and exciting to scientists and non-scientists alike and **amenable** to scientific progress—form the basis for our scientific program over the next several decades. To address these Fundamental Questions, the Space Science Enterprise—guided by the National Academy of Sciences, and in conjunction with the space science community—has laid out . . . detailed Science Objectives— scientific investigations that can be accomplished within the next 5–6 years through one or more space missions and ground-based programs. . . .

Fundamental Questions

1. How did the Universe begin and what is its ultimate fate?
2. How do galaxies, stars, and planetary systems form and evolve?
3. What physical processes take place in extreme environments such as black holes?
4. How and where did life begin?
5. How is the evolution of life linked to planetary evolution and to **cosmic phenomena**?

Amenable: Agreeable to, open to.

Cosmic phenomena: What happens in the cosmos, or universe; also used to refer to the comets, solar eclipses, and meteor showers observable in our solar system.

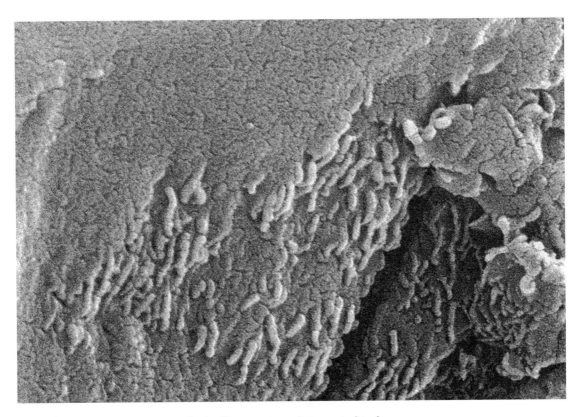

An electron microscope image of tube-like structures interpreted to be microscopic fossils of primitive, bacteria-like organisms that may have lived on Mars more than 3.6 billion years ago. Possible microscopic fossils such as these were found inside of an ancient Martian rock that fell to the Earth as a meteorite. *(NASA)*

6. ***How and why does the Sun vary*** *and how do the Earth and other planets respond?*
7. *How might humans inhabit other worlds?. . .*

Science Objectives
1. *Observe the earliest structure in the Universe.*
2. *Observe the emergence of stars and galaxies in the very early Universe.*
3. *Observe the evolution of galaxies and the* ***intergalactic medium.***
4. *Measure the amount and distribution of* ***dark and luminous matter*** *in the ancient and modern Universe.*

How and why does the Sun vary: How and why does the Sun's brightness and energy output change.

Intergalactic medium: The foglike dust and gas between galaxies.

Dark and luminous matter: Dark matter is unknown matter that may constitute as much as 99 percent of the matter in the universe. Luminous matter is the matter in the universe that can be directly observed, such as stars, gas, and dust.

Theory of General Relativity: Theory stating that measurable properties will differ depending on the relative motion of the observer.

Cosmic rays: Streams of atomic nuclei that enter Earth's atmosphere from outer space at speeds approaching that of light.

Compact objects: Compact objects form when a star dies and leaves behind an extremely compressed interior.

Disks: Seemingly flat figures of a celestial body.

Jets: Streams of material coming from or appearing to come from a celestial object.

Interstellar medium: Dust and gas between the stars in a galaxy.

Plasma: An electrically neutral, usually hot, gas containing positively charged particles and some neutral particles.

In situ: Latin for "in place"; meaning' in its orginal location.

Protoplanetary disks: Disks of matter, including dust and gas, near a star from which plants may eventually form.

Solar wind: A continuous stream of charged atomic particles that radiates from the Sun.

Europa: A large moon of Jupiter.

5. Test the **Theory of General Relativity.**
6. Identify the origin of gamma-ray bursts and high-energy **cosmic rays.**
7. Study **compact objects** and investigate how **disks** and **jets** are formed around them.
8. Study the formation and evolution of the chemical elements and how stars evolve and interact with the **interstellar medium.**
9. Measure space **plasma** processes both remotely and **in situ.**
10. Observe and characterize the formation of stars, **protoplanetary disks**, and planetary systems, and detect Neptune-size planets around other stars.
11. Measure solar variability and learn to predict its effect on Earth more accurately.
12. Study the interactions of planets with the **solar wind.**
13. Characterize the history, current environment, and resources of Mars, especially the accessibility of water.
14. Determine the pre-biological history and biological potential of Mars and other bodies in the solar system.
15. Determine whether a liquid water ocean exists today on **Europa,** and seek evidence of organic or biological processes.
16. Investigate the composition, evolution, and resources of the Moon, small bodies, and Pluto-like objects across the solar system.
17. Complete the inventory and characterize a sample of near-Earth objects down to l-km diameter.
18. Reconstruct the conditions on the early Earth that were required for the origin of life and determine the processes that govern its evolution.
19. Investigate the processes that underlie the diversity of solar system objects. . . .

The NASA Strategic Plan mandates that we "involve the education community in our endeavors to inspire America's Students, create learning opportunities, enlighten inquisitive minds," and "communicate widely the content, relevancy, and excitement of NASA's missions and discoveries to inspire and to increase the understanding and the broad application of science and technology. . . ."

To realize this potential more fully, we have developed a comprehensive, organized approach to making education at all levels and the enhanced public understanding of science integral parts of Space Science missions and research programs. We will work closely with the space science and education communities to develop a variety of

Middle school students speaking through audio and visual means to NASA scientists in Washington, D.C., about numerous research and educational projects, including the Martian meteorite that NASA researchers claim contains fossilized proof that life existed on Mars.
(NASA)

long-term partnerships between educators and space scientists and to ensure that the information, ideas, and materials emerging from the Space Science program are developed in a variety of formats useful to educators and understandable by the public. . . .

Education and Public Outreach Objectives
1. *Have a substantial education and outreach program associated with every Space Science flight mission and research program.*
2. *Increase the fraction of the space community directly involved in education at the pre-college level and in contributing to the broad public understanding of science.*
3. *Develop a presence in every state in the U.S. to serve as a focal point for encouraging and assisting scientists and educa-*

tors to develop partnerships and, in so doing, contribute in a meaningful way to Space Science education and outreach.

4. *Organize a comprehensive, national approach for providing information on and access to the results from the Space Science education and outreach programs.*

5. *Continue, and refine or enhance where appropriate, programs dedicated to the development and support of future scientists and engineers.*

6. *Provide new opportunities for minority universities in particular and for underserved/underutilized groups in general to compete for and participate in Space Science missions and research programs.*

What happened next . . .

In *The Space Science Enterprise Strategic Plan,* NASA gave top priority to missions that had already been approved and funded. Among them were the Hubble Space Telescope (HST), the Advanced X-Ray Astrophysics Facility, the Cassini-Huygens mission to Saturn, and the Mars Surveyor Program (now called the Mars Exploration Program; a series of NASA missions devoted to exploration of Mars).

Launched in 1990, the HST has become one of NASA's greatest accomplishments. The HST orbits Earth in outer space, taking pictures of stars, galaxies, planets, and vast regions previously unknown to humans. Since the space observatory is positioned beyond Earth's atmosphere, it receives images that are brighter and more detailed than those captured by telescopes based on land. Maintenance of the HST, however, is performed by astronaut crews who travel aboard space shuttles for service missions. In 2004, a year after the *Columbia* space shuttle disaster (see entry), NASA grounded its shuttle fleet. The final service mission to the HST was therefore canceled, leaving in doubt the future of the telescope, which was expected to continue operating until 2015. Supporters of the HST immediately began seeking ways to prolong the life of the largest, most successful astronomy project in history.

The Advanced X-Ray Astrophysics Facility was sent into space in 1999. It was later renamed Chandra in honor of Indian American Noble Prize winner Subrahmanyan Chandrasekhar (1910–1995). Positioned in Earth orbit, Chandra is a satellite observatory that detects X rays. Scientists hope to gain a better understanding of black holes, supernovas, dark matter, and the origins of life through analysis of X rays found by Chandra.

The Cassini-Huygens mission was launched in 1997. It is being conducted by the Huygens probe supplied by the European Space Agency (ESA), which is onboard the NASA spacecraft *Cassini.* The probe carries a robotic laboratory that it will use to observe the clouds, atmosphere, and surface of Saturn and its moon, Titan. After traveling billions of miles for seven years, *Cassini* reached Saturn in July 2004 and the Huygens probe began sending back images of the planet and its colorful rings.

The Mars Exploration Program has become one of NASA's most popular endeavors. Initiated in 1964 to explore Mars, the mission began with flybys by Mariner spacecraft to take pictures of the Red Planet. In the early 1970s NASA put spacecraft in orbit around Mars to conduct longer-term studies, and by the mid-1970s landers had been placed on the surface of Mars. In 1997 the Mars rover *Pathfinder* was the first vehicle to move around on the planet. Six years later NASA deployed two technologically advanced rovers, *Spirit* and *Opportunity,* which were capable of traveling longer distances. In 2004 the rovers sent back pictures of craters, hills, and empty landscape, and they collected soil samples that may enable scientists to determine the existence of life on Mars.

NASA offers a variety of education programs for students and teachers around the country. In conjunction with its educational mission, the agency produces books, films, videos, DVDs, television and radio shows, and audio recordings on space science. NASA maintains numerous space science Web sites on the Internet, many of them featuring live images from outer space. The sites also provide information and activity links for students.

Did you know . . .

- In June 2000, the Mars Global Surveyor, an orbiter spacecraft, found evidence of water on Mars. Scientists regard this discovery as a significant step toward solving the mystery of whether life existed on the planet.

- The Chandra X-ray Observatory was instrumental in uncovering evidence that a gamma-ray burst occurred in Earth's Milky Way galaxy a few thousand years ago. A gamma-ray burst is one of the most dramatic events in the natural world.

- President George W. Bush (1946–; served 2001–; see entry) announced a major revitalization of NASA in a speech in January 2004. One of his goals was to send humans to Mars in the future.

- Since the grounding of the space shuttle fleet, scientists have been experimenting with robots that could replace humans on HST service missions.

- In 2004 NASA was operating more than thirty-five space science missions. Twenty more missions were in development, and twenty-five others were under study.

Consider the following . . .

- NASA operates many space science missions that are not widely publicized but yet make significant contributions to knowledge about the universe. Visit the NASA Space Science Missions Web site at http://spacescience.nasa.gov/missions/index.htm (accessed on August, 10, 2004). Browse the "Operating Missions" links and find a little-known mission that you think should receive more publicity. In a brief paper explain the reasons for your choice.

- Do you think it is important to determine whether life exists on Mars? Prepare a short speech in which you present your position on this subject to your science class.

- Space exploration has resulted in technology that we now take for granted, such as satellite communication, global positioning devices, the MRI (Magnetic Resonance Imaging) machine (device that use nuclear protons to take pictures of the interior of the body and the CAT (Computed Axial Tomography) scanner (medical device consisting of X-ray and computer equipment that produce three-dimensional images). Can you think of other examples? Make a list of items and identify the space science project or mission that created each of them.

For More Information

Books

Burrows, William E. *Mission to Deep Space: Voyager's Journey of Discovery.* New York: Scientific American Books for Young Readers, 1993.

Davis, Lucile. *The Mars Rovers.* San Diego: Greenhaven Press, 2004.

Fischer, Daniel. *Mission Jupiter: The Spectacular Journey of the* Galileo *Spacecraft.* Translated by Don Reneau. New York: Copernicus, 2001.

Goodwin, Simon. *Hubble's Universe: A Portrait of Our Cosmos.* New York: Viking Penguin, 1997.

Harland, David M. *Mission to Saturn:* Cassini *and the* Huygens *Probe.* New York: Springer-Praxis, 2002.

Mishkin, Andrew. *Sojourner: An Insider's View of the Mars Pathfinder Mission.* New York: Berkeley Books, 2003.

The Space Science Enterprise Strategic Plan: Origins, Evolution, and Destiny of the Cosmos and Life. In *Exploring the Unknown: Selected Documents in the History of the U.S. Civil Space Program. Volume V: Exploring the Cosmos.* Edited by John M. Logsdon. Washington, DC: National Aeronautics and Space Administration, 2001; also available at *NASA.* http://www.hq.nasa.gov/office/codez/stratplans/1996/science.html (accessed on August 9, 2004).

Periodicals

Feder, Toni. "NASA Sets Ambitious Strategic Plan for Space Science." *Physics Today* (September 1997): pp. 59–60.

"HST, Keck Find a Galaxy from the 'Dark Ages.'" *Astronomy* (May 2004): p. 30.

Web Sites

"Cassini-Huygens: Mission to Saturn and Titan." *Jet Propulsion Laboratory, NASA.* http://saturn.jpl.nasa.gov/home/index.cfm (accessed on August 10, 2004).

"Chandra X-Ray Observatory News." *NASA.* http://chandra.nasa.gov/ (accessed on August 10, 2004).

HubbleSite. http://hubblesite.org (accessed on August 10, 2004).

"Life on Mars?" *MarsNews.com.* http://www.marsnews.com/focus/life/ (accessed on August 10, 2004).

"Mars Exploration Rover Mission." *Jet Propulsion Laboratory, NASA.* http://marsrovers.jpl.nasa.gov/home/ (accessed on August 10, 2004).

"NASA's Mars Exploration Program." *Jet Propulsion Laboratory, NASA.* http://mars.jpl.nasa.gov/missions/ (accessed on August 10, 2004).

"Space Science Missions." *NASA.* http://spacescience.nasa.gov/missions/index.htm (accessed on August 10, 2004).

Other Sources

The Big Bang. World Almanac Video, 1999.

Exploding Stars and Black Holes. PBS Home Video, 1997.

Columbia Space Shuttle Disaster

Excerpts from Columbia Accident Investigation Board Report,
Volume 1

Published in 2003; available at Columbia *Accident Investigation Board*
(CAIB) **and** *NASA* **(Web sites)**

On February 1, 2003, the National Aeronautics and Space Agency (NASA) was dealt a severe blow. The space shuttle *Columbia,* carrying a crew of seven, broke up while attempting to reenter Earth's atmosphere after a sixteen-day mission. It was the first major accident since 1986, when the space shuttle *Challenger* exploded less than two minutes after takeoff, with most of the nation watching on television. The space shuttle program, which had been regarded by many Americans as engaging in "routine" missions, came under intense examination. A thorough investigation was initiated the day following the explosion. The final report, issued on August 26, 2003, faulted NASA for the explosion because the agency had overlooked problems that had been plaguing the aging *Columbia* for years.

Since its founding in 1958, NASA has been successful in accomplishing its missions. Sending human beings into outer space is never a routine exercise, and the space agency has generally been credited with maintaining a good record. In fact, by the turn of the twenty-first century, NASA had made space travel seem to be an everyday occurrence. Nevertheless, for many years critics have charged that NASA officials and engineers have frequently been guilty of arrogance or indifference, which have cost astronauts their lives. Some accidents, such as the fire in the cockpit of the *Apollo 1* spacecraft that killed three astronauts in 1967, were not due to negligence on the part of NASA scientists. Other fatal accidents, such as the *Challenger* disaster in 1986 and the *Columbia* explosion in 2003, were preventable. NASA officials claim that a lack of funding prevented them from performing some necessary repairs, but Congressional reports have found differently.

The *Columbia* mission began amidst problems on launch day, January 16, 2003. When the shuttle lifted off from Cape Canaveral, Florida, a piece of hardened foam insulation dislodged from its external fuel tank and struck the underside of its left wing. The next day, while the *Columbia* was in orbit, NASA engineers discussed whether the foam could have damaged heat-resistant tiles that were necessary to prevent a fire upon reentry. On January 21 and 22, NASA engineer Alan Rodney Rocha begged NASA officials to request spy satellite photos of *Columbia* to evaluate the extent of the damage. His requests were denied. On January 29, senior NASA official William Readdy (1952–) inquired about taking photos, but he did not make a formal request. Consequently, no photos were ever taken by NASA while the *Columbia* was in orbit.

On February 1, *Columbia* attempted reentry into the atmosphere. At 5:53 A.M. PST (Pacific Standard Time; 8:53 A.M. Eastern Standard Time [EST]), sensors on the shuttle indicated that there was trouble. An astronomer in San Francisco, California, shot five photos of the craft as it was breaking up in the atmosphere. One of the photos showed a mysterious "purple streak" trailing the craft. It was later determined to be part of *Columbia*'s on-board camera. One minute later, at 5:54 A.M. PST, a news photographer in California observed pieces of the *Columbia* flying overhead. He also saw a red flare coming from the shuttle. Meanwhile, in Houston, Texas, site of NASA Mission Control, officials had lost radio contact with *Columbia* at 9:00 A.M. EST (6:00 A.M. PST). At the time transmission was lost, NASA engineers were attempting to explain to the crew the nature of the warning signals. The craft was scheduled to land at Cape Canaveral at 9:16 A.M EST (6:16 A.M. PST). At 9:05 A.M. EST (6:05 A.M. PST) residents in north-central Texas

Space shuttle *Columbia* lifts off from Cape Canaveral in Florida. *(NASA)*

President Mourns *Columbia* Crew

The American public responded to the *Columbia* explosion with shock and disbelief. For many, the *Challenger* explosion was still a vivid memory that haunted them every time NASA launched a shuttle. President George W. Bush (1946–; served 2001–) addressed the grieving nation approximately five hours after the *Columbia* broke apart over the southwestern United States. He expressed remorse for the loss of the seven astronauts: Commander Rick D. Husband (1957–2003), a U.S. Air Force colonel and mechanical engineer, had piloted the first shuttle mission to dock with the International Space Station (ISS). Pilot William C. McCool (1961–2003) was a U.S. Navy commander. Payload commander Michael P. Anderson (1959–2003), a U.S. Air Force lieutenant colonel and physicist, was in charge of the onboard science mission. Payload specialist Ilan Ramon (1954–2003) was a colonel in the Israeli Air Force and the first Israeli astronaut. Kalpana Chawla (1961–2003), an Indian-born aerospace engineer, was flying her second mission. Mission specialist David M. Brown (1956–2003) was a U.S. Navy captain and a flight surgeon. Mission specialist Laurel Clark (1961–2003), a U.S. Navy commander and flight surgeon, worked on biological experiments. President Bush reminded the American people that space flight is never "routine" and that "it is easy to overlook . . . the difficulties of navigating the fierce outer atmosphere of Earth."

reported hearing a faint boom and then seeing trails of smoke and debris in the sky. After receiving these reports, the NASA flight director declared a contingency (emergency) and contacted search and rescue teams in the area. None of the astronauts were found. (Later, over 2,000 pieces of debris, including human remains, were found.)

On February 2, NASA administrator Sean O'Keefe (1956–) appointed retired U.S. Navy Admiral Harold Gehman Jr. (1942–) to head the *Columbia* Accident Investigation Board (CAIB). On February 3, the American public was informed that foam shed from *Columbia*'s external tank was likely the "root cause" of the tragedy. Two days later, however, NASA reversed this statement and stated that the debris likely was *not* the cause of the accident. On February 7, in the face of public protest, NASA was forced to allow individuals outside of NASA to participate in the investigation. On February 8, NASA announced that it was examining a picture of *Columbia* taken two days after launch, which showed an object

The seven *Columbia* astronauts killed in the explosion: (clockwise from far left) Kalpana Chawla, David M. Brown, William C. McCool, Michael P. Anderson, Ilan Ramon, Laurel B. Clark, and Rick D. Husband.

(AP/Wide World Photos)

coming off the craft. On February 10, NASA admitted that dozens of scientists had voiced concern about problems with the *Columbia*, particularly in regard to the foam from the external tank. On February 11, Congress began its official investigation, headed by the CAIB. Throughout the following months, NASA was forced to admit it had not heeded the advice of its own engineers. For instance, satellite photos might have provided crucial information for the rescue of *Columbia*'s crew, though a rescue attempt most likely would have failed. NASA continued to undergo intense examination, and on August 26, 2003, the CAIB released its official findings.

The CAIB found that a joint, known as a T-seal, was shifted after foam debris from the external tank hit the left wing. Although the gap was small—.24 x 21.7 inches (0.6 x 55 centimeters)—it was large enough to rip open upon reentry. The report was highly critical of NASA's actions during the *Columbia* flight. The board called into question NASA's organizational techniques used to promote safety. The report called for sweeping changes in NASA's organization and the way it conducts its flights. The space shuttles remain grounded until safety changes are made.

Things to remember while reading excerpts from the Columbia *Accident Investigation Board Report*:

- It took seven months from the time of the accident until the issue of the report. However, the government's report was highly critical of how NASA handled the shuttle flight. For instance, ground controllers did not effectively communicate information to the *Columbia* crew. Although nothing will bring back the seven crew members who died, the U.S. government is serious about preventing another such accident.

- The investigators found that, although NASA frequently complains that the American public finds space flight to be "routine," NASA itself failed to perform the basic preparations necessary for a safe flight. Objections and warnings raised by knowledgeable scientists were largely ignored. The report cited that this was largely due to an overall arrogance on part of NASA officials.

- Although the *Columbia* tragedy affected the American public, there is still support for NASA. According to an Associated Press poll, a majority of Americans are still in favor of space missions.

Columbia Accident Investigation Board Report, *Volume 1*

Report Synopsis

Designated STS-I07, this was the Space Shuttle Program's 113th flight and Columbia*'s 28th. The flight was close to trouble-free. Unfortunately, there were no indications to either the crew onboard* Columbia *or to engineers in Mission Control that the mission was in trouble as a result of a foam strike during* **ascent**. *Mission management failed to detect weak signals that the Orbiter was in trouble and take corrective action.* Columbia *was the first space-rated Orbiter. It made the Space Shuttle Program's first four orbital test flights. Because it was the first of its kind,* Columbia *differed slightly from Orbiters* Challenger, Discovery, Atlantis, *and* Endeavour. *Built to an earlier engineering standard,* Columbia *was slightly heavier, and, although it could reach the high-**inclination orbit** of the International Space Station, its* **payload** *was insufficient to make* Columbia *cost-effective for Space Station missions. Therefore,* Columbia *was not equipped with a Space Station* **docking** *system, which freed up space in the payload bay for longer cargos, such as the science* **modules** *Spacelab and Spacehab. Consequently,* Columbia *generally flew science missions and serviced the Hubble Space Telescope.*

STS-107 was an intense science mission that required the seven-member crew to form two teams, enabling round-the-clock shifts. Because the extensive science cargo and its extra power sources required additional checkout time, the launch sequence and countdown were about 24 hours longer than normal. Nevertheless, the countdown proceeded as planned, and Columbia *was launched from Launch Complex 39-A on January 16, 2003, at 10:39 A.M. Eastern Standard Time (EST).*

At 81.7 seconds after launch, when the Shuttle was at about 65,820 feet and traveling at Mach 2.46 (1,650 miles per hour), a large piece of hand-crafted insulating foam came off an area where the Orbiter attaches to the External Tank. At 81.9 seconds, it struck the leading edge of Columbia*'s left wing. This event was not detected by the crew on board or seen by ground support teams until the next day, during detailed reviews of all launch camera photography and videos. This foam strike had no apparent effect on the daily conduct of the 16-day mission, which met all its objectives.*

Ascent: Rising or mounting upward.

Inclination orbit: Angle at which a celestial body crosses Earth's equator, and its altitude above Earth. A high-inclination orbit means that the path between Earth and the ISS is at such a steep angle that a space shuttle must maintain a high level of thrust, or speed, which can be slowed down by heavy cargo.

Payload: Load carried by an aircraft or spacecraft consisting of things (such as passengers or instruments) necessary to the purpose of the flight.

Docking: Joining of two spacecraft in space.

Modules: Independently operable units that are part of the total structure of a space vehicle.

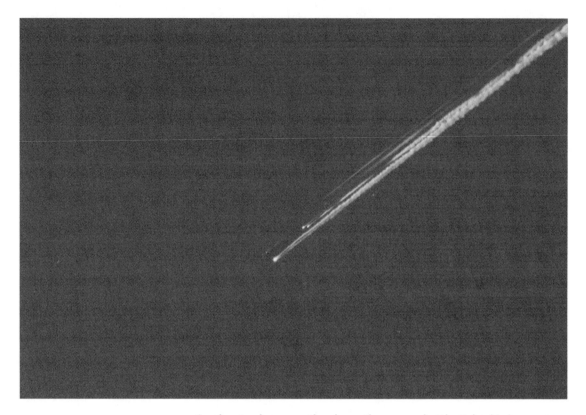

Smoke streaks across the sky as the space shuttle *Columbia* burns up while heading back to Earth. *(© Robert McCullough/Dallas Morning News/Corbis)*

Arbitrarily: Randomly, without a discernible pattern or reason.

Appendices: Supplemental material usually attached at the end of a piece of writing.

The de-orbit burn to slow *Columbia* down for re-entry into Earth's atmosphere was normal, and the flight profile throughout re-entry was standard. Time during re-entry is measured in seconds from "Entry Interface," an **arbitrarily** determined altitude of 400,000 feet where the Orbiter begins to experience the effects of Earth's atmosphere. Entry Interface for STS-107 occurred at 8:44:09 a.m. on February 1. Unknown to the crew or ground personnel, because the data is recorded and stored in the Orbiter instead of being transmitted to Mission Control at Johnson Space Center, the first abnormal indication occurred 270 seconds after Entry Interface. Chapter 2 [of the Board's report] reconstructs in detail the events leading to the loss of *Columbia* and her crew, and refers to more details in the **appendices**. In Chapter 3, the Board analyzes all the information available to conclude that the direct, physical action that initiated the chain of events leading to the loss of *Columbia* and her crew was the foam strike during ascent. This chapter reviews five **analytical paths**—**aerodynamic, thermodynamic, sensor data timeline**, debris reconstruction, and **imaging evidence**—to show that all five independently arrive at the same conclusion. The subsequent impact testing conducted by the Board is also discussed.

That conclusion is that Columbia *re-entered Earth's atmosphere with a pre-existing **breach** in the leading edge of its left wing in the **vicinity** of Reinforced Carbon-Carbon (RCC) panel 8. This breach, caused by the foam strike on ascent, was of sufficient size to allow superheated air (probably exceeding 5,000 degrees Fahrenheit) to penetrate the cavity behind the RCC panel. The breach widened, destroying the insulation protecting the wing's leading edge support structure, and the superheated air eventually melted the thin aluminum wing **spar**. Once in the interior, the superheated air began to destroy the left wing. This destructive process was carefully reconstructed from the recordings of hundreds of sensors inside the wing, and from analyses of the reactions of the flight control systems to the changes in aerodynamic forces.*

By the time Columbia *passed over the coast of California in the pre-dawn hours of February 1, at Entry Interface plus 555 seconds, amateur videos show that pieces of the Orbiter were shedding. The Orbiter was captured on videotape during most of its quick transit over the Western United States. The Board correlated the events seen in these videos to sensor readings recorded during re-entry. Analysis indicates that the Orbiter continued to fly its pre-planned flight profile, although, still unknown to anyone on the ground or aboard Columbia, her control systems were working furiously to maintain that flight profile. Finally, over Texas, just southwest of Dallas-Fort Worth, the increasing aerodynamic forces the Orbiter experienced in the **denser** levels of the atmosphere overcame the **catastrophically** damaged left wing, causing the Orbiter to fall out of control at speeds in excess of 10,000 mph. . . .*

Chapter 7: The Accident's Organizational Causes

In the Board's view, NASA's organizational culture and structure had as much to do with this accident as the External Tank foam. Organizational culture refers to the values, norms, beliefs, and practices that govern how an institution functions. At the most basic level, organizational culture defines the assumptions that employees make as they carry out their work. It is a powerful force that can persist through reorganizations and the reassignment of key personnel.

Analytical paths: Ways of thinking; division of a topic or problem into logical parts and the evaluation of each part individually.

Aerodynamic: The motions of and forces associated with air and other gases, especially as they interact with objects moving through them.

Thermodynamic: Of or operating by mechanical power derived from heat.

Sensor data timeline: A record of how sensing devices recorded events, in the order in which they occurred.

Imaging evidence: Evidence captured by imaging techniques such as film and photography.

Breach: Broken, ruptured, or torn condition or area.

Vicinity: Nearby area.

Spar: Part of the wing that supports the ribs.

Denser: Thicker, having more mass per unit volume.

Catastrophically: Disastrously or tragically.

Debris collected from the space shuttle *Columbia* about two months after the explosion. NASA investigators examined the debris in an attempt to reconstruct the shuttle orbiter and determine the cause of the accident. (© NASA/Corbis)

Bureaucratic: Firmly obedient to official forms, rules, and procedures that complicate and slow effective action.

Deferred: Put off or delayed.

Cumbersome: Burdensome, troublesome.

Vestiges: Remnants, what is left.

Robust: Strongly formed or constructed.

Espoused: Supported.

*Given that today's risks in human space flight are as high and the safety margins as razor thin as they have ever been, there is little room for overconfidence. Yet the attitudes and decision-making of Shuttle Program managers and engineers during the events leading up to this accident were clearly overconfident and often **bureaucratic** in nature. They **deferred** to layered and **cumbersome** regulations rather than the fundamentals of safety.*

*The Shuttle Program's safety culture is straining to hold together the **vestiges** of a once **robust** systems safety program.*

As the Board investigated the Columbia *accident it expected to find a vigorous safety organization, process, and culture at NASA, bearing little resemblance to what the Rogers Commission identified as the ineffective "silent safety" system in which budget cuts resulted in a lack of resources, personnel, independence, and authority. NASA's initial briefings to the Board on its safety programs **espoused** a risk-*

*averse philosophy that empowered any employee to stop an opera-tion at the mere glimmer of a problem. Unfortunately, NASA's views of its safety culture in those briefings did not reflect reality. Shuttle Program safety personnel failed to adequately **assess anomalies** and frequently accepted critical risks without **qualitative** or **quantitative** support, even when the tools to provide more comprehensive assess-ments were available.*

Similarly, the Board expected to find NASA's Safety and Mission Assurance organization deeply engaged at every level of Shuttle man-agement: the Flight Readiness Review, the Mission Management Team, the Debris Assessment Team, the Mission Evaluation Room, and so forth. This was not the case. In briefing after briefing, inter-view after interview, NASA remained in denial: in the agency's eyes, "there were no safety-of-flight issues," and no safety compromises in the long history of debris strikes on the Thermal Protection System. The silence of Program-level safety processes undermined oversight; when they did not speak up, safety personnel could not fulfill their stated mission to provide "checks and balances." A pattern of ac-ceptance prevailed throughout the organization that tolerated foam problems without sufficient engineering justification for doing so.

What happened next . . .

As a result of the CAIB report, NASA administrator O'Keefe grounded all future shuttle missions. In January 2004 Presi-dent Bush announced that the space shuttle fleet will be re-tired from service in 2010. NASA plans to replace the shuttle with the Crew Exploration Vehicle, which is expected to con-duct its first manned mission by 2014 (see George W. Bush entry).

Did you know . . .

- After the explosion, many Americans feared that terrorists had somehow been involved. Terrorism was quickly ruled out as a possible cause of the accident.

- On March 26, 2003, the United States House of Repre-sentatives's Science Committee approved funds for the construction of a memorial at Arlington National Cemetery for the *Columbia* crew. A similar memorial was built for the *Challenger* crew.

- On January 6, 2004, NASA announced that the landing site for the Mars Rover *Spirit* would be called Columbia Memorial Station. NASA also announced that a series of hills on Mars are being named for individual *Columbia* crew members.

Consider the following . . .

- Although NASA has come under considerable fire for the *Challenger* and *Columbia* tragedies, the space agency has been extremely successful. Do you think flights should resume? Why or why not? Should NASA continue to use the existing shuttles, many of which are nearly thirty years old, or is it a good idea to build new crafts for a new age of exploration?

- Many people are still very angry that NASA officials might have been able to prevent the 1986 and 2003 shuttle accidents. Do you think that there should be a non-government agency that investigates NASA's work so as to help prevent another accident? Why or why not?

- Ask your parents or teacher where they were when the space shuttle *Challenger* exploded. Ask them how they felt and if they think space flight should continue. Do you remember the *Columbia* disaster? How did it make you feel?

For More Information

Books

Cabbage, Michael, and William Harwood. *Comm Check: The Final Flight of Shuttle* Columbia. New York: Free Press, 2004.

Cole, Michael D. *Columbia Space Shuttle Disaster: From First Liftoff to Tragic Final Flight.* Berkeley Heights, NJ: Enslow Publishers, 2003.

Periodicals

Cowen, R. "*Columbia* Disaster." *Science News* (February 8, 2003): pp. 83–84.

"A Fall to Earth." *U.S. News & World Report* (2003 Special Commemorative Issue): pp. 24–25.

Web Sites

Columbia Accident Investigation Board Report, Volume 1. NASA: Washington, DC, 2003. Available at *CAIB.* http://www.caib.us/news/report/default.html (accessed on August 10, 2004); also available at *NASA.* http://www.nasa.gov/columbia/home/CAIB_Vol1.html (accessed on August 10, 2004).

"NASA Honors the STS–107 Crew and Their Dedication to the Spirit of Exploration and Discovery." *NASA.* http://www.nasa.gov/columbia/home/index.html (accessed on August 10, 2004).

"Space Shuttle *Columbia* Disaster." *Wikipedia.* http://en.wikipedia.org/wiki/Columbia_disaster (accessed on August 10, 2004).

George W. Bush

Remarks on a New Vision for Space Exploration Program
Presented on January 14, 2004

The U.S. space program began in 1958 with the formation of the National Aeronautics and Space Administration (NASA). At that time the United States and the former Soviet Union had been engaged in a period of hostile relations known as the Cold War (1945–91) for more than a decade, since the end of World War II (1939–45). Not only were the two superpowers involved in an arms race for military superiority, they were also competing for dominance in space. In 1957 the Soviet Union had launched the *Sputnik 1* satellite to study the atmosphere of Earth, sending shock waves through American society. *Sputnik* was a sign that the Soviet Union was moving ahead in the Cold War. The United States responded by creating NASA, which integrated U.S. space research agencies and established a manned space program.

The first stage of the program was Project Mercury, which developed the basic technology for manned space flight and investigated a human's ability to survive and perform in space. On May 5, 1961, astronaut Alan Shepard (1923–1998) flew a Mercury capsule for fifteen minutes in Earth orbit over the Atlantic Ocean, becoming the first American in space. Shepard was not the first human to perform this achievement, how-ever: Less than a month earlier, on April 12, Soviet cosmonaut (astronaut) Yuri Gagarin (1934–1968) had made a nearly complete orbit of Earth. Americans saw Gagarin's flight as a potentially fatal blow to the prestige of the United States.

Immediately confronting the Soviet challenge, in May 1961 U.S. president John F. Kennedy (1917–63; served 1961–63; see entry) made a speech before a joint session of Congress. He announced that the United States would put a man on the Moon within the next ten years. In 1962 astronaut John Glenn (1921–) made three orbits of Earth aboard the Mercury spacecraft *Friendship 7.* Two years later NASA initiated Project Gemini, which provided astronauts with experience in returning to Earth from space as well as practice in successfully linking space vehicles and "walking" in space. Gemini also involved the launching of a series of unmanned satellites, with the goal of gaining information about the Moon and its surface to determine whether humans could survive there. Gemini was the transition between Mercury's short flights and Project Apollo, which would safely land a human on the Moon.

The first Apollo mission ended tragically in January 1967, when three astronauts died in a launchpad fire in their module. The next Apollo missions were unmanned flights that tested the safety of the equipment. The first manned flight was *Apollo 7* in 1968, and the last was *Apollo 17* in 1972. The most famous was *Apollo 11,* which successfully landed astronauts Neil Armstrong (1930–) and Edwin "Buzz" Aldrin (1930–) on the Moon in 1969 (see Michael Collins and Edwin E. Aldrin Jr. entry). After *Apollo 17* the United States did not undertake any other moon flights.

Interest in further moon exploration steadily waned in the early 1970s, so NASA concentrated its efforts on the Large Space Telescope (LST) project. Initiated in 1969, the LST was an observatory (a structure housing a telescope, a device that observes celestial objects) that would continuously orbit Earth. An immediate result of the LST project was the introduction of the space shuttle, a reusable vehicle that would launch the LST into orbit. Technical issues and lack of funding caused a series of delays before the LST was finally approved by Congress in 1977. Collaborating with the European Space

Agency, NASA began building the telescope, which was first renamed the Space Telescope and then the Hubble Space Telescope (HST). The HST was assembled and ready for launch in 1985, but the midair explosion of the *Challenger* forced the temporary grounding of all space shuttles. The HST was finally lifted into space in 1990. Over the next several years the observatory's powerful camera took spectacular pictures of the universe, enabling scientists to make many astronomical advances and discoveries.

At the turn of the twenty-first century NASA was still operating the HST, but it had been designed to have a life span of only fifteen years. Astronauts made periodic visits to the orbiting telescope to do maintenance work and install new equipment. Three service missions had been completed by 2003, and the fourth and final mission was scheduled for 2006. It was canceled after the accident of the space shuttle *Columbia,* which broke apart over the western United States on February 1, 2003 (see *Columbia* Space Shuttle Disaster entry). All seven crew members were killed. The day after the accident NASA administrator Sean O'Keefe (1956–) organized the *Columbia* Accident Investigation Board (CAIB). In August 2003 the CAIB issued a final report, stating that the most immediate cause of the crash was a piece of insulating foam that had separated from the shuttle's left wing during takeoff. The missing foam left a hole through which leaking gas was ignited by intense heat from the rocket that propelled the *Columbia.* The board concluded that shuttle flights were becoming increasingly dangerous and that a minimum number of shuttles should be flown only when necessary. The report further cited deficiencies within NASA and a lack of government oversight of the space agency.

Although the HST has been considered a great success, NASA's primary project is the International Space Station (ISS). The largest international scientific collaboration in history, the ISS represented the future of space exploration when construction began in 1998. Often described as an orbiting "house" or "hotel," a space station is a craft in which people can live for extended periods of time while conducting research and scientific experiments. Astronauts travel to and from the station on space shuttles. The ISS involves the efforts of seventeen countries: the United States, the eleven member nations of the European Space Agency, Canada,

Japan, Russia, and Brazil. The ISS was scheduled to be completed in 2006, when astronauts will have assembled a total of one hundred separate parts during forty-five missions—while the station is orbiting 240 miles (384 kilometers) above Earth. By 2004 eight crews had stayed on the ISS for months at a time. The previous year, however, the space station met the same fate as the HST, when further ISS construction was halted after the crash of *Columbia.*

By 2004 the U.S. manned space program had reached a turning point: NASA had not conducted exploration of the Moon for nearly thirty-two years, space shuttles were grounded, and the future was uncertain for both the HST and the ISS. Scientists, politicians, and the American public began to question the future of NASA itself. On January 14, 2004, in a speech at NASA headquarters in Washington, D.C., President George W. Bush (1946–; served 2001–) announced plans for a major revitalization of the U.S. space program.

Things to remember while reading President Bush's Remarks on a New Vision for Space Exploration Program:

- The president commits the nation to exploration of the solar system, both by humans and robots (electronic devices programmed to perform human activities), beginning with a return to the Moon. The program will eventually be expanded to include trips to Mars and to other destinations in space.

- Bush outlines new objectives for NASA, stressing a commitment to affordable, sustainable, and safe manned space flight. He also announces that construction of the ISS will be completed and that the space shuttle will be replaced by a new Crew Exploration Vehicle.

- The president mentions "Commander Mike Foale's introduction." British-born NASA astronaut Michael Foale (1957–) was the commander of the Expedition-8 crew who was living aboard the ISS at the time of Bush's speech. ("Expedition-8" was the eighth crew to live on the ISS for an extended period of time.) Foale introduced the president to the NASA audience via a video link from the ISS. After a six-month stay on the space station—from October 2003 until April 2004—Foale set a new U.S. record for the length of time spent in space: 374 days, 11 hours, and 19 minutes.

President Bush's Remarks on a New Vision for Space Exploration Program

*Thanks for the warm welcome. I'm honored to be with the men and women of NASA. I thank those of you who have come in person. I welcome those who are listening by video. This agency, and the dedicated professionals who serve it, have always reflected the finest values of our country—daring, discipline, **ingenuity**, and unity in the pursuit of great goals.*

*America is proud of our space program. The risk takers and **visionaries** of this agency have expanded human knowledge, have revolutionized our understanding of the universe, and produced technological advances that have benefited all of humanity.*

Inspired by all that has come before, and guided by clear objectives, today we set a new course for America's space program. We will give NASA a new focus and vision for future exploration. We will build new ships to carry man forward into the universe, to gain a new foothold on the moon, and to prepare for new journeys to worlds beyond our own.

*I am comfortable in delegating these new goals to NASA, under the leadership of [NASA administrator] Sean O'Keefe. He's doing an excellent job. I appreciate **Commander Mike Foale's introduction**— I'm sorry I couldn't shake his hand. Perhaps, Commissioner, you'll bring him by—Administrator, you'll bring him by the Oval Office when he returns, so I can thank him in person.*

I also know he is in space with his colleague, Alexander Kaleri [1956–], who happens to be a Russian cosmonaut. I appreciate the joint efforts of the Russians with our country to explore. I want to thank the astronauts who are with us, the courageous spacial entrepreneurs who set such a wonderful example for the young of our country.

Ingenuity: Inventiveness, cleverness.

Visionaries: People who have imaginative ideas of what could be.

Commander Mike Foale's introduction: British-born NASA astronaut Michael Foale (1957–), commander of the Expedition-8 crew who was living aboard the ISS at the time of Bush's speech, introduced the president.

President George W. Bush announces his proposal for the U.S. space program during a speech at NASA headquarters in Washington, D.C.
(© Kevin LaMarque/Reuters/Corbis)

And we've got some veterans with us today. I appreciate the astronauts of yesterday who are with us, as well, who inspired the astronauts of today to serve our country. I appreciate so very much the members of Congress being here. [Texas Congressman] Tom DeLay [1947–] is here, leading a House delegation. Senator [Bill] Nelson [1942–] [of Florida] is here from the Senate. I am honored that you all have come. I appreciate you're interested in the subject—it is a subject that's important to this administration, it's a subject that's mighty important to the country and to the world.

*Two centuries ago, Meriwether Lewis [1774–1809] and William Clark [1770–1838] left St. Louis to explore the new lands acquired in the **Louisiana Purchase**. They made that journey in the spirit of discovery, to learn the potential of vast new territory, and to chart a way for others to follow.*

*America has ventured forth into space for the same reasons. We have undertaken space travel because the desire to explore and understand is part of our character. And that quest has brought **tangible** benefits that improve our lives in countless ways. The*

Louisiana Purchase: Land purchased by the United States from France in 1803; extended west from the Mississippi River to the Rocky Mountains.

Tangible: Real, substantial.

Space shuttle astronauts listen as President George W. Bush announces his vision for future space exploration. One goal in Bush's plan calls for replacing aging space shuttles with a new generation spacecraft. *(© Kevin LaMarque/Reuters/Corbis)*

Global Positioning System (GPS): A system used to determine a position on Earth's surface by comparing radio signals from several satellites.

CAT (Computed Axial Tomography) scanners: Medical devices consisting of X-ray and computer equipment that produce three-dimensional images.

MRI (Magnetic Resonance Imaging) machines: Devices that use nuclear protons to take pictures of the interior of the body.

*exploration of space has led to advances in weather forecasting, in communications, in computing, search and rescue technology, robotics, and electronics. Our investment in space exploration helped to create our satellite telecommunications network and the **Global Positioning System**. Medical technologies that help prolong life—such as the imaging processing used in **CAT scanners** and **MRI machines**—trace their origins to technology engineered for the use in space.*

Our current programs and vehicles for exploring space have brought us far and they have served us well. The Space Shuttle has flown more than a hundred missions. It has been used to conduct important research and to increase the sum of human knowledge. Shuttle crews, and the scientists and engineers who support them, have helped to build the International Space Station.

Telescopes—including those in space—have revealed more than one hundred planets in the last decade alone. **Probes** have shown us stunning images of the rings of Saturn and the outer planets of our solar system. Robotic explorers have found evidence of water—a key ingredient for life—on Mars and on the moons of Jupiter. At this very hour, the **Mars Exploration Rover Spirit** is searching for evidence of life beyond the Earth.

Yet for all these successes, much remains for us to explore and to learn. In the past thirty years, no human being has set foot on another world, or ventured farther upward into space than 386 miles—roughly the distance from Washington, D.C., to Boston, Massachusetts. America has not developed a new vehicle to advance human exploration in space in nearly a quarter century. It is time for America to take the next steps.

Today I announce a new plan to explore space and extend a human presence across our solar system. We will begin the effort quickly, using existing programs and personnel. We'll make steady progress—one mission, one voyage, one landing at a time.

Our first goal is to complete the International Space Station by 2010. We will finish what we have started, we will meet our obligations to our fifteen international partners on this project. We will focus our future research aboard the station on the long-term effects of space travel on human biology. The environment of space is hostile to human beings. Radiation and weightlessness pose dangers to human health, and we have much to learn about their long-term effects before human crews can venture through the vast voids of space for months at a time. Research on board the station and here on Earth will help us better understand and overcome the obstacles that limit exploration. Through these efforts we will develop the skills and techniques necessary to sustain further space exploration.

To meet this goal, we will return the Space Shuttle to flight as soon as possible, consistent with safety concerns and the recommendations of the Columbia Accident Investigation Board. The Shuttle's chief purpose over the next several years will be to help finish assembly of the International Space Station. In 2010, the Space Shuttle—after nearly 30 years of duty—will be retired from service.

Our second goal is to develop and test a new spacecraft, the Crew Exploration Vehicle, by 2008, and to conduct the first manned mission no later than 2014. The Crew Exploration Vehicle will be capable of ferrying astronauts and scientists to the Space Station after the shuttle is retired. But the main purpose of this spacecraft will be

Probes: Devices that send information from outer space to Earth.

Mars Exploration Rover
Spirit: A remote-controlled, six-wheeled robot that was placed on Mars in January 2004 and programmed to explore the surface of the planet.

to carry astronauts beyond our orbit to other worlds. This will be the first spacecraft of its kind since the Apollo Command Module.

Our third goal is to return to the moon by 2020, as the launching point for missions beyond. Beginning no later than 2008, we will send a series of robotic missions to the lunar surface to research and prepare for future human exploration. Using the Crew Exploration Vehicle, we will undertake extended human missions to the moon as early as 2015, with the goal of living and working there for increasingly extended periods. **Eugene Cernan,** who is with us today— the last man to set foot on the lunar surface—said this as he left "We leave as we came, and God willing as we shall return, with peace and hope for all mankind." America will make those words come true.

Returning to the moon is an important step for our space program. Establishing an extended human presence on the moon could vastly reduce the costs of further space exploration, making possible ever more ambitious missions. Lifting heavy spacecraft and fuel out of the Earth's gravity is expensive. Spacecraft assembled and provisioned on the moon could escape its far lower gravity using far less energy, and thus, far less cost. Also, the moon is home to abundant resources. Its soil contains raw materials that might be harvested and processed into rocket fuel or breathable air. We can use our time on the moon to develop and test new approaches and technologies and systems that will allow us to function in other, more challenging environments. The moon is a logical step toward further progress and achievement.

With the experience and knowledge gained on the moon, we will then be ready to take the next steps of space exploration; human missions to Mars and to worlds beyond. Robotic missions will serve as trailblazers—the advanced guard to the unknown. Probes, **landers** and other vehicles of this kind continue to prove their worth, sending spectacular images and vast amounts of data back to Earth. Yet the human thirst for knowledge ultimately cannot be satisfied by even the most vivid pictures, or the most detailed measurements. We need to see and examine and touch for ourselves. And only human beings are capable of adapting to the inevitable uncertainties posed by space travel.

As our knowledge improves, we'll develop new power generation, **propulsion,** life support, and other systems that can support more distant travels. We do not know where this journey will end, yet we know this: human beings are headed into the cosmos.

Eugene Cernan (1934–): Commander of *Apollo 17,* the last U.S. manned mission to the Moon (December 6–19, 1972).

Landers: Space vehicles designed to land on celestial bodies.

Propulsion: Forward motion; driving force.

Robotic explorers, such as the Remote Manipulator System, have captured vivid images, such as this one of Earth with a solar sunburst behind it; yet "we need to see and examine and touch for ourselves," President George W. Bush proposed. *(NASA)*

And along this journey we'll make many technological breakthroughs. We don't know yet what those breakthroughs will be, but we can be certain they'll come, and that our efforts will be repaid many times over. We may discover resources on the moon or Mars that will boggle the imagination, that will test our limits to dream.

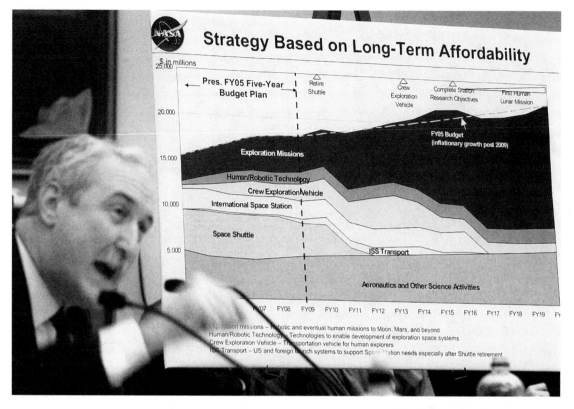

NASA administrator Sean O'Keefe discusses how NASA plans to spend its long-term budget during a House Science Committee hearing to review President George W. Bush's proposed space exploration initiative. *(© Jason Reed/Reuters/Corbis)*

And the fascination generated by further exploration will inspire our young people to study math, and science, and engineering and create a new generation of innovators and pioneers.

This will be a great and unifying mission for NASA, and we know that you'll achieve it. I have directed Administrator O'Keefe to review all of NASA's current space flight and exploration activities and direct them toward the goals I have outlined. I will also form a commission of private and public sector experts to advise on implementing the vision that I've outlined today. This commission will report to me within four months of its first meeting. I'm today naming former Secretary of the Air Force, Pete Aldridge [1938–], to be the Chair of the Commission. Thank you for being here today, Pete. He has tremendous experience in the Department of Defense and the aerospace industry. He is going to begin this important work right away.

We'll invite other nations to share the challenges and opportunities of this new era of discovery. The vision I outline today is a journey, not a race, and I call on other nations to join us on this journey, in a spirit of cooperation and friendship.

Achieving these goals requires a long-term commitment. NASA's current five-year budget is $86 billion. Most of the funding we need for the new endeavors will come from reallocating $11 billion within that budget. We need some new resources, however. I will call upon Congress to increase NASA's budget by roughly a billion dollars, spread out over the next five years. This increase, along with refocusing of our space agency, is a solid beginning to meet the challenges and the goals we set today. It's only a beginning. Future funding decisions will be guided by the progress we make in achieving our goals.

We begin this venture knowing that space travel brings great risks. The loss of the Space Shuttle Columbia was less than one year ago. Since the beginning of our space program, America has lost twenty-three astronauts, and **one astronaut from an allied nation**— men and women who believed in their mission and accepted the dangers. As one family member said, "The legacy of Columbia must carry on—for the benefit of our children and yours." The Columbia's crew did not turn away from the challenge, and neither will we.

Mankind is drawn to the heavens for the same reason we were once drawn into unknown lands and across the open sea. We choose to explore space because doing so improves our lives, and lifts our national spirit. So let us continue the journey.

May God bless.

One astronaut from an allied nation: Israeli astronaut Ilan Ramon (1954–2003), one of seven crew members who died in the *Columbia* crash.

What happened next . . .

Although service missions to the HST had been canceled, the telescope continued to send spectacular images back to Earth. Its life span was originally expected to end in 2005, but it was extended until 2010. Without servicing and repair, however, the components of the observatory will eventually wear out. Since the HST was built to dock with a space shuttle, a spacecraft other than the shuttle could not be used for a service mission. The HST had become so popular with scientists and the American public that by early 2004 there was an outpouring of concern about the fate of the observatory. In response, NASA administrator O'Keefe asked the National Academy of Science (NAS) to study possible ways to prolong its life. NAS then appointed a committee of former astronauts, professors, scientists, and engineers to explore alternatives to the space shuttle.

In April 2004, NASA astronaut Edward Michael Fincke (1967–) and Russian cosmonaut Gennady I. Padalka (1958–) arrived at the ISS for a six-month repair mission, the first such visit since the grounding of U.S. space shuttles. Flying to the space station aboard a Soyuz spacecraft (Russian space shuttle), the two men made up a smaller crew than the usual minimum number of three. Occupancy of the ISS was limited to two people until NASA shuttles began flying again and delivering spare parts and supplies. (As an international effort, the ISS requires specific tasks and duties of each participating nation. These tasks and duties cannot easily be assumed by another nation.) The absence of a third crew member meant that Fincke and Padalka would have to leave the space station vacant when they worked outside. Usually the third crew member stays onboard to tend the station and to be available in the event of an emergency.

On June 24 Fincke and Padalka attempted to conduct a spacewalk to repair an electrical circuit board that provides power to one of four gyroscopes (spinning wheels that orient and stabilize the station). The spacewalk was aborted (stopped before completion) because of oxygen-supply problems on Fincke's spacesuit. On July 1, with both wearing Russian spacesuits, Fincke and Padalka successfully completed the spacewalk. They encountered little difficulty as they made the necessary repairs to the circuit board while remaining in constant contact with ground controllers. They even had extra time to install handrails on the exterior of the ISS, for use on future spacewalks.

On June 24, the same day Fincke and Padalka aborted their spacewalk, O'Keefe announced a major reorganization of the U.S. space agency. Acting on recommendations from the com-

A First Private Manned Space Flight

On June 23, 2004, American test pilot Mike Melvill successfully flew the rocket plane SpaceShipOne 62.5 miles (100 kilometers) over the Mojave Desert in California. This was an important event in the history of space exploration because Melvill was a private citizen and SpaceShipOne was built by Scaled Composites, a private company. Prior to this time, space explorers had been employed by national space agencies and spacecraft had been designed and constructed with government funds.

SpaceShipOne was carried to 50,000 feet (15,240 meters) by a jet called White Knight, then the rocket plane glided for a few seconds until Melvill ignited its engines.

SpaceShipOne rose to Mach 3, or three times the speed of sound. Once the craft had reached weightlessness, Melvill released some M&M candy pieces into the cockpit and watched them float for three minutes. Although his flight was successful, Melvill later reported that he had to cut it short. As SpaceShipOne ascended into space, it twice rolled 90 degrees and went twenty miles off course within only a few seconds. Melvill was forced to switch to a backup system in order to keep the rocket plane under control. His achievement with SpaceShipOne was hailed as a significant milestone toward more extensive privately funded space exploration.

mission appointed by President Bush, O'Keefe proposed the merging of the existing seven NASA centers into four directorates: Exploration Systems (human and robotic space research), Space Operations (human spaceflight, rocket launching, and space communications), Aeronautics Operations (aviation technology), and the Science Directorate (space science and earth science). Under its new structure NASA would also encourage involvement of private companies in space exploration. The first step in this direction had already been made the previous day, on June 23, when test pilot Mike Melvill (1941–) successfully flew the privately built SpaceShipOne 62.5 miles (100 kilometers) over the Mojave Desert in California (see box on this page).

Did you know . . .

- Scientists have been experimenting with robots that could replace humans on repair missions to the HST.

- The ISS is being assembled in three phases, which involve shuttle missions with specific goals, such as delivering and assembling parts, transporting crews, delivering cargo and supplies, and maintaining and servicing the station. When the shuttle fleet was grounded in 2004, twenty-eight missions had been completed and construction was in the third phase.

- President Bush's plans for the space program, as well as for certain aspects of the NASA reorganization, must be approved by the U.S. Congress. By mid-2004 the approval process was being stalled by such issues as funding problems related to a federal government budget deficit, financing of the war in Iraq, and increased expenditures for a new Medicare health insurance program. Scientists were also questioning whether the NASA Science Directorate would receive adequate attention from both the government and NASA.

Consider the following . . .

- Politicians and scientists are debating the future of the HST. One side argues that NASA should not attempt to extend the life span of the orbiting telescope because it drains funds from more vital NASA projects such as the ISS and future Moon and Mars missions. The other side argues that the HST is NASA's most reliable and successful endeavor, so every effort should be made to keep it in space. What do you think? Support your position with research on each side of the issue.

- Politicians and scientists are also debating the value of the ISS. One side says the space station is a waste of scarce U.S. taxpayer funds, which could be more effectively used for the new NASA goals envisioned by President Bush. The other side, stressing the need for global cooperation, believes that the ISS provides an opportunity for the United States to continue working with other nations. What is your position on this issue? Support your view with evidence from each side.

- Mike Melvill's privately sponsored flight on SpaceShipOne has been hailed as the future of space exploration. What is your opinion of private space endeavors? Explore the question through further reading, then take a stand.

For More Information

Books

Bond, Peter. *The Continuing Story of the International Space Station.* New York: Springer-Verlag, 2002.

Goodwin, Simon. *Hubble's Universe: A Portrait of Our Cosmos.* New York: Viking Penguin, 1997.

Periodicals

"Hubble's Gifts." *Kids Discover* (May 2004): pp. 10–11.

Reichhardt, Tony. "NASA Seeks Robotic Rescuers to Give Hubble Extra Lease on Life." *Nature* (March 25, 2004): p. 353.

Sietzen, Frank Jr. "A New Vision for Space." *Astronomy* (May 2004): pp. 48+.

Web Sites

Coren, Michael. "Private Craft Soars in Space, History." *CNN.com.* http://www.cnn.com/2004/TECH/space/06/21/suborbital.test/ (accessed on August 9, 2004).

"The Hubble Project." *NASA.* http://hubble.nasa.gov (accessed on August 9, 2004).

"ISS Spacewalk a Success." *Spacetoday.net.* http://www.spacetoday.net/Summary/2442 (accessed on August 9, 2004).

"President Bush Announces New Vision for Space Exploration Program." *The White House.* http://www.whitehouse.gov/news/releases/2004/01/20040114-3.html (accessed on August 9, 2004).

"Where Is the International Space Station?" *NASA.* http://science.nasa.gov/temp/StationLoc.html (accessed on August 9, 2004).

Where to Learn More

Books

Aaseng, Nathan. *The Space Race*. San Diego, CA: Lucent, 2001.

Andronik, Catherine M. *Copernicus: Founder of Modern Astronomy*. Berkeley Heights, NJ: Enslow, 2002.

Asimov, Isaac. *Astronomy in Ancient Times*. Revised ed. Milwaukee: Gareth Stevens, 1997.

Aveni, Anthony. *Stairways to the Stars: Skywatching in Three Great Ancient Cultures*. New York: John Wiley and Sons, 1997.

Baker, David. *Spaceflight and Rocketry: A Chronology*. New York: Facts on File, 1996.

Benson, Michael. *Beyond: Visions of the Interplanetary Probes*. New York: Abrams, 2003.

Bille, Matt, and Erika Lishock. *The First Space Race: Launching the World's First Satellites*. College Station, TX: Texas A&M University Press, 2004.

Bilstein, Roger E. *Orders of Magnitude: A History of the NACA and NASA, 1915–1990*. Washington, DC: National Aeronautics and Space Administration, 1989.

Boerst, William J. *Galileo Galilei and the Science of Motion*. Greensboro, NC: Morgan Reynolds, 2003.

Bredeson, Carmen. *NASA Planetary Spacecraft: Galileo, Magellan, Pathfinder, and Voyager.* Berkeley Heights, NJ: Enslow, 2000.

Caprara, Giovanni. *Living in Space: From Science Fiction to the International Space Station.* Buffalo, NY: Firefly Books, 2000.

Catchpole, John. *Project Mercury: NASA's First Manned Space Programme.* New York: Springer Verlag, 2001.

Chaikin, Andrew L. *A Man on the Moon: The Voyages of the Apollo Astronauts.* New York: Penguin, 1998.

Christianson, Gale E. *Edwin Hubble: Mariner of the Nebulae.* Chicago, IL: University of Chicago Press, 1996.

Clary, David A. *Rocket Man: Robert H. Goddard and the Birth of the Space Age.* New York: Hyperion Press, 2003.

Cole, Michael D. *The Columbia Space Shuttle Disaster: From First Liftoff to Tragic Final Flight.* Revised ed. Berkeley Heights, NJ: Enslow, 2003.

Collins, Michael. *Carrying the Fire: An Astronaut's Journeys.* New York: Cooper Square Press, 2001.

Davies, John K. *Astronomy from Space: The Design and Operation of Orbiting Observatories.* Second ed. New York: Wiley, 1997.

Dickinson, Terence. *Exploring the Night Sky: The Equinox Astronomy Guide for Beginners.* Buffalo, NY: Firefly Books, 1987.

Dickson, Paul. *Sputnik: The Shock of the Century.* New York: Walker, 2001.

Ezell, Edward Clinton, and Linda Neuman Ezell. *The Partnership: A History of the Apollo-Soyuz Test Project.* Washington, DC: National Aeronautics and Space Administration, 1978.

Florence, Ronald. *The Perfect Machine: Building the Palomar Telescope.* New York: HarperCollins, 1994.

Fox, Mary Virginia. *Rockets.* Tarrytown, NY: Benchmark Books, 1996.

Gleick, James. *Isaac Newton.* New York: Pantheon Books, 2003.

Hall, Rex, and David J. Shayler. *The Rocket Men: Vostok and Voskhod, the First Soviet Manned Spaceflights.* New York: Springer Verlag, 2001.

Hall, Rex D., and David J. Shayler. *Soyuz: A Universal Spacecraft.* New York: Springer Verlag, 2003.

Hamilton, John. *The Viking Missions to Mars.* Edina, MN: Abdo and Daughters Publishing, 1998.

Harland, David M. *The MIR Space Station: A Precursor to Space Colonization.* New York: Wiley, 1997.

Harland, David M., and John E. Catchpole. *Creating the International Space Station.* New York: Springer Verlag, 2002.

Holden, Henry M. *The Tragedy of the Space Shuttle Challenger*. Berkeley Heights, NJ: MyReportLinks.com, 2004.

Jenkins, Dennis R. *Space Shuttle: The History of the National Space Transportation System*. Third ed. Cape Canaveral, FL: D. R. Jenkins, 2001.

Kerrod, Robin. *The Book of Constellations: Discover the Secrets in the Stars*. Hauppauge, NY: Barron's, 2002.

Kerrod, Robin. *Hubble: The Mirror on the Universe*. Buffalo, NY: Firefly Books, 2003.

Kluger, Jeffrey. *Moon Hunters: NASA's Remarkable Expeditions to the Ends of the Solar System*. New York: Simon and Schuster, 2001.

Kraemer, Robert S. *Beyond the Moon: A Golden Age of Planetary Exploration, 1971–1978*. Washington, DC: Smithsonian Institution Press, 2000.

Krupp, E. C. *Beyond the Blue Horizon: Myths and Legends of the Sun, Moon, Stars, and Planets*. New York: Oxford University Press, 1992.

Launius, Roger D. *Space Stations: Base Camps to the Stars*. Washington, DC: Smithsonian Institution Press, 2003.

Maurer, Richard. *Rocket! How a Toy Launched the Space Age*. New York: Knopf, 1995.

Miller, Ron. *The History of Rockets*. New York: Franklin Watts, 1999.

Murray, Charles. *Apollo: The Race to the Moon*. New York: Simon and Schuster, 1989.

Naeye, Robert. *Signals from Space: The Chandra X-ray Observatory*. Austin, TX: Raintree Steck-Vaughn, 2001.

Orr, Tamra B. *The Telescope*. New York: Franklin Watts, 2004.

Panek, Richard. *Seeing and Believing: How the Telescope Opened Our Eyes and Minds to the Heavens*. New York: Penguin, 1999.

Parker, Barry R. *Stairway to the Stars: The Story of the World's Largest Observatory*. New York: Perseus Publishing, 2001.

Reichhardt, Tony, ed. *Space Shuttle: The First 20 Years—The Astronauts' Experiences in Their Own Words*. New York: DK Publishing, 2002.

Reynolds, David. *Apollo: The Epic Journey to the Moon*. New York: Harcourt, 2002.

Ride, Sally. *To Space and Back*. New York: HarperCollins, 1986.

Shayler, David J. *Gemini: Steps to the Moon*. New York: Springer Verlag, 2001.

Shayler, David J. *Skylab: America's Space Station*. New York: Springer Verlag, 2001.

Sherman, Josepha. *Deep Space Observation Satellites*. New York: Rosen Publishing Group, 2003.

Sibley, Katherine A. S. *The Cold War.* Westport, CT: Greenwood Press, 1998.

Slayton, Donald K., with Michael Cassutt. *Deke! An Autobiography.* New York: St. Martin's Press, 1995.

Sullivan, Walter. *Assault on the Unknown: The International Geophysical Year.* New York: McGraw-Hill, 1961.

Tsiolkovsky, Konstantin. *Beyond the Planet Earth.* Translated by Kenneth Syers. New York: Pergamon Press, 1960.

Voelkel, James R. *Johannes Kepler and the New Astronomy.* New York: Oxford University Press, 1999.

Walters, Helen B. *Hermann Oberth: Father of Space Travel.* Introduction by Hermann Oberth. New York: Macmillan, 1962.

Ward, Bob. *Mr. Space: The Life of Wernher von Braun.* Washington, DC: Smithsonian Institution Press, 2004.

Wills, Susan, and Steven R. Wills. *Astronomy: Looking at the Stars.* Minneapolis, MN: Oliver Press, 2001.

Winter, Frank H. *The First Golden Age of Rocketry: Congreve and Hale Rockets of the Nineteenth Century.* Washington, DC: Smithsonian Institution Press, 1990.

Wolfe, Tom. *The Right Stuff.* New York: Farrar, Straus, and Giroux, 1979.

Web Sites

"Ancient Astronomy." *Pomona College Astronomy Department.* http://www.astronomy.pomona.edu/archeo/ (accessed on September 17, 2004).

"Ancients Could Have Used Stonehenge to Predict Lunar Eclipses." *Space.com.* http://www.space.com/scienceastronomy/astronomy/stonehenge_eclipse_000119.html (accessed on September 17, 2004).

"The Apollo Program." *NASA History Office.* http://www.hq.nasa.gov/office/pao/History/apollo.html (accessed on September 17, 2004).

"The Apollo Soyuz Test Project." *NASA/Kennedy Space Center.* http://www-pao.ksc.nasa.gov/kscpao/history/astp/astp.html (accessed on September 17, 2004).

"Apollo-Soyuz Test Project." *National Aeronautics and Space Administration History Office.* http://www.hq.nasa.gov/office/pao/History/astp/index.html (accessed on September 17, 2004).

"The Apollo-Soyuz Test Project." *U.S. Centennial of Flight Commission.* http://www.centennialofflight.gov/essay/SPACEFLIGHT/ASTP/SP24.htm (accessed on September 17, 2004).

"Biographical Sketch of Dr. Wernher Von Braun." *Marshall Space Flight Center.* http://history.msfc.nasa.gov/vonbraun/index.html (accessed on September 17, 2004).

"Cassini-Huygens: Mission to Saturn and Titan." *Jet Propulsion Laboratory, California Institute of Technology.* http://saturn.jpl.nasa.gov/index. cfm (accessed on September 17, 2004).

"CGRO Science Support Center." *NASA Goddard Space Flight Center.* http:// cossc.gsfc.nasa.gov/ (accessed on September 17, 2004).

"Chandra X-ray Observatory." *Harvard-Smithsonian Center for Astrophysics.* http://chandra.harvard.edu/ (accessed on September 17, 2004).

"Cold War." *CNN Interactive.* http://www.cnn.com/SPECIALS/cold.war/ (accessed on September 17, 2004).

The Cold War Museum. http://www.coldwar.org/index.html (accessed on September 17, 2004).

"The Copernican Model: A Sun-Centered Solar System." *Department of Physics and Astronomy, University of Tennessee.* http://csep10.phys.utk. edu/astr161/lect/retrograde/copernican.html (accessed on September 17, 2004).

"Curious About Astronomy? Ask an Astronomer." *Astronomy Department, Cornell University.* http://curious.astro.cornell.edu/index.php (accessed on September 17, 2004).

European Space Agency. http://www.esa.int/export/esaCP/index.html (accessed on September 17, 2004).

"Explorer Series of Spacecraft." *National Aeronautics and Space Administration Office of Policy and Plans.* http://www.hq.nasa.gov/office/pao/ History/explorer.html (accessed on September 17, 2004).

"Galileo: Journey to Jupiter." *Jet Propulsion Laboratory, California Institute of Technology.* http://www2.jpl.nasa.gov/galileo/ (accessed on September 17, 2004).

"The Hubble Project." *NASA Goddard Space Flight Center.* http://hubble. nasa.gov/ (accessed on September 17, 2004).

HubbleSite. http://www.hubblesite.org/ (accessed on September 17, 2004).

"International Geophysical Year." *The National Academies.* http://www7. nationalacademies.org/archives/igy.html (accessed on September 17, 2004).

"International Space Station." *Boeing.* http://www.boeing.com/defense space/space/spacestation/flash.html (accessed on September 17, 2004).

"International Space Station." *National Aeronautics and Space Administration.* http://spaceflight.nasa.gov/station/ (accessed on September 17, 2004).

"Kennedy Space Center: Apollo Program." *NASA/Kennedy Space Center.* http://www-pao.ksc.nasa.gov/kscpao/history/apollo/apollo.htm (accessed on September 17, 2004).

"Kennedy Space Center: Gemini Program." *NASA/Kennedy Space Center.* http://www-pao.ksc.nasa.gov/kscpao/history/gemini/gemini.htm (accessed on September 17, 2004).

"Kennedy Space Center: Mercury Program." *NASA/Kennedy Space Center.* http://www-pao.ksc.nasa.gov/history/mercury/mercury.htm (accessed on September 17, 2004).

"The Life of Konstantin Eduardovitch Tsiolkovsky." *Konstantin E. Tsiolkovsky State Museum of the History of Cosmonautics.* http://www.informatics.org/museum/tsiol.html (accessed on September 17, 2004).

"Living and Working in Space." *NASA Spacelink.* http://spacelink.nasa.gov/NASA.Projects/Human.Exploration.and.Development.of.Space/Living.and.Working.In.Space/.index.html (accessed on September 17, 2004).

"Mars Exploration Rover Mission." *Jet Propulsion Laboratory, California Institute of Technology.* http://marsrovers.jpl.nasa.gov/home/index.html (accessed on September 17, 2004).

Mir. http://www.russianspaceweb.com/mir.html (accessed on September 17, 2004).

Mount Wilson Observatory. http://www.mtwilson.edu/ (accessed on September 17, 2004).

"NASA: Robotic Explorers." *National Aeronautics and Space Administration.* http://www.nasa.gov/vision/universe/roboticexplorers/index.html (accessed on September 17, 2004).

NASA's History Office. http://www.hq.nasa.gov/office/pao/History/index.html (accessed on September 17, 2004).

National Aeronautics and Space Administration. http://www.nasa.gov/home/index.html (accessed on September 17, 2004).

National Radio Astronomy Observatory. http://www.nrao.edu/ (accessed on September 17, 2004).

"Newton's Laws of Motion." *NASA Glenn Learning Technologies Project.* http://www.grc.nasa.gov/WWW/K-12/airplane/newton.html (accessed on September 17, 2004).

"Newton's Third Law of Motion." *Physics Classroom Tutorial, Glenbrook South High School.* http://www.glenbrook.k12.il.us/gbssci/phys/Class/newtlaws/u2l4a.html (accessed on September 17, 2004).

"One Giant Leap." *CNN Interactive.* http://www.cnn.com/TECH/specials/apollo/ (accessed on September 17, 2004).

"Paranal Observatory." *European Southern Observatory.* http://www.eso.org/paranal/ (accessed on September 17, 2004).

"Project Apollo-Soyuz Drawings and Technical Diagrams." *National Aeronautics and Space Administration History Office.* http://www.hq.nasa.gov/office/pao/History/diagrams/astp/apol_soyuz.htm (accessed on September 17, 2004).

"The Race for Space: The Soviet Space Program." *University of Minnesota.* http://www1.umn.edu/scitech/assign/space/vostok_intro1.html (accessed on September 17, 2004).

"Remembering *Columbia STS-107.*" *National Aeronautics and Space Administration.* http://history.nasa.gov/columbia/index.html (accessed on September 17, 2004).

"Rocketry Through the Ages: A Timeline of Rocket History." *Marshall Space Flight Center.* http://history.msfc.nasa.gov/rocketry/index.html (accessed on September 17, 2004).

"Rockets: History and Theory." *White Sands Missile Range.* http://www.wsmr.army.mil/pao/FactSheets/rkhist.htm (accessed on September 17, 2004).

Russian Aviation and Space Agency. http://www.rosaviakosmos.ru/english/eindex.htm (accessed on September 17, 2004).

Russian/USSR spacecrafts. http://space.kursknet.ru/cosmos/english/machines/m_rus.sht (accessed on September 17, 2004).

"Skylab." *NASA/Kennedy Space Center.* http://www-pao.ksc.nasa.gov/kscpao/history/skylab/skylab.htm (accessed on September 17, 2004).

Soyuz Spacecraft. http://www.russianspaceweb.com/soyuz.html (accessed on September 17, 2004).

"Space Race." *Smithsonian National Air and Space Museum.* http://www.nasm.si.edu/exhibitions/gal114/gal114.htm (accessed on September 17, 2004).

"Space Shuttle." *NASA/Kennedy Space Center.* http://www.ksc.nasa.gov/shuttle/ (accessed on September 17, 2004).

"Space Shuttle Mission Chronology." *NASA/Kennedy Space Center.* http://www-pao.ksc.nasa.gov/kscpao/chron/chrontoc.htm (accessed on September 17, 2004).

"Spitzer Space Telescope." *California Institute of Technology.* http://www.spitzer.caltech.edu/ (accessed on September 17, 2004).

"Sputnik: The Fortieth Anniversary." *National Aeronautics and Space Administration Office of Policy and Plans.* http://www.hq.nasa.gov/office/pao/History/sputnik/ (accessed on September 17, 2004).

"Tsiolkovsky." *Russian Space Web.* http://www.russianspaceweb.com/tsiolkovsky.html (accessed on September 17, 2004).

United Nations Office for Outer Space Affairs. http://www.oosa.unvienna.org/index.html (accessed on September 17, 2004).

"Vanguard." *Naval Center for Space Technology and U.S. Naval Research Laboratory.* http://ncst-www.nrl.navy.mil/NCSTOrigin/Vanguard.html (accessed on September 17, 2004).

"Voyager: The Interstellar Mission." *Jet Propulsion Laboratory, California Institute of Technology.* http://voyager.jpl.nasa.gov/ (accessed on September 17, 2004).

"Windows to the Universe." *University Corporation for Atmospheric Research.* http://www.windows.ucar.edu/ (accessed on September 17, 2004).

W. M. Keck Observatory. http://www2.keck.hawaii.edu/ (accessed on September 17, 2004).

Index

Boldface indicates main entries and their page numbers; illustrations are marked by (ill.)